MW01640085

Law and Society
Recent Scholarship

Edited by Melvin I. Urofsky

A Series from LFB Scholarly

The Corporate Free-Speech Movement

Cognitive Feudalism and the Endangered Marketplace of Ideas

Robert L. Kerr

LFB Scholarly Publishing LLC
New York 2008

Library of Congress Cataloging-in-Publication Data

Kerr, Robert L.
The corporate free-speech movement : cognitive feudalism and the endangered marketplace of ideas / Robert L. Kerr.
p. cm. -- (Law and society)
Includes bibliographical references and index.
ISBN 978-1-59332-293-9 (alk. paper)
1. Corporate speech--United States. 2. Corporations--Political activity--Law and legislation--United States. I. Title.
KF4772.K46 2008
342.7308'53--dc22

2008011184

ISBN 978-1-59332-293-9

Printed on acid-free 250-year-life paper.

Manufactured in the United States of America.

"In a democracy, the economic is subordinate to the political,
a lesson that our ancestors learned long ago,
and that our descendants will undoubtedly have to relearn
many years hence."

Chief Justice William Rehnquist,
writing in 1980 in dissent
in *Central Hudson v. Public Service Commission*

Table of Contents

Acknowledgements

I would like to express my appreciation for funding provided in support of this research through the Association for Education in Journalism and Mass Communication's Baskett Mosse Award, the University of Oklahoma Research Council, and the Gaylord College Junior Faculty Research Program.

It is a research project that began some nine years ago in the narrower efforts that produced my dissertation, first book, and related journal articles that are noted in this book's reference section. As those endeavors proceeded, I came to realize that my findings were akin to those of the blind men in the fable about their encounter with the elephant. Like them, I was recognizing and assessing only parts of a much larger beast — which I ultimately came to conceptualize as the corporate free-speech movement. Thus, this book is my attempt to capture in print a representation of the entire creature and what its influence has meant in American law and political culture.

CHAPTER ONE

The Age of Cognitive Feudalism

The pages ahead draw upon law, history, economics, and philosophy to advance the proposition that recent decades have seen an ominous turn away from democratic governance in American political culture. The evidence and arguments put forth suggest the nature of the forces behind that transformation are such that the period examined can justifiably be characterized historically as an age of cognitive feudalism. Part I articulates that thesis more fully and traces the relevant historical and legal developments. Part II puts forth a unified set of theoretical constructs that provide predictive support for the likelihood of outcomes this study asserts. Part III focuses upon the most current dynamics and implications of a historical process still unfolding.

It is a complex argument, grounded in years of scholarship and assembled in full in this book. But the broad conceptual outlines can be expressed in metaphorical shorthand by referencing one of the most familiar narratives in American popular consciousness. Let us imagine that George Bailey never let Clarence the Angel bring him back to life in Bedford Falls. Imagine that classic film, *It's a Wonderful Life*, culminating not with George's return, but instead with idyllic Bedford Falls transformed into Pottersville — the bleak locale glimpsed earlier in the film, a vision of what Bedford Falls would have been if Jimmy Stewart's character George had never lived.

In the film, Pottersville is a place of Hogarthian squalor and vice dominated by one interest: the short-term fiscal concerns of the local financier, Mr. Potter. Bars, gambling, graft, and prostitution dominate both the economy and social relations in Pottersville. It stands in sharp contrast to the Rockwellian shops, churches, and neighborly values of Bedford Falls — all fostered through community-wide participation in the savings and loan that George Bailey struggles to keep afloat. In the way that Mr. Potter's character relentlessly seeks to advance his sole interest in short-term financial gain over the broader, diverse interests of the rest of the townspeople, he provides a cinematic manifestation of the profit imperative — a concept crucial to the ideas developed on the pages ahead. They will document the way that media discourse and legal efforts in recent decades have synthesized the profit imperative with rhetoric of liberty, equality, and freedom of speech, elevating it to a more dominant role in political culture.

The stirring history of free speech in America has given us inspirational accounts of the courageous efforts that have built a tradition of expansive First Amendment rights. The nation's commitment to freedom of expression has been dramatized time and again in episodes of resistance against government efforts to censor the voices of citizens. Early Americans rejected the repressive Sedition Act of 1798. Nineteenth-century abolitionists persevered in the face of legal restrictions on communicating their message. Time and again, citizens opposed to wars have challenged laws passed to silence their criticism. Those who dared to speak out against the terror of McCarthyism helped eventually bring it to an end. Among the achievements of the civil rights movement were landmark court rulings that struck down attempts to punish the speech activities of its participants.

But a more recent chapter in First Amendment history unfolded with a very different cast of players from any of those earlier episodes. Beginning in the latter part of the twentieth century, another campaign began moving forward in the name of free speech, and in the years since then it has achieved spectacular success. It has focused fundamentally on the championing of corporate spending as free "speech." One of the most vigorous recent demonstrations of the rhetoric of the corporate free-speech movement and its vast economic resources was unleashed in a high-profile false-advertising case brought against the Nike Corporation. Nike's response focused not on establishing the truth of the messages in question, but on arguing that they were political speech not subject to false-advertising regulation. When the appeal in *Nike, Inc. v. Kasky* reached the U.S. Supreme Court in 2003, a crowd of interested parties lined up front and center with friend-of-the-court briefs to invoke all the core ideological tenets established by the corporate free-speech movement over the course of preceding decades.

Central to the movement's message is an insistence that it violates First Amendment freedoms to place any restrictions on corporate media spending done to influence political processes. In its *Nike* brief, the Association of National Advertising declared that the case raised "fundamental issues that go to the core of the First Amendment — the freedom of public debate about political, economic and social issues." It is vital to the nation that the courts protect "the ability of corporations to participate in robust debate on matters of public concern," said the Business Roundtable. Several such briefs hammered home another bedrock axiom of the corporate free-speech movement — that restrictions on corporate political spending are assaults on the liberties of *individual* Americans. The *Nike* case, said the Center for the Advancement of Capitalism, "directly challenges the right of individuals, when acting through a corporation, to engage in unshackled speech." Corporate giants are only seeking to participate "as an equal in ongoing public debate," insisted Pfizer, Inc. So it is wrong to "suppress corporations' speech and discriminate against them," explained the United States Chamber of Commerce. To do so would "deprive the public of potentially valuable information and opinion," said the National Association of Manufacturers, as well as "impoverish the public debate on important issues," added the Product Liability Advisory Council.[1]

Those basic themes have been reiterated time and again in media and legal discourse aimed at expanding First Amendment rights and public support for corporate political spending. They ring of basic common sense and fair play, of time-honored American values, indeed of patriotic fervor. In its *Nike* brief, ExxonMobil told the Court that "Nike's speech and speech by corporations on other matters of public concern . . . merits the highest level of First Amendment protection and is entitled to the same 'breathing space' as speech on matters of public concern by other speakers." The rhetoric and the podium could not have been more familiar for the company. No player in the corporate free-speech movement has played a more prominent role in articulating its positions than has Mobil Oil (as the company was known before its merger with Exxon in 1999).

Ultimately, the Supreme Court decided not to issue a ruling in *Nike, Inc. v. Kasky* and returned it to the lower courts for further proceedings, whereupon Nike settled out of court. The case, discussed fully in Chapter Nine, has been widely characterized as a devastating blow to the right of the corporation to "speak." To the contrary, this book asserts that the aggressive, well-funded corporate effort to redefine the meaning of the First Amendment more likely today stands closer to victories in the nation's highest court even beyond those already achieved. Quite arguably, that effort over the course of recent decades has positioned American constitutional jurisprudence on the brink of a shift with the potential to further recast the marketplace of ideas along more feudalistic lines.

The campaign driving that transformation has focused through law and media discourse on advancing acceptance of an understanding of democratic decisionmaking that radically departs from American tradition. Fundamentally, that understanding reflects a concept of democratic processes as something to be shaped by the few rather than by the many. It represents the basis of a broader ideology in which key components of American democracy have been reworked with functional qualities that are more feudal than democratic.

Thus, the phenomenon this book puts forth under the rubric of *cognitive feudalism*. The fuller meaning of that term is articulated in the following chapters, but essentially it is proposed here to describe a marketplace of ideas that is not truly a free market. The influence of the marketplace-of-ideas concept in American First Amendment jurisprudence and political culture cannot be overemphasized. Especially since 1919, when Justice Oliver Wendell Holmes asserted in *Abrams v. United States* that "the best test of truth is the power of the thought to get itself accepted in the competition of the market," the concept has been formally established as the guiding principle in modern First Amendment law.[2]

Basically, the marketplace-of-ideas concept holds that the best means available for assessing the truth of an idea is to see how it fares in a marketplace of truly free competition. Hence, government diminishes available truth when it suppresses competition in ideas. More than any other rationale, the Court has emphasized that concept in explaining the reasoning of its First Amendment cases over the past century. The court's reliance on the marketplace-of-ideas concept is consistent with its deep roots in democratic political theory. English poet and essayist John Milton established the most often cited early articulation in his *Areopagitica* in 1644, asserting the value of letting truth and falsehood "grapple . . . in a free and open encounter." The concept was further advanced in the work of other English political thinkers who were influential in shaping the thinking of the American founders. Thomas Jefferson in his First Inaugural Address extolled "the safety with which error of opinion be tolerated where reason is left free to combat it." Such ideas have proliferated in American political rhetoric and are now entrenched in First Amendment jurisprudence. Courts in the United States have commonly declared, as a federal appellate judge recently did in summarizing the significance of the marketplace concept in American law, that the principle justifies "freedom of speech on the ground that the truth will prevail, and many of the most important cases under the First Amendment recite this position. The Framers undoubtedly believed it. As a general matter it is true."[3]

This book focuses its analysis on the nature of freedom within that marketplace. It presents the case that a marketplace of ideas in which one idea or interest is significantly advantaged over all others is in reality no marketplace at all. Such a marketplace is characterized by an inequitable distribution of opportunities. It is a market structured through law to maintain domination by a small number of favored participants, leaving others who would trade in the market at a disadvantage. A free marketplace of ideas advances democratic decisionmaking that reflects the interests of the citizenry at large. A market that structurally favors a few participants advances government shaped more by feudal deference to the interests of the advantaged powers.

On its face, it is a preposterous notion to suggest that Americans would embrace such changes to their system of democracy. How could the citizens of a nation "founded in liberty and dedicated to the proposition that all men are created equal" turn over self government to a handful of feudal lords? And of course, they wouldn't — at least not if proposed straightforwardly on those terms.

The changes discussed here, however, have been effected through a process far more sophisticated and nuanced in its reconstruction of the meaning of American democracy. Its roots can be traced to historical developments that began to unfold most clearly with the dramatic rise of the modern business corporation after the Civil War. Over the course of the twentieth century, mass media began to play an ever-greater role in shaping the way that developed societies negotiate meaning. Corporate efforts to influence public opinion assumed a more central role in that process as the century proceeded — the focal point of Chapter Two. Then in the 1970s, a focus on redefining the First Amendment through ideological strategies emerged as a prominent theme in those efforts, as detailed in Chapter Three.

Much conventional wisdom maintains that the past quarter-century or so was a time in which American political winds brought forth an age of less government and lower taxes, a revival of family values, an expansion of individual freedoms and opportunities. Certainly, many millions of Americans were told that was what they were voting for over those years. But the evidence suggests that the outcome of all that was closer to the opposite. Indeed, it seems more accurate that the past few decades witnessed not a "conservative" revolution, but a profit-imperative revolution. The actual concerns of middle America were more often drowned out in the marketplace of ideas as the restructuring of government focused instead more greatly on the relentless, short-term fiscal dictates of corporate interests.

Evidence offered in Chapter Four, for example, indicates that both government spending and the share of the tax burden most Americans pay grew dramatically over recent decades. Corporate profits skyrocketed while corporate taxes plummeted. More and more of the load was shifted to the middle class, considerably eroding its standard of living by many measures. Political rhetoric espousing love of country was accompanied by increasing numbers of Americans having their jobs shipped out of the country. Wages for most stagnated, while the costs of healthcare, housing, and education soared. With record numbers of families in bankruptcy, or teetering on the edge by the dawn of the twenty-first century, and so much popular media dominated by flash and trash, "family values" in actuality seemed to flourish in political hype more than anywhere else. And as economic mobility ground close to a halt in recent decades, the range of individual freedoms and opportunities that once represented the American Dream grew soberingly narrower by many indicators.

CORNERING THE MARKETPLACE OF IDEAS

If indeed Americans have experienced a country headed in the opposite direction from that in which majorities thought they were taking it with their votes, how could such a thing happen? This book argues that the contradictions derive to a great extent from the highly consequential shift in corporate strategy that can be identified as beginning most strikingly in the 1970s. That shift involved both heightened efforts to exert more effective corporate influence on government directly, as well as campaigns in media and in the courts to effect fundamental changes in the role that the corporation should occupy in American life and law.

Critical to the advancement of those efforts was a remarkably successful bid to corner to a great degree the very marketplace of ideas through an ideological campaign grounded in the stirring rhetoric of First Amendment rights. By promoting its objectives as vital to protecting the most precious fundamental rights of American citizens, the corporate free-speech movement steadily and solidly advanced its own interests over the course of the latter decades of the twentieth century.

That movement came into being at a time when corporate interests had been stung by the developments of the latter 1960s and early 1970s. A series of major regulatory initiatives was enacted during that period with the aim of more greatly protecting the environment, consumers, and workers, and that body of regulation was implemented through vigorous executive and judicial enforcement. The trends in the direction of such actively democratic governance from that period would prove relatively short-lived, however. They would usher in not more of the same but a stunningly successful counter-revolution. The sixties proved only a prelude to the greatest escalation of corporate initiatives to reshape American democracy that the nation had ever seen, as big business rapidly evolved the manner in which it engaged the political process. Over the course of the 1970s, for example, the number of corporations with public-affairs offices in Washington quintupled, so that more than 80 percent of the Fortune 500 companies had such offices operating in the nation's capital by 1980.

That period was also marked by sharply heightened coordination among corporate interests. The most prominent venture in that process was the 1972 formation of the Business Roundtable, an advocacy organization of the chief executive officers from virtually every major corporation in every American industry joined together to establish a unified political voice. The Roundtable's direct lobbying of legislators by CEOs, campaign-finance spending, and media activities designed to shape public opinion all were focused on mobilizing business interests in the formation of public policy. The new organization quickly grew as powerful as much longer-established entities such as the National Association of Manufacturers and the United States Chamber of Commerce, and would prove instrumental in defeating a series of major regulatory bills in Congress as well as lobbying to influence the drafting of many others.

Broadly speaking of course, there is nothing new in reporting that corporations have tremendous economic and political power or that they have engaged in efforts to expand that power. Scholars, journalists, activists, and other observers have in fact been pointing that out virtually over the entire course of the development of the modern business corporation during the past century and a half. What the evidence and arguments presented in these pages focus upon, however, is one of the most recent, extraordinary, and successful evolutions in the *nature* of corporate power.

For the 1970s were also the years when the corporate free-speech movement won landmark battles in the U.S. Supreme Court to endow political media spending by corporations with the powerful protections of the First Amendment. Until that time, the Constitution's protection for political expression had been recognized only for human individuals. Subsequent court cases additionally enhanced the role of corporate spending in American political discourse. As detailed in later chapters, the corporate free-speech movement has not yet won *absolute* First Amendment rights for corporate political media spending. But the Supreme Court majority that has resisted taking that step has shrunk in recent years. The early twenty-first century changes in the justices on the Court may in fact have reduced that majority to a minority even as this is written. So the establishing of corporate political media spending as a right even more fully protected from regulation by the First Amendment may come down to simply how long it takes dispositive cases on the subject to reach the High Court.

The 1970s were also the period in which the most prominent and prolific voice of the early corporate free-speech movement stormed upon the stage. Chapter Three includes analysis of the Mobil Oil Corporation's editorial-advocacy campaign of the seventies, a body of discourse that represents the nexus of the most definitive components of corporate ideological strategies that have been employed in a variety of venues since then. Historically, that campaign represents the richest set of texts for documenting the fundamentals of the corporate free-speech movement. In those messages, Mobil vigorously essayed to legitimize corporate political media spending as an activity fully embraced by the First Amendment. The corporate role in democratic processes was consistently framed as identical to that of the individual citizen, constructing an ideology that represented the corporation not as the *subject* of democratic decisionmaking but as a vital participant *within* such processes.

A worried nation struggled through the seventies to deal with recession, energy crises, double-digit inflation, crumbling industries, failure in Vietnam, and the corruption of Watergate. Big business focused on articulating the corporate profit imperative as not just the answer to the difficulties of the times but indeed as the only truly legitimate source of direction for American democracy. In essence, the message promised that where democracy had taken the nation off course, business would put matters right again. The basic rhetoric, assumptions and worldview promoted with ever-greater intensity in such messages as Mobil's over the course of the Seventies would become staples of political discourse. The Mobil campaign and the rise of the ideological movement it championed foretold the rise of a political culture largely focused on establishing a business-as-democracy theme as the fundamental guiding force in American democracy over the course of the period examined in these pages.

PROFIT IMPERATIVE AND COGNITIVE FEUDALISM

The theoretical mechanism through which the logic of the corporate free-speech movement translates into domination of the marketplace of ideas is laid out in chapters Five, Six, and Seven, but it can be summarized briefly here. Because the corporate form of business organization is endowed through legislative action with powerful economic advantages — particularly limited liability, perpetual life, and favorable treatment of the accumulation and distribution of assets — corporate managers wield significantly enhanced power to attract capital and to maximize return on shareholders' investments. As individuals with First Amendment rights, the corporate managers already have the same opportunities as any other citizen in the democracy to fully express all ideas, convey all information, argue all opinions as they may choose. Yet when government extends First Amendment rights to political spending by those managers from their corporate treasuries, it overwhelmingly advantages that spending in democratic decisionmaking. The significant, government-endowed advantages provided to the corporate form in the *economic* marketplace are thus transferred directly to the *political* marketplace of ideas.

To be clear, this book does not seek to discredit the function that profit-seeking serves in economic processes. The concern is with the implications of structurally and inordinately advantaging one entity in the marketplace of ideas — an entity that is created in law to prioritize one interest over all others. A business operating under the corporate form of organization is compelled to do all it can to pursue a course of action most likely to provide the greatest immediate fiscal gain. In that context, the profit imperative is not a function of greed. It is simply a fundamental obligation of the corporate charter.

Basically, under U.S. law, fiduciary responsibility requires corporate managers to prioritize the immediate interests of their companies, which essentially means maximizing shareholder profits at all times. American industrialists as mighty as Henry Ford have been forced to yield to this unwavering dictate when they sought to deviate from it — the iconic automaker being barred by the courts from implementing a plan to cut stockholders' dividends so he could sell his Model T's for a lower price.[4] In recent decades, more than ever, corporations that have failed to maximize stockholder profits have found themselves punished on Wall Street and in greater jeopardy of takeover. As Nobel Prize winning economist Milton Friedman so famously titled his influential 1970 essay, "The Social Responsibility of Business is to Increase its Profits." In Friedman's articulation of the dynamics of corporate law, "a corporate executive is an employee of the owners of the business. He has direct responsibility to his employers . . . which generally will be to make as much money as possible while conforming to the basic rules of the society."[5] Peter Drucker, one of the most widely recognized scholars in the study of corporate management, declared that "the first 'social responsibility' of business is then to make enough profit to cover the costs of the future. If this 'social responsibility' is not met, no other 'social responsibility' can be met."[6]

This is not to say that it is impossible for corporations ever to contribute to the greater social good, or that many people working at corporations do not sincerely wish to benefit society. But such impulses far too often must succumb to the overriding force of organizational dictates. It is not that the corporation is either good or evil, but rather that it simply is what it was designed to be, by law — the most effective profit-maximizing organism ever invented.

So for practical purposes today, corporate managers can pursue notions of social responsibility only in such instances when they may convince investors that the actions contribute directly to profitability.[7] But Wall Street has in recent decades increasingly demanded both immediate and maximized return on investment, punishing management by beating down stock prices of any company whose short-term profits have failed to meet expectations. Much recent analysis has asserted that the relentless quest for short-term financial gain has contributed to a process of sharply concentrating economic and political power in ever fewer hands. The process tends to be self-perpetuating. The concentration of such power intensifies its ability and motivation to concentrate its might further, even to the point of exceeding the power of any other institution to serve as a countervailing social force. In isolation, the profit imperative advances short-term fiscal gain at the expense of other interests and values — moral values, family values, community values, health values, environmental values. Certainly it can undermine the values of democratic governance and the quest for truth — as Franklin Roosevelt cautioned: "The liberty of democracy is not safe if we tolerate the growth of private power to the point that it is stronger than the democratic state itself." When Dwight Eisenhower warned Americans about the military-industrial complex endangering liberty and democratic processes, he was highlighting the threat of the profit imperative being allowed to dominate other interests in the name of national defense.[8]

In more contemporary developments, the profit imperative has found no problem with taking jobs from American workers and giving them to workers in countries where conditions mandate much lower wage scales. The profit imperative, left to its own devices, does not mind doing business with dictators — indeed, in many ways may prefer doing so. The profit imperative has tended to be quite comfortable with government accumulating massive debt in order to legislate expensive tax breaks, incentives, contracts, and subsidies for corporate interests. So in the context of the marketplace of ideas, the profit imperative must be moderated through real competition with other interests. Through democratic processes, the profit imperative can be restrained from its excesses, as long as it is not advantaged by government over other interests.

What this book argues therefore is essentially what Adam Smith argued: That the profit impulse can be harnessed for the better or for the worse. When *some* are advantaged by government in a marketplace, most of society is the worse for it. But when government works to maintain free markets — rather than providing advantages to some competitors — then society is the better for it. Smith's fundamental principles are central to the theoretical constructs that form the thesis of the chapters of Part II. As laid out particularly in Chapter Five, the line of reasoning that Smith focused upon the economic marketplace is employed in terms of the political marketplace of ideas. The latter is intrinsically relevant to American political culture because of the commanding role that marketplace-of-ideas theory has long played in shaping First Amendment jurisprudence in the United States.

In addition to the seminal economics of Adam Smith, the core conceptual framework of this book also draws most significantly upon two other influential theoretical foundations. One is the legal doctrine articulated extensively by the late Supreme Court Chief Justice William Rehnquist (Chapter Six). The other is the metaphorical model for connecting law and democracy asserted by First Amendment philosopher Alexander Meiklejohn (Chapter Seven). The three paradigms represented by those bodies of thought each provide elements vitally relevant to a unified understanding of the societal impact of constitutional protection for corporate political media spending.

Building upon those three schools of economic, legal, and philosophical thought, this book constructs a unified theoretical basis for placing recent trends in American political culture in context. That is, it seeks to explain the apparent contradictions between recent political rhetoric and reality in terms of a proposed understanding of marketplace-of-ideas theory. That understanding suggests conditions described here as cognitive feudalism are the probable result when corporate competitors are constitutionally advantaged in that marketplace. Literally speaking, a market in which some competitors are provided overwhelming structural advantages is no market at all. It is not a *free* market at least, because real freedom of competition is replaced by governing forces more feudal than free.

That assertion brings us to the broad historical parallel that this book hypothesizes: In much the way that feudal populations found their lives constrained within the parameters of the fiefdoms that dominated the terms of existence in that age, Americans in recent decades have increasingly found their world to be framed within parameters constructed to a greater degree than ever before by this age's dominant business corporations. Political and economic power has been concentrated ever more greatly in the hands of a relative few, translating into a society characterized more by deference to those centers of power than by democratic decisionmaking. With democratic governance weakened, relationships between individuals and sources of power have grown more feudal and have tended to erode the sovereignty of the people. In a marketplace of ideas with one interest significantly advantaged over all others, the free-market function has declined. What is left is what this book describes as cognitive feudalism.[9]

Why are these theoretical constructs important? As with any useful theory, a set of ideas is put forth as providing a valid explanation for a significant phenomenon, and observations are offered in support of the ideas. With the marketplace of ideas dominated by corporate political media spending, it becomes far more difficult to know which representations of reality are closer to truth and which are simply constructed by big business in order to advance the profit imperative. Techniques for manipulating public opinion have grown so advanced that through elaborate, sophisticated, extensive communication campaigns, money can create the appearance of information just as reasonable and relevant as information that is generated without such an agenda. The marketplace of ideas cannot function freely enough to sort out truth as intended, because some competitors are advantaged by government over most others. Therefore, the theoretical constructs of this book provide a basis for explaining which among competing versions of reality can be considered the more probable when government advantages corporate political spending in the marketplace of ideas.

Again, decrying the vast reach of corporate influence is not new. But what *is* new is the way that recent ideological strategies have been employed to engender acceptance for such corporate dominance. Critical in that effort has been the corporate free-speech movement and its reworking of the marketplace of ideas so as to tilt the market in favor of its interests over all others. Certainly of course, people continue to have other influences in their lives besides that driving theme of corporate ideology. The argument here is not that the profit imperative has come to dictate *all* understanding and behavior in American society, but that it has reached a level of influence more greatly in excess of what is healthy for democracy than ever before.

It is one thing to say that sellers should be free to promote their goods and services. It is another to say sellers with vast resources — many more extensive and overwhelming than most governments today — should be free to dominate democratic decisionmaking in order to promote their goods and services. The great danger emerging from the age of cognitive feudalism is its relentless push toward a world in which the very nature of humanity is being shaped by corporate interests — rather than the nature of the corporation being shaped by human interests.

This study endeavors to remain outside the current popular obsession with dichotomously categorizing all thought as either "liberal" or "conservative." Although many assertions in these pages challenge the political culture that has dominated recent decades, the challenge focuses on excessive concentration of power — whether it be in big business, big government, or both.[10] Much campaign rhetoric central to recent corporate ideological strategies has been categorized as "conservative" in the conventional terms of current parlance. Yet the success of those strategies in legitimizing the dominance of corporate interests in democratic decisionmaking has contradicted fundamental tenets of conservatism — most particularly by accelerating the centralization of power in American life on a greater order of magnitude than ever before. That dominance has in fact translated into much bigger *government* — precisely the opposite of what successful campaign rhetoric of recent decades has most often promised. And in a great many ways it is the very interests of countless citizens who call themselves conservative today that are most systematically undermined through the dominance of the profit imperative.

THE SOVEREIGNTY OF THE FEW

Thus, the corporate free-speech movement is characterized here as a significant component of broader societal trends that in recent decades have served to transform the quality of democratic decisionmaking to a historically significant degree, trending away from a sovereignty of the many toward a sovereignty of the few. The pages ahead examine an array of tangible examples by which the dominance of the profit imperative in the marketplace of ideas seems to have played out in dramatic ways during that period. To reemphasize though, the intention is not to indiscriminately condemn either profits or business corporations. Rather, the ultimate objective is to propose a vision of a society in which the nature of the corporation would be shaped by human interests — rather than the nature of humanity being shaped by corporate interests.

Certainly it would be impossible to legislate away all potential negative societal/political influences that may be associated with the corporate form of organizing business activity. But the assertion here is that evidence indicates First Amendment protection for corporate political media spending represents a dynamic of overwhelming proportion. As chapters, Eight, Nine, and Ten detail, a close split on the Supreme Court between justices who want to limit the First Amendment rights of such spending and those who want to expand it may be shifting in favor of the latter. The positions of those two camps reflect very different understandings of the way the marketplace of ideas works. Ideas — certainly the ideas of Supreme Court justices — can have consequences that change the course of history. So the ideas that are the focus of this book go far beyond theory. They hold the potential for truly staggering impact upon the lives of all Americans.

Even though debate on the full purpose of the First Amendment can never be resolved once and for all, it seems difficult to justify using that body of constitutional law to structure a marketplace of ideas in which one interest is advantaged overwhelmingly above all others. The chapters that follow articulate a philosophical and legal basis for advancing a political marketplace characterized instead by ongoing and truly free debate among as many interests as possible. In order for the marketplace of ideas to function as a free market, the ultimate interest of the business corporation must be one of many competing interests — not the interest that is provided with a structurally dominant role by government through constitutional law. To that end, the profit imperative must compete with other interests on an ongoing basis. And it must do so democratically, not feudally.

[1] The briefs highlighted were all filed in *Nike, Inc. v. Kasky*, 539 U.S. 654 (2003).

[2] See *Abrams v. United States*, 250 U.S. 616, 630 (1919) (Holmes, J., dissenting). For a recent discussion of Holmes' assertion as "the germ of modern free-speech law," see Richard A. Posner, *Law, Pragmatism, and Democracy* (Cambridge, Mass.: Harvard University Press, 2003), 360-61.

[3] This discussion of the significance of the marketplace-of-ideas concept was drawn in particular from W. Wat Hopkins, "The Supreme Court Defines the Marketplace of Ideas," *Journalism & Mass Communication Quarterly* 73, no. 1 (Spring 1996): 40-52; John Milton, *Areopagitica: A Speech of Mr. John Milton, for the Liberty of Unlicensed printing, to the Parliament of England* (1644; reprint, London: A. Millar, 1738), 51; John Gabriel Hunt, ed., *The Essential Thomas Jefferson* (New York: Gramercy, 1984), 199; Jeffery A. Smith, *Printers and Press Freedom: The Ideology of Early American Journalism* (New York: Oxford University Press, 1988), 31-41; Laurence H. Tribe, *American Constitutional Law*, 2d ed. (Mineola, N.Y.: Foundation, 1988), 785-86; *American Booksellers Association v. Hudnut*, 771 F.2d 323, 330 (7th Cir. 1985), affirmed 475 U.S. 1001 (1986).

[4] See *Dodge v. Ford Motor Co.*, 204 Mich. 459 (1919).

[5] Friedman argued against corporations "spending other people's money" in the name of social responsibility. "Insofar as his actions in accord with his 'social responsibility' reduce returns to stockholders, he is spending their money. Insofar as his actions raise the price to customers, he is spending the customers' money. Insofar as his actions lower the wages of some employees, he is spending their money." See Milton Friedman, "The Social Responsibility of Business is to Increase its Profits," *The New York Times Magazine*, 13 September 1970, in W. Michael Hoffman and Jennifer Mills Moore, *Business Ethics: Readings and Cases in Corporate Morality* (New York.: McGraw-Hill, 1984), 126-127.

[6] See Peter F. Drucker, "The New Meaning of Corporate Social Responsibility," *California Management Review* 26, no. 2 (winter 1984): 62.

[7] Even in the area of corporate philanthropic giving, which usually involves tax advantages for the donor, the courts have emphasized that such actions must by justified as advancing corporate interests. See, for example, *A.P. Smith v. Barlow*, 13 N.J. 145, 161 (1953), a seminal case on the subject.

[8] For a broader discussion of these trends and the concerns they raise, see Joel Balkan, *The Corporation: The Pathological Pursuit of Profit and Power* (New York: Free Press, 2004), 33-58; Ted Nace, *Gangs of America: The Rise of Corporate Power and the Disabling of Democracy* (San Francisco: Berrett-Koehler, 2003), 5, 172-73; David C. Korten, *When Corporations Rule the World*, 2ed. (Bloomfield, Conn.: Kumarian Press, 2001), 21-23; Robert

Kuttner, *Everything for Sale: The Virtues and Limits of Markets* (New York: Alfred A. Knopf, 1997), 39-67, 328-62; Ann Zimmerman, "Costco's Dilemma: Be Kind to Its Workers, or Wall Street?" *The Wall Street Journal*, 26 March 2004, sec. B, p. 1; Lawrence E. Mitchell and Geneva Overholser, "Higher Profits, Lower Costs: To What End?" Nieman Foundation for Journalism, 21 February 2006, accessed 22 February 2006 at: http://www.niemanwatchdog.org /index.cfm?fuseaction=background.view&backgroundid=0075; Frances Moore Lappe, Transcript of Interview, *NOW*, 9 December 2005, Accessed 12 December 2005 at: http://www.pbs.org/now/transcript/transcriptNOW149_full. html.

[9] To be clear, this conceptualization does not argue a *literal* feudalization of current American society, but rather a significant heightening of many basic dynamics historically characteristic of feudalism. For fuller discussion of such dynamics as referenced here, see: Clifford R. Backman, *The Worlds of Medieval Europe* (New York: Oxford University Press, 2003), 176-78; Jerry L. Singman, *Daily Life in Medieval Europe* (Westport, Conn.: Greenwood Press, 1999), x-xi, 2-8; Frank Barlow, *The Feudal Kingdom of England, 1042-1216*, 5th ed. (New York: Addison Wesley Longman, 1999), 6; Susan Reynolds, *Fiefs and Vassals: The Medieval Evidence Reinterpreted* (New York: Oxford University Press, 1994), 17, 20. For a discussion of the concept of the modern corporation as "feudal estate," see Marjorie Kelly, *The Divine Right of Capital: Dethroning the Corporate Aristocracy* (San Francisco: Berrett-Koehler, 2001), 41-50.

[10] It is instructive to consider that one of the parties filing an amicus brief in support of Nike in the case discussed earlier in this chapter was the American Civil Liberties Union, invariably characterized as "liberal" in popular discourse. In asserting that the matter "should be resolved through public debate and not in a courtroom," the ACLU reflexively embraced the simplistic First Amendment notion that all voices in such debate stand on equal footing with corporate political spending. See Brief for the American Civil Liberties Union, 3, *Nike, Inc. v. Kasky*, 539 U.S. 654 (2003) (No. 02-575). As Ted Nace put it in *Gangs of America*, 173-74, many monovisioned First Amendment defenders such as the ACLU fall into the trap of "seeing only the actors who remain in the game" once corporate political spending is constitutionally advantaged in the marketplace of ideas: "Thus it is the rights of these actors — corporations and the relatively few wealthy individuals who can match the resources of corporations — that the ACLU ends up defending."

CHAPTER TWO

Setting the Stage

The process that gave rise to the corporate free-speech movement in the 1970s has deep roots in the nation's history. Although the corporation did not take its place as a dominant institution until after the Civil War, Americans' concerns about the societal impact of organizing businesses in corporate form began much earlier. As the rise of the modern corporation began to reconfigure not only the nation's economic system but many legal, political, and cultural institutions as well, it soon collided with a deeply held distrust among the citizenry.

They saw in the second half of the nineteenth century a dramatically expanded use of the corporate form of organizing business, driven by abandonment of the inherited European tradition requiring an act of governmental charter in order to acquire corporate status. Within a relatively short period of time, such changes made incorporation routinely available to the largest business enterprises the world had ever seen. A nation accustomed to small operations rarely valued at more than $1 million now looked upon Standard Oil capitalized at $122 million by 1900, and just a few years later, American Tobacco at $500 million. The 1901 merger creating U.S. Steel represented a $1.4 billion transaction. The reinvention and expansion of the corporate form on such a previously unimagined scale sent shockwaves through American society and soon generated a backlash that would challenge the legitimacy of big business and lead in time to the rise of big government.

For many Americans, the staggering influence of the massive new business corporations loomed as a threat to societal balance, the very sort of excessive centralized power that American founders had sought to prevent. In barely a generation's time, corporate consolidation transformed the business landscape and seemed to have dwarfed traditional institutions of family, church, and local community. During one seven-year period at the turn of the century, a wave of mergers reduced 4,227 companies to a mere 257 corporations. By 1904, a group of 318 corporations controlled roughly two-fifths of the country's manufacturing assets. Through mergers and trusts, corporations were acquiring the ability to fix market shares and ensure profit margins within industries to an unprecedented degree. While the economy expanded and overall standard-of-living rose, wealth disproportionately pooled among a handful of citizens at the top. It engendered a level of alarm in public opinion that historian Roland Marchand documented as "a crisis of legitimacy" for big business.[1]

Efforts to rein in the excesses of the giant corporations and trusts began in the late nineteenth century, launching what would become the country's first major period of regulatory activity. A House committee report declared that "the concentration of wealth, money, and property in the United States under the control and in the hands of a few individuals or great corporations has grown to such an enormous extent that unless checked it will ultimately threaten the perpetuity of our institutions." That early series of major legislative efforts aimed at moderating the societal impact of big business included the Interstate Commerce Act in 1887, the Sherman Antitrust Act in 1890, the Tillman Act in 1907, and the Federal Trade Commission and Clayton Acts in 1914. "If we will not endure a king as a political power we should not endure a king over the production, transportation, and sale of the necessaries of life," said Senator John Sherman, sponsor of the Sherman Act.[2]

By the early part of the twentieth century, a series of Supreme Court decisions on balance had upheld enough of the regulatory legislation to bestow government with power on a scale relatively closer to that of big business.[3] Over the first decade and a half of the new century, a period of reform now called the Progressive Era saw the landmark 1911 breakup of Standard Oil and the American Tobacco Company by the Supreme Court for engaging in restraint of trade and monopoly.[4] More broadly, the period was highlighted by a flourishing of popular democracy, including the secret ballot, popular initiative and referendum, presidential primary elections, and women's right to vote. The creation of the Food and Drug Administration in 1906 represented the first consumer-protection legislation in American history.[5]

The turn of the century at the same time brought dramatic changes in social life and media influence. The middle-class American public of that time was experiencing the world in very different ways from the eighteenth-century public that was shaped by the American Revolution. Since that earlier time, the focus of American social life had shifted from the town square to the home parlor, contributing to greater isolation for most Americans and to the development of a disembodied public sphere that was shaped not by discourse among citizens but by the increasing influence of mass media. As the twentieth century approached, readership of chain newspaper and national-circulation magazines rose sharply, meaning that increasing numbers of Americans received identical constructions of mediated reality on a daily basis.[6]

Turn-of-the-century mass media were characterized by a "remarkable literature of indignation." Ida Tarbell's *The Standard Oil Company* and Henry Demarest Lloyd's *Wealth Against Commonwealth*, both targeting John D. Rockefeller and his Standard Oil Company, the largest corporation in the world, were among the most prominent.[7] It was becoming clear to the corporate giants that in addition to their business strategies they must develop strategies for influencing public opinion. Although most of the earliest efforts were rather clumsy, they would later begin to evolve into more effective public-relations campaigns. Also, academics of the day were beginning to respond to the historic social trends with concepts for managing modern democratic societies through the use of mass media. Soon they would begin contributing more sophisticated techniques to corporate efforts to influence public opinion.[8]

AN ABIDING AND WIDESPREAD FEAR

The deep-rooted intensity of feeling to which those early corporate public-opinion efforts were responding was grounded in a distrust of excessive concentrations of economic power, something that is reflected in cultural and political discourse back to the founding of the nation. While considering the intent behind the Sherman Act, in deciding a 1966 case, Supreme Court Justice Hugo Black wrote that "from this country's beginning there has been an abiding and widespread fear of the evils which flow from monopoly — that is the concentration of economic power in the hands of a few." Indeed, Thomas Jefferson had declared in 1816, "I hope we shall . . . crush in its birth the aristocracy of our monied corporations which dare already to challenge our government to a trial of strength, and bid defiance to the laws of our country."[9]

The business corporation as it is known today did not exist in the eighteenth century, but the origins of corporate forms for organizing large enterprises date to imperial Rome and the medieval church. Both those institutions maintained authority by requiring that associations and corporate bodies obtain official sanction. "In every state of society, from Rome to the present day, where social, economic and business life tends to become complex and intricate, and where the need for cooperation and collective endeavor becomes manifest," Maurice Wormser concluded in his history of the corporation, "there the idea of the corporation bursts forth into being and use, as irrepressible as a natural force."[10]

At the time of the American founding in 1776, Great Britain had banned corporations since the devastating 1720 collapse of the corrupt South Sea Company — a scandal that demonstrated long in advance of Enron how investors could be defrauded on a massive scale through a shell game of creative bookkeeping and promotion by corporate management. European "joint-stock" companies had begun forming centuries before, merchant enterprises bestowed by the crown with limited liability and monopoly powers. Their names became known around the world, with such operations as the Dutch United East India Company and the British East India Company controlling vast international trade empires, the London Company founding Virginia, the Massachusetts Bay Company colonizing New England, and the Hudson's Bay Company establishing much of what is now Canada.[11]

Early corporations in the United States followed the inherited British tradition of requiring an act of governmental charter in order to acquire corporate status, although only a handful of business corporations operated in America in the eighteenth century. Most businesses in the early days of the nation were either family owned or partnerships, rather than operated through corporate charters. From the 1780s into the mid-nineteenth century, business corporations in the United States were most often created for large endeavors such as canals, turnpikes, toll bridges, banks, insurance companies, and municipal water services. Some debate at the 1787 Constitutional Convention focused on giving only the federal government the power to charter corporations, but many states were opposed and ultimately no mention of the subject was included in the Constitution. The authority to grant corporate charters would over time be exercised almost exclusively by state legislatures.

The appeal of the corporate form lay in its ability to concentrate within a single entity virtually unlimited economic power by combining the capital of large numbers of investors. Limited liability meant that individual investors could not be held responsible for obligations of the corporation beyond their own personal investment. If a corporate venture failed, the rest of an investor's property remained safe from the company's creditors. An incorporated business took on a separate legal existence from its owners, a separation that simplified both financing (through the sale of ownership shares) and keeping businesses intact over multiple generations of owners.

The magnitude of such advantages over citizens operating businesses as individuals or through unincorporated partnerships proved immeasurable. Over the next several decades, the corporate instrument would come to dominate business organization in the United States. But all along the way, the gathering momentum of that process generated strong reaction from many quarters. Concerns focused on the impact that growing corporate power could have on democratic governance. For a nation founded as an experiment in democracy, it appeared that the use of a legal device for concentrating financial resources for public purposes was being appropriated to leverage unmatchable economic and political resources behind private agendas that prioritized profits over the public interest. In an 1855 corporation case, Supreme Court Justice James Moore Wayne observed that "combinations of these classes in society . . . united by the bond of a corporate spirit . . . unquestionably desire limitations upon the sovereignty of the people. . . . But the framers of the constitution were imbued with no desire to call into existence such combinations, nor dread of the sovereignty of the people."[12]

Nineteenth century journalist Ambrose Bierce's *The Devil's Dictionary* listed for the word "corporation" this definition: "An ingenious device for obtaining individual profit without individual responsibility."[13] In *Gain*, Richard Powers' remarkable historical novel on the corporation in American life, he reflected upon the experience of a nineteenth century businessman trying to come to grips with his partners' decision to incorporate the family soap factory (one that in

Powers' fictional account later evolves into a global multinational bearing a strong resemblance to Procter and Gamble):

> The very word smacked of failure. Incorporating would betray all that he and his brothers had worked these three decades to assemble. Back when the merchant Clares still wrinkled their noses at the stink of manufacturing, incorporation evoked universal hostility and suspicion. . . . Corporate franchises played fast and loose, a kind of cheating that nobody cottoned to, least of all the American capitalist. . . . If an owner couldn't manage his own firm without special privileges, he had no right to stay in business. . . . [Yet] when risks were distributed and liability defrayed, what might collective humanity not accomplish? . . . Civilization had stumbled upon that institution, one that might take it anywhere at all. . . . The limited-liability corporation: the last noble experiment, loosing an unknowable outcome upon its beneficiaries. Its success outstripped all rational prediction until, gross for gross, it became mankind's sole remaining endeavor.[14]

That passage is grounded solidly in nonfiction — the legal transformation of the corporate form over the course of the nineteenth century into an entity with few limitations on its operations and a great many constitutional rights previously guaranteed only to human individuals. Particularly after the Civil War, rapidly growing railroad corporations — mammoth, capital-intensive ventures — influenced legislatures to overhaul state laws of incorporation. The traditional special-charter procedures restricting corporate activity to designated purposes were steadily abandoned in favor of standardized, general-incorporation acts. By the turn of the century incorporation was routinely available to virtually any business by completing relatively minimal administrative procedures. States began competing feverishly to attract business, racing to eliminate ever more restrictions on corporate activity. No longer was business incorporation required to be for narrowly defined purposes, for limited times, or restricted to particular locations. Controls on mergers and acquisitions were lifted, as were rules against one company owning stock in another.

Gradually, corporate interests accumulated a series of victories before the Supreme Court as well, redefining the status of the corporation in American law. In 1809, corporations were determined to have the same access to the courts as individuals. A decade later, the Court protected corporate charters from arbitrary alterations by government, asserting that a corporation "is no more a state instrument than a natural person exercising the same powers would be." Twenty years after that, the Court limited constitutional protection available to the business corporation by ruling that a corporation was not a citizen within the meaning of Article Four's provision entitling citizens of each state to all privileges and immunities of citizens in the other states.[15] But after the Fourteenth Amendment was enacted in 1868, prohibiting states from depriving "any person of life, liberty, or property without due process of law," or denying "any person . . . equal protection of the laws," the Supreme Court in 1886 and 1889 "quietly accepted the proposition that a corporation was a 'person' within these guarantees."[16]

Supreme Court Justice Stephen Johnson Field, who served on the Court from to 1863 to 1897, regularly advanced that broadened understanding of corporate personhood to assert Fourteenth Amendment protections of corporate property rights. After the Court in 1876 upheld state regulations on excessive railroad and grain-elevator rates, he condemned any restrictions placed upon corporate activity as tantamount to holding that "all property and all business in the State are held at the mercy of a majority of its legislature."[17] In later years, Field's reasoning found a majority on the Court as it moved into several decades dominated by a doctrine in which legislative regulations on working conditions, wages, and other aspects of business were struck down regularly.

That period is often referred to as the "Lochner era," after the Supreme Court case *Lochner v. New York*, in which a state law setting the maximum work week for bakery employees at 60 hours was declared unconstitutional. Declaring that the protections of the due-process clause of the Fourteenth Amendment included "liberty of contract," the Court held that government could not interfere with the right of companies and citizens to enter into any contract as they may desire.[18] That doctrine and its emphasis on liberty of contract and substantive due process would dominate the Court well into the nineteen thirties. It paralleled the age when English philosopher Herbert Spencer's social Darwinism popularized a laissez-faire school of thought that condemned social legislation as contradicting laws of nature that dictate the weak must be weeded out in order to advance the survival of the fittest.[19]

A minority on the Court argued that all individuals are not masters of their own fate and that government had an obligation to protect their freedom of choices in some areas of life, including labor law. The Lochner majority would endure for some four decades, however. It was an era when "the realities of capitalism had decoupled the promise of human freedom from the consequences of economic freedom," in the assessment of economist Richard Parker.[20]

THE QUEST FOR A CORPORATE SOUL

The early decades of the twentieth century were also the time when both corporate efforts to shape public opinion and public relations as a profession began playing influential roles in American life. The two were brought into being by the same social and economic forces, historians conclude, and have developed in relationship to each other ever since. Merle Curti declared that the rise of the public relations specialist was inevitable once modern society became characterized by large organizations with critical needs to influence public opinion. Scott Cutlip wrote that the practice of public relations was produced most directly from the conflict that developed between the phenomenal growth in corporate power late in the nineteenth century and the corresponding growth of public concern over corporate influence on society. The concerns about big business focused upon the growing perception of the lack of a corporate "soul," Marchand found, with citizens worried most about the inability of the giant corporations to maintain a personal relationship with human beings as anything more than "units of consumption."[21]

Corporate interests had good reason to try and respond to such concerns. Economic historians have documented the significant role that public opinion has played in shaping government regulation of business activity in the United States. "What Americans have believed, since our beginnings, about the proper relationship between the people as a nation and the people as individuals going about their business," Albro Martin wrote, "is one of the three or four great pillars of the edifice we call history." Edward Kirkland called the Sherman Anti-

Trust Act "as much a political and social measure as an economic one." William Letwin argued that "economic doctrines have never as much influenced the making of American economic policy as have political and constitutional considerations." For Thomas McCraw, "Regulation is best understood as a political settlement, undertaken in an effort to keep peace within the polity."[22]

Early efforts on the part of big business to influence public opinion met with mixed success, but a landmark campaign launched in 1908 by American Telephone and Telegraph is considered the forerunner of modern corporate-advocacy messages. It promoted a theme of universal service by emphasizing language and images that represented AT&T as working endlessly to make that service something all Americans could count on anywhere and anytime. The campaign has been credited with diminishing support for government antitrust efforts against AT&T during that period. Two other early and particularly influential campaigns also were built around themes of corporate giants as vital benefactors of society. General Motors emphasized images of family and community in its "Making the Nation a Neighborhood" campaign, and General Electric represented electricity as the pinnacle of human advancement with its "Lighting the World" campaign.

Companies such as G.E., Eastman Kodak, National Cash Register, Standard Oil, U.S. Rubber, and Goodyear Tire and Rubber were part of a movement in the early twentieth century promoted as "New Capitalism." Its proponents "sought to demonstrate that corporations could be good without the coercive push of governments and unions." Pioneer advertising executive Bruce Barton promoted General Motors as a metaphor for the American family, "something personal, warm and human," with ads that told stories about people who drove GM vehicles — preachers, pharmacists, country doctors — to help other people in need. Distinctive corporate logos, such as those of Campbell's Soup, Heinz Pickles, and Quaker Oats, became a more prominent component of marketing efforts, including the promotion of characters like Uncle Ben, Aunt Jemima, and Old Grand-Dad.[23]

As the United States prepared to enter World War I, George Creel, a journalist and close advisor to President Woodrow Wilson, was a leader among Washington insiders who feared that the great numbers of recent immigrants to the United States would not support the war effort. When Wilson appointed Creel civilian director of the Committee for Public Information, he organized a propaganda effort that employed the forces of public relations, advertising, and entertainment to successfully promote the war as vital to saving the world for democracy. Although the effort produced a backlash of distrust and suspicion after the war among Americans who learned about manipulative and misleading techniques the CPI often employed, its effectiveness proved influential in future public-relations effort. After the war, business leaders recognized in the CPI's success that greater opportunities were available to sell their ideas and policies along with their goods and services. The institutionalization of public relations in the management structure and strategy of large corporations quickly gained even wider acceptance.[24]

The CPI veteran who went on to the greatest success in the business world was Edward Bernays. So influential was his role in shaping corporate communications efforts that he is commonly referred to today as the "father" of public relations. He had worked earlier in life as an entertainment publicist, and his CPI experience led him to write: "If today's leaders cannot do what they want without the approval of the masses, propaganda provides a useful tool for gaining that approval. This was well established by the success of government propaganda in World War I." Bernays' thinking was also shaped by his interest in social psychology. A double nephew to Sigmund Freud — Bernays' mother was Freud's sister, while his father's sister was Freud's wife — Bernays had deep discussions with the pioneer psychoanalyst on theories of how unconscious drives influence human behavior. Biographer Larry Tye concluded that Bernays "borrowed his uncle's insights into symbols and other forces that motivate people" in developing his concepts on public relations. But "while Freud sought to liberate people from their subconscious drives and desires . . . [Bernays] sought to exploit those passions." In Bernays' 1923 *Crystallizing Public Opinion*, he emphasized that individuals were influenced by the "herd" mentality of groups and that the values of groups tend to be represented by stereotypes that can be utilized by public-relations practitioners to influence public opinion.[25]

Bernays warned business leaders that they must defend themselves against the "menace" of government regulation and taxation and continually take measures to prevent public interference with their operations. The key to influencing public opinion, he wrote, was to enlist ideas already held by key publics and to associate those ideas with the interests that one seeks to promote. Those who understand the "conscious and intelligent manipulation of the organized habits and opinions of the masses . . . constitute an invisible government which is the true ruling power of our country," he wrote in *Propaganda*, a later book. "Good government can be sold to a community just as any other commodity can be sold." Cultural historian Stuart Ewen called Bernays' 1947 essay, "The Engineering of Consent," in which he further elaborated upon how to "open doors to the public mind" through mass media, "one of the clearest articulations of the assumptions and strategies that have guided public relations practices in the U.S." since that time.[26]

SHIFTING BALANCE OF POWER

The ability of all American institutions to engineer consent was challenged considerably by the Great Depression. Deep doubt and mistrust were created toward both government and business by the economic suffering and social dislocation that characterized the 1930s. Government was first to respond effectively as Franklin Roosevelt proved a natural publicist for his New Deal programs after being elected president in 1932. Roosevelt promoted the federal government as the means to redress imbalances created by corporate business excess, on which he publicly blamed the Great Depression. The overriding theme of his New Deal emphasized judging economic activity on the basis of the degree to which it served the greater good of the nation. Although not all New Deal programs were successfully instituted, on balance the period resulted in much greater government regulation of business and financial markets, as well as unprecedented government support for the rights of organized labor. The Social Security system, unemployment insurance, public welfare for the destitute, and minimum-wage and overtime laws were all established. The shift in federal policy has been described by legal scholar Arthur Miller as implementation of the positive state, "a shorthand term for the express acceptance by the federal government — and thus by the American people — of an affirmative responsibility for the economic well-being of all."[27]

At the Supreme Court, 1937 proved to be a watershed year, signaling the end of the *Lochner* era and shifting the balance of power between big business and big government. The Court upheld the constitutionality of a state minimum-wage law in *West Coast Hotel Company v. Parrish*, declaring, "Liberty implies the absence of arbitrary restraint, not immunity from reasonable regulations and prohibitions imposed in the interests of the community." In his majority opinion, Chief Justice Charles Evans Hughes, pointed out how the Great Depression had made clear the cost to the greater society of an unrestrained profit imperative. "There is an additional and compelling consideration which recent economic experience has brought into a strong light. The exploitation of a class of workers who are in an unequal position with respect to bargaining power and are thus relatively defenseless against the denial of a living wage is not only detrimental to their health and well being but casts a direct burden for their support upon the community. What these workers lose in wages the taxpayers are called upon to pay," Hughes wrote. "The community is not bound to provide what is in effect a subsidy for unconscionable employers. The community may direct its law-making power to correct the abuse which springs from their selfish disregard of the public interest."[28]

The same year, the Court upheld the National Labor Relations Act of 1935, a major piece of New Deal legislation. The act provided regulatory protections for unions, including a ban on employer interference with organizing efforts and government-supervised elections within factories to determine whether workers wanted a union. Chief Justice Hughes again grounded the case in terms of government protecting a marketplace of competing interests. "Employees have as clear a right to organize and select their representatives for lawful purposes as the respondent has to organize its business and select its own officers and agents," he wrote. "Discrimination and coercion to prevent the free exercise of the right of employees to self-organization and representation is a proper subject for condemnation by competent legislative authority." The Court's 1937 rulings set in motion a doctrine that allowed Congress to pass legislation affecting virtually every aspect of the conduct of business. The developments of the New Deal era meant that "the national government had assumed authority to regulate business in order to check the market power of large corporations," wrote business historians George David Smith and Davis Dyer.[29]

Bruce Barton, the advertising guru who was a preacher's son and later successfully ran for Congress, warned corporate leaders that they could not expect to win back public opinion simply by criticizing the New Deal. He told them that, from then on, big business would be required to court public opinion in the same way that politicians did. Corporations began to emphasize social responsibility in various individual campaigns, but even more significantly, many began working to coordinate their efforts to a greater degree. This occurred most prominently through the National Association of Manufacturers, a trade organization dating back to the nineteenth century, which was revamped in the early 1930s to focus on winning public support for big business. Such moves came partly in response to the New Deal and more broadly to fears of growing government regulation, greater public awareness of corporate efforts to influence public opinion, and widening popular support for socialism as the answer to the economic woes of the period. To that end, NAM organized groups of community leaders across the nation into grassroots networks that promoted the role of business in American life. Through its "American Way" campaign, NAM utilized extensive media messages to construct ideological themes of free enterprise as the protector of the freedom of individuals against what was characterized as the oppression of government.[30]

World War II saw improvement in public opinion toward American corporate giants as they provided industrial and organizational might that helped drive the successful war effort and served as demonstrations of their patriotism. And once again the wartime effort provided wider training in public-relations techniques, as more than 100,000 Americans worked in the Office of War Information and other government publicity offices. Many of those workers went on find employment in corporate public relations as the business community grew more successful in influencing government in the post-World War II era. The improved public image of big business in the postwar era was enhanced by soaring affluence in the United States and the corporations' ongoing image campaigns to promote their support for civic causes and for democracy, especially during the Cold War. The Hill and Knowlton advertising agency was prominent among those involved in substantial efforts during that time to amplify the voice of industry and educate Americans on the role of big business. President Dwight D. Eisenhower's administration has been described by historian Robert Griffith as "the corporate commonwealth," promoting "a deeply conservative image of a good society in which conflict would yield to cooperation, greed to discipline, coercion to self-government." Indeed, the postwar decades were characterized by widely shared economic advancement, with huge corporate expansion and a rising standard of living for more Americans than ever before. The concentration of wealth owned by the top one percent of the population fell from forty-five percent in 1929 to twenty percent by 1971. Economist John Kenneth Galbraith wrote in 1952 that corporate economic might had been successfully balanced by "the countervailing power of those who are subject to it" through the strengthening of labor unions, government regulatory bodies, and civic institutions.[31]

To whatever degree that pronouncement of such a happy state of affairs was indeed the case at that point in American history, it was not to last. After the relative stability of the Eisenhower era, the government-business relationship went through a far more tumultuous and contentious evolution in the 1960s and '70s, leading to an effort on the part of big business far beyond the scale of any previous to address what it viewed as a political and social imbalance unfavorable to business interests. Most significantly, it would focus aggressively and effectively on the marketplace of ideas and would in time evolve into the most consequential development in the history of corporate efforts to shape public opinion.

A NEW BLUEPRINT FOR BIG BUSINESS

The sixties are well remembered for the sharp rise in public-interest activism, sparked at least in part by corporate roles in environmental, consumer, and civil-rights problems. That was followed by the economic decline of seventies — the nation's worst since the 1930s. The downturn was characterized by energy shortages, skyrocketing inflation, and greatly increased competition for U.S. corporations from Japan, Germany, and other nations recovering from their World War II devastation. The period brought the enactment of a number of major regulatory initiatives as well as vigorous executive and judicial enforcement. A broad and energized public-interest movement drove the push for cleaner air, safer automobiles, labeling of food, lending reform, and other consumer protections.[32]

Consumers were demanding and getting such concessions from corporations as safety features, toll-free complaint lines, and more generous warranties, while even business-school students were joining the clamor on college campuses for greater social consciousness from big business. "Not since the trust-busting days of Theodore Roosevelt has the force of public opinion intruded so emphatically on the business community's patterns of operation," declared *The New York Times*. Environmental and consumer concerns were becoming a more prominent factor of business life than ever before. A series of major power, mining, paper, and chemical plants were canceled or altered over environmental issues in 1969, and Ford Chairman Henry Ford II called environmental issues the biggest problem facing the auto industry. Monsanto President Edward Bock said, "If efforts to correct social problems fail, long-range corporate progress will be limited."[33]

The regulations of the era represented a break from the past in that a great number of the new laws were not industry-specific, as had typically been the case before, but applied to business in general. Further distinguishing those years from previous periods of heightened regulatory activity, business historian David Vogel concluded, "was a quantitative and qualitative increase in the scope and intrusiveness of federal controls over corporate social performance . . . and most critically, in sharp contrast to both the Progressive Era and the New Deal, government social regulatory policy became far more politicized." Evidence of public disapproval of business in the early seventies was reflected in polling on the subject. Yankelovich polls showed the number of Americans who agreed that business was striking a fair balance between profits and the public interest dropped from 70 percent in 1968 to 32 percent by 1972. Harris polls found that the number of Americans expressing confidence in the leaders of major companies dropped from 55 percent in 1966 to 27 percent by 1971.[34]

For a while, the situation created considerable confusion and disarray among various industries and trade associations that in the past had had relatively fewer occasions to create ongoing political alliances that crossed industry lines. In time, however, the fact was driven home to big business that new means of collective influence were needed to focus on the legislative process more effectively. Over the course of the seventies, big business dramatically overhauled its manner of engaging that process. More than half of the 80 percent of the Fortune 500 companies with their own Washington offices by 1980 created them after 1970. Between 1974 and 1982, the number of corporate political-action committees soared from 89 to 1,467. By the end of the seventies, persons employed by private industry to represent its interests in the nation's capital outnumbered federal employees in the Washington metropolitan area. "Legislators have tended to be more receptive to the public interest than they might have been to business," an executive of the National Association of Manufacturers told *Consumer Reports* magazine. "We are attempting to balance the scales." Political journalist Thomas Byrne Edsall in his history of the period wrote that "the political stature of business rose steadily from the early 1970s, one of its lowest points in the nation's history, until, by the end of the decade, the business community had achieved virtual dominance of the legislative process in Congress."[35]

The unprecedented mobilization of business interests focused on successfully defeating major regulatory bills in Congress and effectively lobbying to influence the drafting of others. But most significant historically was the heightened focus by corporate interests on actively reshaping the marketplace of ideas. In 1972, General Motors Chief Executive Officer R.C. Gerstenberg effectively offered a blueprint for the strategy that would be stressed by big business in seeking to influence public opinion. In a *New York Times* op-ed column, Gerstenberg argued that the low estimation of business responsibility that Americans had expressed in recent years was due to citizens' lack of understanding of the free-enterprise system. Business must respond quickly to remedy that situation, he declared. "Recent experience teaches us that the importance of public opinion should never be underestimated, that legislation follows opinion, and uninformed opinion can lead to bad legislation and to unreasonable controls and restraints by government. We in the auto industry have seen a great deal of this in recent years," Gerstenberg said. "The business community has a job to do. . . . Individually and collectively, we must speak out more than we have. We must reach new audiences outside of the business community."[36]

Such contentions were articulated with ever-greater frequency by corporate leaders in the seventies. For the U.S. Chamber of Commerce, the clarion call for coordinated political activism by the business community came in a report written by corporate attorney Lewis F. Powell —less than six months before taking his seat as a justice on the Supreme Court. "Few elements of American society today have as little influence in government as the American businessman, the corporation, or even the millions of corporate stockholders," he wrote. "Current examples of the impotency of business, and of the near-contempt with which businessmen's views are held, are the stampedes by politicians to support almost any legislation related to 'consumerism' or to the 'environment.' " Powell called for corporations to wage through advertising and other public discourse "a sustained, major effort to inform and enlighten the American people," not only separately but with a level of coordination beyond any ever mounted at that time. "Strength lies in organization, in careful long-range planning and implementation, in consistency of action over an indefinite period of years, in the scale of financing available only through joint effort, and in the political power available only through united action and national organizations," he wrote.[37]

One entirely new joint effort in corporate political power proved so effective so quickly that by the mid seventies *Business Week* called it "the most powerful voice of business in Washington." The Business Roundtable was formed in 1972 by some 200 of the chief executive officers from the nation's largest corporations in order to establish a unified political voice representing their diverse business interests. They had concluded that the wave of federal business regulation enacted over the previous decade required a different form of response. The Roundtable's activities included one-on-one lobbying of legislators by the CEOs directly, campaign-finance spending through political-action committees, and media activities designed to shape public opinion. All were focused on the organization's ultimate goal of playing "an active and effective role in the formation of public policy." The Roundtable's corporate membership consisted of virtually every important company in every industry, including General Electric, Westinghouse, U.S. Steel, ALCOA, Exxon, IBM, Xerox, AT&T, American Express, Mobil, Merrill Lynch, Bechtel, International Harvester, Boeing, Bank of America, Citibank, Coca-Cola, Nabisco,

General Foods, Quaker Oats, Du Pont, Dow Chemical, Monsanto, Allied Chemical, Johnson and Johnson, Shell, Procter and Gamble, Merck, Ford, General Motors, Chrysler, Sears, Firestone, Goodyear, and Texaco.[38]

The prowess of organizing diverse business interests into a unified political front was demonstrated almost from the start. John D. Harper, a chairman of the Roundtable in the early seventies, said the organization was formed because the American corporation was under heavy fire from opponents, with "no one rushing to the defense of this endangered species." Combining their considerable resources to meet what they perceived as an attack on big business, the CEOs "launched a new-style political activism on several fronts" designed to regain lost ground and curb the influence of the public-interest movement and organized labor. "Less than a decade later, all their objectives had been accomplished," business historian Scott Bowman concluded. Putting it more bluntly, *Fortune* magazine declared that the Roundtable quickly made itself "the biggest and baddest lobbying group in Washington . . . the Green Berets of business influence."[39]

For all its clout in Washington, however, it would not be the Business Roundtable that found the public voice to express the most revolutionary vision of the corporate role in American life. The experience of the Progressive, New Deal, and sixties eras had all demonstrated for corporate powers the deep, ongoing disjunction between their interests and the widely held distrust of concentrated economic power that had been a part of the nation's psyche since its very founding. That distrust, with its enduring narrative power as a source of authority and meaning in American lives, had yet to be truly overcome. Beyond all the expanded political activity of the seventies, what was really needed was a new way of defining freedom in popular discourse — a campaign with ideological force and consistency that would represent the corporation as *synonymous* with democracy, rather than a threat to it. Although variations on that theme had appeared in earlier business discourse, a truly compelling and comprehensive assertion had yet to be established. But the player who would do just that was about to step onstage and take the spotlight.

Mobil would become such a prominent champion of the corporate free-speech movement in the 1970s that historian Walter Berns titled an essay he published at the end of the decade "The Corporation's Song:

Book and Lyrics by Hobbes, Locke, and Madison. Music by Mobil Oil?"[40] As the next chapter will detail, the company's campaign of editorial advocacy would prove to be the most influential of its kind in history. Mobil was never a plaintiff or a defendant in a First Amendment case in the seventies, and its concept of the corporate citizen was not itself ever literally reviewed by the Supreme Court. Yet by the end of the decade, neither had the Court in its landmark series of pronouncements on corporate political media spending contradicted the theory that the corporation was every bit as legitimate a part of democratic processes as were human individuals. Mobil in its advocacy campaign caught an ideologically powerful wave at just the right moment and went on to ride it farther and more flamboyantly than any other figure in the corporate free-speech movement.

[1] See Roland Marchand, *Creating the Corporate Soul: The Rise of Public Relations and Corporate Imagery* (Berkeley: University of California Press, 1998); George David Smith and Davis Dyer, "The Rise and Transformation of the American Corporation," in Carl Kaysen, ed., *The American Corporation Today* (New York: Oxford University Press, 1996); James Willard Hurst, *The Legitimacy of the Business Corporation in the Law of the United States, 1780-1970* (Charlottesville: University of Virginia Press, 1970); Thomas K. McCraw, "Business & Government: The Origins of the Adversary Relationship," *California Management Review* 26, no. 2 (winter 1984): 33-52.

[2] See Thomas K. McCraw, *Prophets of Regulation: Charles Francis Adams, Louis D. Brandeis, James M. Landis, Alfred E. Kahn* (Cambridge: Belknap Press of Harvard University Press, 1984); H.R. Rep. No. 627, 63d Congress, at 19 (1914); 21 Congressional Record 2457 (1890) (statement of Senator Sherman).

[3] See in particular *Munn v. Illinois*, 94 U.S. 113 (1876); *U.S. v. Trans-Missouri Freight Association,* 166 U.S. 290 (1897); *U.S. v. Northern Securities,* 193 U.S. 197 (1904); and *Muller v. Oregon,* 208 U.S. 412 (1908).

[4] See *Standard Oil v. United States*, 221 U.S. 1 (1911) and *United States v. American Tobacco*, 221 U.S. 106 (1911). The legislative history behind the antitrust laws reflects an effort by the drafters to write the provisions with deliberately broad language in an effort to eliminate loopholes for escaping the intent of the Congress. See Keith Conrad, "Media Mergers: First Step in a New Shift of Antitrust Analysis?" 49 *Federal Communication Law Journal* 675 (1997): 684-88; Gary Minda, "Interest Groups, Political Freedom, and Antitrust: A Modern Reassessment of the Noerr-Pennington Doctrine," 41 *Hastings Law Journal* 905 (1990): 908-09. That intent has been characterized as an effort to enact the " 'Magna Carta of free enterprise,' guaranteeing to 'each and every business, no matter how small,' the freedom to compete." Wesley A. Cann, Jr., "Section 7 of the Clayton Act and the Pursuit of Economic 'Objectivity': Is There Any Role for Social and Political Values in Merger Policy?," 60 *Notre Dame Law Review* 273 (1985): 280 (quoting *United States v. Topco*, 405 U.S. 596, 610 (1972)).

[5] For a fuller discussion of the remarkable reforms of the Progressive Era, see, for example, Kenneth Fox, *Better City Government: Innovation in American Urban Politics, 1850-1937* (Philadelphia: Temple University Press, 1977); Morton Keller, *Affairs of State: Public Life in Late Nineteenth-Century America* (Cambridge, Mass.: Harvard University Press, 1977); Martin J. Schiesl, *The Politics of Efficiency: Municipal Administration and Reform in America, 1880-1920* (Berkeley: University of California Press, 1977); Jon C. Teaford, *The Unheralded Triumph: City Government in America, 1870-1900* (Baltimore: Johns Hopkins University Press, 1984); Nell Irvin Painter, *Standing at Armageddon: The United States, 1877-1917* (New York: Norton,

1987); Morton Keller, *Regulating a New Economy: Public Policy and Economic Change in America, 1900-1933* (Cambridge, Mass.: Harvard University Press, 1990); John Whiteclay Chambers II, *The Tyranny of Change: America in the Progressive Era, 1890-1920* (New York: St. Martin's Press, 1992); Sean Dennis Cashman, *America in the Gilded Age: From the Death of Lincoln to the Rise of Theodore Roosevelt*, (New York: New York University Press, 1993); Morton Keller, *Regulating a New Society: Public Policy and Social Change in America, 1900-1933* (Cambridge, Mass.: Harvard University Press, 1994); Charles W. Calhoun, ed., *The Gilded Age: Essays on the Origins of Modern America* (Wilmington, Del.: Scholarly Resources, 1996); Mark Wahlgren Summers, *The Gilded Age: or, The Hazard of New Functions* (Upper Saddle River, N.J.: Prentice-Hall, 1997); Sidney M. Milkis and Jerome M. Mileur, eds., *Progressivism and the New Democracy* (Amherst, Mass.: University of Massachusetts Press, 1999).

[6] See Stuart Ewen, *PR! A Social History of Spin* (New York: Basic, 1996).

[7] See Albro Martin, "Uneasy Partners: Government-Business Relations in Twentieth-Century American History," in Robert F. Himmelberg, ed., *Government-Business Cooperation, 1945-1864*, vol. 9 of *Business and Government in America Since 1870* (New York: Garland, 1994), 233-37. It was Rockefeller who had pioneered the use of the trust as a means of structuring business by which leading producers in an industry would exchange certificates for common stock in each other's corporations. See Eleanor M. Fox and Lawrence A. Sullivan, "Antitrust — Retrospective and Prospective: Where Are We Coming From? Where Are We Going?," 62 *New York University Law Review* 936, 939 (1987); David Millon, "The Sherman Act and the Balance of Power," 61 *Southern California Law Review* 1219, 1219 (1988).

[8] See Scott M. Cutlip, *The Unseen Power: Public Relations, A History* (Hillsdale, N.J.: Lawrence Erlbaum, 1994), 1-3.

[9] See *United States v. Von's Grocery*, 384 U.S. 270, 274 (1966); Letter to Tom Logan, Nov. 1816, in Paul Leicester Ford, *The Works of Thomas Jefferson*, vol. 12 (New York: G.P. Putnam's Sons, 1905), 42.

[10] See I. Maurice Wormser, *Frankenstein Incorporated* (New York: Whittlesey House, 1931), 7-8.

[11] For a broader discussion of the early history of the corporation, see Jack Beatty, ed., *Colossus: How the Corporation Changed America* (New York: Broadway, 2001); William G. Roy, *Socializing Capital: The Rise of the Large Industrial Corporation in America* (Princeton, N.J.: Princeton University Press, 1997); Scott Bowman, *The Modern Corporation and American Political Thought: Law Power and Ideology* (University Park: Pennsylvania State University Press, 1996); Mansel G. Blackford and K. Austin Kerr, *Business Enterprise in American History*, 2d ed. (Boston, Mass.: Houghton Mifflin, 1990); Ronald E. Seavoy, *The Origins of the American Business Corporation,*

1784-1855: Broadening the Concept of Public Service During Industrialization (Westport, Conn.: Greenwood Press, 1982); Edward Merrick Dodd, *American Business Corporations Until 1860* (Cambridge, Mass.: Harvard University Press, 1934); Joseph S. Davis, *Essays in the Earlier History of American Corporations* (Cambridge, Mass.: Harvard University Press, 1917); John P. Davis, *Corporations*. (1905; reprint, New York: Capricorn Books, 1961).

[12] See *Dodge v. Woolsey*, 59 U.S. 331, 377-78 (1855).

[13] See Ambrose Bierce, *The Unabridged Devil's Dictionary*, David E. Schultz and S.T. Joshi, eds. (Athens, Ga.: University of Georgia Press, 2000).

[14] See Richard Power, *Gain* (New York: Picador, 1999), 155-59.

[15] See *Bank of the United States v. Deveaux*, 9 U.S. 61 (1809); *Dartmouth College v. Woodward*, 17 U.S. 518, 636 (1819); *Bank of Augusta v. Earle*, 38 U.S. 519 (1839).

[16] See James Willard Hurst, *The Legitimacy of the Business Corporation in the Law of the United States, 1780-1970* (Charlottesville: University of Virginia Press, 1970), 64-65, in reference to *Santa Clara County v. Southern Pacific Railroad* 118 U.S. 394 (1886) and *Minneapolis and St. Louis Railroad v. Beckwith* 129 U.S. 26 (1889). For further discussion of that dramatic evolution of the understanding of corporate personhood in U.S. law, see Gregory A. Mark, "The Personification of the Business Corporation in American Law," 54 *University of Chicago Law Review* 1441 (1987).

[17] See *Munn v. Illinois*, 94 U.S. 113, 140 (1905) (Field, J., dissenting).

[18] See *Lochner v. New York*, 198 U.S. 45 (1877).

[19] In his most popular book, Spencer wrote that "when regarded not separately, but in connection with the interests of universal humanity, . . . harsh facilities are seen to be full of the highest beneficience — the same beneficience which brings to early graves the children of diseased parents, and singles out the low-spirited, the intemperate, and the debilitated as the victims of an epidemic." Herbert Spencer, *Social Statics, or, The Conditions Essential to Human Happiness Specified, and the First of Them Developed* (New York: D. Appleton, 1872), 354. See also Mike Hawkins, *Social Darwinism in European and American Thought, 1860-1945* (New York: Cambridge University Press, 1997); Karen Orren, *Belated Feudalism: Labor, the Law, and Liberal Development in the United States* (New York: Cambridge University Press, 1991; Richard Hofstadter, *Social Darwinism in American Thought, 1860-1915* (Philadelphia: University of Pennsylvania Press, 1945).

[20] "This case is decided upon an economic theory which a large part of the country does not entertain," wrote Justice Oliver Wendell Holmes. "The Fourteenth Amendment does not enact Mr. Herbert Spencer's *Social Statics*." See *Lochner v. New York*, 198 U.S. 45, 75 (1877). (Holmes, J., dissenting). See also Richard Parker, *John Kenneth Galbraith: His Life, His Politics, His*

Economics (New York: Farrar, Straus and Giroux, 2005), 654; Cass R. Sunstein, "Lochner's Legacy," 87 *Columbia Law Review* 873 (1987).

[21] See Merle Curti, *The Growth of American Thought*, 3d ed. (New Brunswick, N.J.: Transaction, 1964), 501; Cutlip, *The Unseen Power: Public Relations, A History*, 1-3; Marchand, *Creating the Corporate Soul*, 8-9.

[22] See Albro Martin, "Uneasy Partners," 233-234; Edward C. Kirkland, "The Robber Barons Revisited," in Robert F. Himmelberg, ed., *The Rise of Big Business and the Beginnings of Antitrust and Railroad Regulation, 1870-1900*, vol. 1 of *Business and Government in America Since 1870* (New York: Garland, 1994), 166; William Letwin, *A Documentary History of American Economic Policy Since 1789* (Garden City, N.Y.: Anchor Books, 1961), xxix-xxx; Thomas K. McCraw, *Prophets of Regulation*, 302.

[23] See Kim McQuaid, "Young, Swope and General Electric's 'New Capitalism': A Study in Corporate Liberalism, 1920-33," *American Journal of Economics and Sociology* 36 (1977); Naomi Klein, *No Logo* (New York: Picador, 1999), 6-7.

[24] See Ewen, *PR! A Social History of Spin*, 102 27.

[25] See Larry Tye, *The Father of Spin: Edward L. Bernays and the Birth of Public Relations* (New York: Crown, 1998), 8-9, 193, 197; Edward L. Bernays, *Propaganda* (New York: Liveright, 1928), 27-28;

[26] See Edward L. Bernays, *Crystallizing Public Opinion* (New York: Liveright, 1923), 141-3; Edward L. Bernays, *Propaganda* (New York: Liveright, 1928), 9, 105; Edward L. Bernays, *The Engineering of Consent* (Norman: University of Oklahoma Press, 1955). Also on Bernays' influence on the practice of public relations, see Stuart Ewen, *PR! A Social History of Spin* (New York: Basic, 1996), 12-13, 131-46, 373-98.

[27] See Ewen, *PR! A Social History of Spin*, 233-46; Arthur Selwyn Miller, *The Supreme Court and American Capitalism* (New York: The Free Press, 1968), 73-74, 85, 90-91.

[28] See *West Coast Hotel Company v. Parrish,* 300 U.S. 379, 392, 399-400 (1937). In the first instance, Hughes was quoting from the Court's earlier opinion in *Chicago, B. & Q. R. Co.* v. *McGuire*, 219 U.S. 549, 567 (1911).

[29] See *National Labor Relations Board v. Jones & Laughlin Steel*, 301 U.S. 1, 33 (1937); Mansel G. Blackford and K. Austin Kerr, *Business Enterprise in American History*, 2d ed. (Boston: Houghton Mifflin, 1990), 334-5; Smith and Dyer, "The Rise and Transformation of the American Corporation," 50-51.

[30] For discussion of this period of corporate efforts to influence public opinion, see Marchand, *Creating the Corporate Soul*, 202-49, 322-23; and Ewen, *PR! A Social History of Spin*, 288-336.

[31] See Karen S. Miller, *The Voice of Business: Hill & Knowlton and Postwar Public Relations* (Chapel Hill: University of North Carolina Press,

1999); Robert Griffith, "Dwight D. Eisenhower and the Corporate Commonwealth," in Robert F. Himmelberg, ed., *Government-Business Cooperation, 1945-1864*, vol. 9 of *Business and Government in America Since 1870* (New York: Garland, 1994), 100, 133-34; Kevin Phillips, *Wealth and Democracy: A Political History of the American Rich* (New York: Broadway Books, 2002), 68-82.; John Kenneth Galbraith, *American Capitalism: The Concept of Countervailing Power*, rev. ed. (White Plains, N.Y.: M.E. Sharpe, 1980), 108-34.

[32] See Jack Beatty, ed., *Colossus: How the Corporation Changed America* (New York: Broadway, 2001), 357-71, 377-81, 468-86, 489.

[33] See Isadore Barmash, "That Angry Voice? It's a Consumer's," *The New York Times*, 11 January 1970, sec. 12, p. 29; John S. Fielden, "Making Executives of Students Will Take More than Haircut," *The New York Times*, 11 January 1970, sec. 12, p. 27; Gladwin Hill, "Industrialists Get Word: Environment," *The New York Times*, 11 January 1970, sec. 12, p. 22; "12 Business Leaders Answer Questions on the Future," *The New York Times*, 11 January 1970, sec. 12, p. 35-36.

[34] See David Vogel, "The 'New' Social Regulation in Historical and Comparative Perspective," in Thomas K. McCraw, ed., *Regulation in Perspective: Historical Essays* (Cambridge, Mass.: Harvard University Press, 1981), 155-59; Seymour Martin Lipset and William Schneider, "How's Business? What the Public Thinks," *Public Opinion* 1:3 (August 1978): 41.

[35] See Kim McQuaid, "Big Business and Public Policy in Contemporary United States," in Robert F. Himmelberg, ed., *Regulatory Issues Since 1964*, vol. 11 of *Business and Government in America Since 1870* (New York: Garland, 1994), 177-9; James Q. Wilson, "The Corporation as a Political Actor," in Carl Kaysen, ed., *The American Corporation Today* (New York: Oxford University Press, 1996), 413-22; Thomas Byrne Edsall, *The New Politics of Inequality* (New York: W.W. Norton, 1984), 107-108, 131; David Vogel, *Fluctuating Fortunes: The Political Power of Business in America* (New York: Basic Books, 1989), 195-98; "Business Lobbying: Threat to the Consumer Interest," *Consumer Reports*, September 1978, p. 527.

[36] See R.C. Gerstenberg, "To Tell the Truth," *The New York Times*, 29 December 1972, sec. 1, p. 23.

[37] In a speech at the David A. Clarke School of Law in 2001, Supreme Court Justice Ruth Bader Ginsberg characterized the impact of the report: "Powell's idea took hold as an array of public interest legal foundations were established to represent 'conservative' or business groups, for example, the Washington Legal Foundation, the Pacific Legal Foundation, the Mountain States Legal Foundation." See "In Pursuit of the Public Good: Lawyers who Care," Joseph L. Rauh Lecture, 9 April 2001, Supreme Court of the United States website, accessed 31 May 2006 at: http://www.supremecourtus.gov/publi

cinfo/speeches/sp_04-09-01a.html#foot14. The U.S. Chamber of Commerce distributed the "Powell Memorandum" to its national membership in its August 23, 1971, *Washington Report* under the headline "Confidential Memorandum: Attack on American Free Enterprise System." It has been widely distributed in recent years, including on the Media Transparency website at: http://www.mediatransparency.org/story.php?storyID=22.

[38] See "Business' Most Powerful Lobby in Washington," *Business Week*, 20 December 1976, p. 60; "Business Roundtable History," The Business Roundtable, accessed 10 July 2004 at: http://www.businessroundtable.org/aboutUs/history.html.

[39] See Patrick J. Akard, "Corporate Mobilization and Political Power: The Transformation of U.S. Economic Policy in the 1970s," *American Sociological Review* 57:5 (October 1992): 602; "The Embattled Businessman," *Newsweek*, 16 February 1976, p. 58; Bowman, *The Modern Corporation and American Political Thought*, 145; "The Fallen Giant," *Fortune*, 8 December 1997, 156.

[40] See Walter Berns, "The Corporation's Song: Book and Lyrics by Hobbes, Locke, and Madison. Music by Mobil Oil?" in *Prosperity and Freedom: The Founding Fathers, Commerce, and the Corporation* (Washington, D.C.: American Enterprise Institute, 1981), 1-10.

CHAPTER THREE

An Ideology Blossoms

The president of Pizza Hut, the largest pizza chain in the country and a division of the Yum Brands conglomerate, was asked in a business-section interview a few years ago about a bill that had been introduced in the U.S. Congress that would require fast-food restaurants to print nutritional information on their menus. His answer: "This is an interesting debate, especially in a country like the United States, that prides itself on individual freedom. What role does the government play in mandating what people eat?" The manner in which a question about proposed regulations on corporate behavior was instantly reframed as a threat of government taking away the freedoms of individual Americans was reflective of a much broader trend. Over the course of the latter decades of the twentieth century, such rhetorical strategies were established as a standard practice, so much so that they are second nature for corporate spokespersons today.[1]

The question asked of the pizza executive, for example, concerned a regulation that in actuality had nothing to do with "mandating what people eat." Providing nutritional information would, if anything, provide diners with the means to make better-informed choices. Greater information for consumers would seem logically to suggest *more* freedom of choice, not less. Yet with only a few potent words, the fast-food executive instinctively and quite efficiently redefined the question so as to represent the regulation in question as an imminent danger to individual freedom. The development and systemized deployment of such discourse has proven a compelling strategy. After all, who among us could want government "mandating" away the right to eat whatever we wish or to take away any of countless other "freedoms" that — through similar rhetoric — have been purported to be threatened?

Certainly, associating American freedoms with corporate interests is not something that has only been invented in recent years. The technique was quite famously employed by public-relations pioneer Edward Bernays in 1929, for example, to link the women's rights movement with the American Tobacco Company's marketing efforts. After he landed the Lucky Strikes cigarettes account, Bernays attracted much media attention by promoting a parade down Fifth Avenue in New York in which he had the women marchers light up "torches of freedom" to celebrate their right to smoke in public — still a social taboo at the time. The "American Way" images from the Depression-era campaign of the National Association of Manufacturers are still widely republished decades later. After Franklin Roosevelt's 1941 speech urging American support for Britain against Nazi Germany, in which he held fourth the four freedoms at stake — freedom of speech, freedom of religion, freedom from want, and freedom from fear — businesses launched a "fifth freedom" campaign (promoting "free enterprise") against Roosevelt's New Deal economic programs.

Yet it was not until the decade of the seventies that the strategy truly began to be articulated fully and extensively enough to be established as an integral, sociocultural phenomenon with broad ideological impact. Aided propitiously by events and trends of the day, and aggressively advanced in media and legal discourse, the priorities of the profit imperative were more successfully than ever before synthesized with the values of liberty, equality, and freedom of speech. Thus a new core narrative was formed, one that steadily gathered symbolic power to imbue the times with a sense of meaning and direction. The process would make it a conceptual fixture in the core rhetoric and thinking of the political culture that dominated the American scene more than any other in the latter twentieth and early twenty-first centuries.

It would seem to defy logic that consumers could be persuaded to reject government actions requiring companies to, for example, provide them with basic, factual information about products. All else being equal, the reverse expectation would seem more likely— that citizens would *support* legislation that would allow them to know more about the things they are buying. However, they could potentially grow relatively more likely to reject legislation favoring consumer interests if an ideology could be popularly advanced that would compellingly frame corporate interests as *consumer* interests — rather than as the interests of corporate managers. Certainly of course, there could be times when corporate interests *would* parallel those of consumers. But it would be impossible for that *always* to be the case. And yet, the latter is essentially the proposition that Mobil Oil advanced in its remarkable editorial-advocacy campaign of the 1970s.

Over the course of the 1970s, Mobil contributed more than any other player to the construction of an ideology of corporate citizenship. The corporate citizen was consistently and creatively represented as simply another decent, hardworking, ordinary citizen, trying to go about its business, but persecuted by the destructive forces of government every step of the way. Thus, it followed from that understanding, when human citizens reject government regulation of corporate activity they are protecting *themselves* from government persecution. They are defending the most fundamental freedoms and protections guaranteed to them by the Constitution. Because if the corporation is no more than another fellow citizen, that line of reasoning suggests, then its freedom too must be defended. With history-altering intensity particularly over the course of the seventies, that understanding of the corporation's role in American democracy was synergized crucially with social and political forces gathering momentum over the same period. The result was a perfect storm that swept through with such lasting impact it would contribute significantly to the forging of a political culture that would dominate public affairs for decades.

After close to a century of evolving corporate efforts to influence public opinion and political decisionmaking in the United States, Mobil launched the most openly promoted and fully articulated corporate assault on the marketplace of ideas that the nation had ever seen. In an advocacy campaign showcased on the op-ed page of *The New York Times*, Mobil conceptualized and marketed a role in democratic processes for corporate giants like itself no less than identical to that of the individual citizen — particularly in terms of the protections of the First Amendment. No set of texts from the corporate free-speech movement's seminal decade provide a richer documentation of the definitive components of the ideological strategies that have been employed in so many venues since then. Much of the basic anti-government/pro-business rhetoric, assumptions and worldview that it promoted with ever-greater zeal over the course of the decade has since been formed into staple elements of political discourse.

That is not to suggest that Mobil can be considered the sole source of such discourse. But it did generate a sizable body of messages that best outlines the basic corporate ideological strategies utilized in the seventies to reformulate the meaning of the First Amendment and the marketplace of ideas. Mobil's vision relentlessly and creatively represented the corporation not as the subject of democratic decisionmaking but as a vital participant within such processes. The oil company was hardly alone in that belief or the effort to make it a reality, but its editorial-advocacy campaign of the 1970s was unprecedented and unmatched during that period in its emphasis on advancing the right and practice of corporate media spending to influence political and social decisionmaking. That campaign provided the most definitive harbinger of the impending arrival of the age of cognitive feudalism. Beyond its role in helping institutionalize an altered understanding of American democracy, Mobil's messages provided a prescient vision of what lay ahead in American political culture. It championed the rise of an ideological movement almost exclusively focused on establishing the corporate profit imperative as the fundamental guiding force in American democracy during the period examined here.

A series of landmark U.S. Supreme Court rulings in decade of the 1970s would also immeasurably enhance the role of corporate media spending in American political discourse. Although later Court rulings have thus far stopped short of providing such spending with First Amendment rights *identical* to political expression by human citizens, the difference between the two in constitutional law was diminished dramatically by the rulings of the seventies. Thus, the decade represents a period in which corporate efforts to reshape the fundamental nature of the marketplace of ideas advanced significantly, providing corporate political media spending much greater legitimacy in American democracy.

THE CHAMP OF ADVOCACY ADVERTISING

In September of 1980, Mobil published a paid message in the lower righthand corner of *The New York Times* op-ed page thanking the newspaper's management for "a great contribution to the free market of ideas." The statement was not a general comment of approval on the *Times*' editorial product but rather a very personal expression of gratitude for providing the "soapbox" ten years before that had enabled

Mobil to become the most prominent corporate voice of the 1970s. Over the course of the decade, the oil company made the *Times* op-ed page the focus of its groundbreaking advocacy strategy to promote interests that went far beyond its immediate business objectives. The campaign now holds a prominent place in both the history of strategic communication and in intellectual history — the history of ideas. As a public relations vehicle, it remains one of the most conspicuous works of its kind. Robert Heath's 1997 assessment of Mobil as "the most visible — and feistiest — corporate practitioner of advocacy communication" for the past quarter century is typical of its characterization in corporate-advocacy literature. Less analysis, however, has focused specifically upon considering the campaign in terms of its broader historical significance, particularly Mobil's efforts to reframe understanding of the marketplace of ideas in First Amendment theory and practice.[2]

In the Mobil messages, corporate political media spending was represented as a natural and vital component of the free debate that the First Amendment exists to foster. Mobil's vision of the corporation as citizen, politically engaged through expression of free speech and other rights and obligations of citizenship, was at the time a radical assertion regarding the role of the corporation in American society, as even Mobil acknowledged. In its 1980 op-ed spot thanking the *Times*, the company recalled: "When we began, advocacy, or 'public issue' advertising was . . . of rather dubious legitimacy in some eyes. That corporations had ideas as well as products seemed to trouble a fair number of people. That the corporation has the same right as anyone else to express its ideas, they found it even harder to accept." Today, those paid advocacy messages of Mobil's, published most prominently on the editorial pages of *The New York Times* and packaged similarly to the other opinions and commentaries published there, represent an abundant body of historical artifacts, corporate messages focused almost exclusively on efforts to influence political and social outcomes. Although other corporations produced advocacy messages in the seventies, none spoke so regularly on so many issues of public policy as Mobil did during that period. And the Mobil campaign inspired a sharp rise in the numbers and extensiveness of corporate advocacy campaigns from that time forward.[3]

That campaign played out at a time in American history when energy crises, declining productivity and rising inflation were slowing the U.S. economy "like a sudden crashing of the gears into reverse," in the assessment of historian Os Guinness. Philip Jenkins titled his 2006 history of the era *Decade of Nightmares*. In 1973 *Fortune* magazine described what the nation was facing as a "siege economy." Political debate centered on what should be done to resolve the tangle of dilemmas that dragged on through virtually the entire decade. Time and again, Mobil aggressively weighed in on the debate. The circumstances of the seventies also frequently made Mobil itself a prominent story, as its annual earnings quadrupled over the course of the decade to reach what was then an all-time high of more than $2 billion. The unimaginable immensity of oil-industry profits in the face of widespread consumer pain became a major political issue.[4]

A generation of young people that had begun to loudly reject materialism and many other elements of mainstream society vital to the health of big business in the previous decade was now coming of age. Causes such as those inspired by consumer-activist Ralph Nader and environmentalist Rachel Carson were rapidly gaining momentum. It was a time when it appeared American society could well be ready to back another significant wave of legislative corporate reform, as in the Progressive and New Deal eras. Instead, electoral majorities went on to regularly embrace candidates espousing the basic tenets of the pro-corporate, anti-government, anti-regulatory ideology promoted by Mobil in the seventies. With relatively few exceptions, that trend dominated the remaining decades of the twentieth century and has continued to do so for the most part in the early years of the twenty-first century.

As detailed in Chapter Two, corporate efforts to influence public opinion widely intensified in the 1970s from a great many sources, in reaction to political developments of the immediately preceding years. Very much in that vein, the successful public-interest reform efforts of the sixties and early seventies were a key factor in Mobil's decision to launch its editorial-advocacy campaign. Mobil was then one of the half-dozen largest oil companies in the business, having been formed out of the divestiture of parts of John D. Rockefeller's gargantuan Standard Oil Trust after its ordered breakup as an illegal monopoly was upheld by the Supreme Court in 1911. Crucial to both the development of the editorial-advocacy campaign and a broader effort by Mobil to establish a brash public image was the rise of Herbert Schmertz to vice president for public affairs at Mobil in 1969 and election to the board of directors in 1976. In Schmertz, Mobil found an aggressive, articulate practitioner of public relations who said he saw no "fundamental difference between individuals and institutions." He relentlessly argued the case for corporate First Amendment rights and became the architect of the Mobil editorial-advocacy campaign on *The New York Times* op-ed page. Former Mobil Chairman of the Board and Chief Executive Officer Rawleigh Warner, Jr., recalls a conversation in which he told Schmertz that if Mobil didn't more actively express its viewpoints, "we leave the marketplace to our enemies. We were fortunate that at about that time the *Times* opened up its op-ed page and Herb recognized that was the perfect venue for us."[5]

Midway through 1970, the *Times* announced that it was overhauling the structure of its editorial-page section. The biggest change would take place on the page following the editorial page. Publisher Arthur Ochs Sulzberger announced that it would henceforth be "designed to afford a greater opportunity than has heretofore existed" in the newspaper for commentary "on subjects covering the whole range of human affairs, but with specific attention to current political and social issues." The five regular columnists of the *Times* — James B. Reston, C.L. Sulzberger, Tom Wicker, Russell Baker, and Anthony Lewis — would be moved to the new op-ed page, but space would be allotted for at least two opinion pieces daily that were submitted by outside writers. Additionally, the lower, right-hand quarter of the page would be made available to advertisers who wanted to publish opinions and commentaries.[6]

Although Mobil ran a few messages sporadically in the *Times* op-ed advertising corner in 1970 and 1971, its editorial-advocacy campaign did not really start to take form and gain momentum until 1972. Beginning in January of that year, Mobil began purchasing the *Times*' Thursday op-ed ad space every week, a practice the oil company would continue through the rest of the decade. Other corporations would purchase the space at times in the seventies to disseminate their messages, but none would use it in a way that was as stylistically harmonious with the content and purpose of the rest of the op-ed page and the editorial page that preceded it each day. The vast majority of Mobil's messages took on both the appearance and the role traditionally borne by newspaper editorials and commentary. Most of Mobil's op-ed spots consisted of a small headline, a block of text (on average more than 400 words in length, and quite often in the neighborhood of 1,000 words), and nothing more. They were not labeled as advertisements (nor were other *Times* op-ed ads of the seventies).

Looking back, Schmertz, says that a motivating factor for the company was to compete with news media of the day. "The media was abrogating to itself all First Amendment claims, which we certainly did not agree with," he said. Schmertz, who worked at Mobil until 1988, recalls that Mobil management backed the editorial-advocacy campaign enthusiastically because of what it saw as "too many attempts by the media to control the agenda and make public policy." So the company saw the *Times* op-ed page as a podium from which Mobil could launch its own agenda-setting and policy-shaping efforts in a highly visible manner.[7]

Although more than half of the company's op-ed messages of the seventies dealt with issues related to petroleum and various energy matters, a great many others addressed separate subjects. Mobil published messages in the *Times* op-ed advertising position on at least 445 occasions between 1970 and 1980. Three-quarters of the messages were advocacy or issue ads, rather than what could be considered to be corporate-image ads — messages that are intended to contribute in some general way to a positive public image of the corporation, not to advocate a specific action or position regarding a political or social issue. Just over fifty-nine percent of those messages dealt with petroleum or energy-related issues, but the rest dealt with other topics.

The Mobil messages stood out considerably from most of the other corporate messages that were published in the *Times* op-ed advertising spot during the seventies. *Newsweek* said midway through the decade that "nobody has worked harder . . . [at advocacy advertising] than Mobil." Even after the oil company's efforts sparked an increase in corporate-advocacy advertising, Mobil's campaign remained the undisputed leader of the pack. At the end of the decade, *Ad Forum* reported that an increasing number of corporations had "joined the fray," and corporate spending on advocacy advertising climbed from $154 million in 1970 to more than $500 million by 1979. But Mobil was recognized as "the clear-cut leader" in corporate advocacy messages "from the beginning," according to John E. O'Toole, president of the Foote, Cone, and Belding agency. *Fortune* magazine called Mobil "the champ of advocacy advertising." *Ad Forum* called Mobil "the leading practitioner of 'issue' or 'advocacy' advertising" throughout the seventies. A 1978 Yankelovich, Skelley, and White survey found that 90 percent of administration, congressional, and other government officials read the Mobil op-ed ads. "No other major advertising campaign generated as much controversy or major media coverage," said *Marketing and Media Decisions* magazine of the first decade of the oil company's editorial-advocacy campaign.[8]

"When you're selling ideas, the results are especially hard to quantify," Schmertz said in 1986. "But it's clear that through our op-ed ads, we've managed to bring some of our views into the public consciousness. We have won a certain degree of credibility with various key publics." Mobil shareholders surveyed by the company reported that the second-most important reason for buying Mobil stock was a "belief that Mobil will be active in protecting their investment from hostile government intervention and legislation." A number of scholarly assessments have documented in various ways the Mobil campaign's significance as persuasive corporate communication. In the broadest terms of its significance in American history, however, it would be Mobil's aggressive efforts to rework First Amendment law and reframe the corporation as literally no different from other citizens in shaping the marketplace of ideas that would come to stand as its most enduring impact.[9]

THE IDEOLOGY OF CORPORATE CITIZENSHIP

Over the course of the seventies, the Mobil editorial-advocacy campaign in a great variety of ways represented the corporation as the concerned, engaged, rational citizen idealized in the theoretical norms of citizenship in a classical republic— working for the common good, responsible to one's fellow man, involved in both civic concerns and democratic processes. And within that broader discourse, the most significant and revealing element was Mobil's framing of the corporation as a vital democratic participant. That dominant theme was characterized by language that recurringly and forcefully equated the corporate role in democratic processes with the role of the individual citizen.

For Mobil, the sort of corporate participation that it championed was represented unequivocally as what big business was *supposed* to do in the American system. "We have participated in the energy dialogue in order to help an informed public make rational judgments," a Mobil op-ed spot declared. "This, we believe, is our right and our responsibility in a pluralistic — and open — society." By 1974, that theme had begun to resonate even more clearly of First Amendment concepts associated with the individual's right to free expression. The language in those messages represented corporate messages as a vital source of ideas in American democracy. With increasing intensity over the course of the seventies, Mobil's op-ed messages reflected a rhetorical coalescing of the corporation into the discursive process idealized in marketplace-of-ideas concepts but previously considered most often in terms of human individuals.[10]

"An oil company has to find some way of speaking its mind and letting the public know what's going on, especially now," said a 1974 Mobil op-ed message, one of the first of a series of "Musings of an Oil Person" spots that were presented in a first-person style and formatted as one solid text block with no indentations, suggesting a stream of consciousness. It went on to empathize with the anger of Americans who that year were often finding themselves waiting in long lines to pay high prices for gasoline. Addressing the crisis, the reflective text concluded, would take information as much as action: "Dammit, we're a can-do company in a can-do country. . . . Give people the facts. Give them genuine information. Speak out. Persuade them to listen." Another op-ed message from that series both lauded the function of a free marketplace of ideas and warned of the dangers of denying corporations a role in the debate: "Who tells the [oil-industry] critics when they're wrong? What if their biases have the unintended result of clobbering the energy consumer?"[11]

Those elements would be developed and focused even more sharply and compellingly as the decade proceeded and Mobil evolved its core message. In the mid-seventies, Mobil called for more corporations to speak out, to recognize what it considered to be a duty to compete not only in the economic marketplace but also in the political marketplace: "For a long time now, we've been raising our voice in ads like this one," said one op-ed spot. "The trouble is, not enough other businesses follow suit." Increasingly equating the interests of the corporation with the interests of the people in its op-ed messages, Mobil also called more often for readers to contact their legislators. When government threatened the rights of the corporation — which was how Mobil invariably characterized regulatory efforts — it was threatening the rights of individuals. "When the bill comes before the full Senate, we sincerely hope that passion and politicking will yield to reason," Mobil said after a 1976 bill aimed at breaking large oil companies into smaller operations made it out of committee. "If some politicians won't listen to reason, perhaps they'll listen to the people. What's needed now is a public outcry. Isn't it time you spoke up? Your future may depend on it." A couple of weeks later, Mobil said, "We trust that the American public will see through the hollow rhetoric of those who would break up the oil companies. . . . Write your Senator — before it is too late." Although several legislative efforts in the seventies sought to force the largest oil companies to divest themselves either horizontally (of non-oil businesses) or vertically (of all but a single petroleum operation — production, transportation, refining, or marketing), all were defeated in the end.[12]

Mobil regularly replied to criticisms of its motives for seeking to influence public policy with depictions of what it declared to be the company's commitment to fostering democratic debate. In 1979, President Jimmy Carter said the real reason for Mobil's outspoken opposition to his plan to decontrol oil prices was its desire to kill his proposed windfall-profits tax on the oil companies. Mobil responded with an op-ed spot that further condemned Carter's plan and concluded: "As we see it, our responsibility is to continue to speak out on the issues." After Mobil's op-ed messages opposing a proposed mid-seventies bill barring Americans from participating in the Arab boycott of Israel drew sharp criticism, the company contended that it sought only "free and open debate . . . on the bill, . . . the right of the American people, all the people, to debate freely and openly any issue that could have a pronounced effect upon their lives." A later Mobil spot on the subject insisted: "Our only purpose in the ads and letters we have written has been to bring to the American people our interpretation of this legislation. If we are wrong, we would be happy to find that out. If we are correct, a useful service will have been performed."[13]

By 1979, Mobil was more unequivocally than ever encouraging corporate participation in the marketplace of ideas as imperative if vital information was going to reach the American people. "Only by knowing all the facts can Americans make informed judgments," one of its op-ed spots said, contending that legislators, government officials, and the press would not supply all the facts that corporate contributors like Mobil could provide. In performing that function, Mobil maintained, its ultimate purpose was advancing democratic decisionmaking: "Once the people are informed, they, through their government, can make the necessary decisions to balance environmental concerns on the one hand and energy needs and related economic problems on the other." Mobil even considered purchasing its own newspaper in the late seventies, looking into the *Oakland Tribune* and *Denver Post* when they were up for sale, and the *Long Island Press* after the Newhouse chain decided to close it. In the end, Mobil decided against buying a newspaper because it was not convinced it could run one profitably enough.[14]

In one late-1979 op-ed spot, Mobil published what now stands as the most concise articulation of its manifesto justifying the corporation as a vital participant in democratic processes protected by the First Amendment. The statement summarized the core assertions of Mobil's editorial-advocacy framing of the corporation as politically engaged citizen. "Mobil provokes, needles, challenges . . . to stir free-wheeling dialogue in the public prints. Saying what we think needs saying on issues that matter to people. Inflation. Jobs. Energy. Environment," it declared. "Voices of business balance other voices. Stifling any voice distorts the democratic process. The people must be able to weigh all the evidence . . . so future decisions in our participatory democracy will be based on the noblest wisdom of the past — the First Amendment."[15] It was during those latter years of the decade that the recurring energy price hikes and inflation of the seventies reached even greater levels of urgency in their political impact. Over the course of 1979 and 1980, the Organization of Petroleum Exporting Countries (OPEC) raised the price of crude oil by almost 150 percent. "Out of Gas" signs began to appear in front of service stations around the country in late 1978, as gasoline once again fell into short supply and prices began to rise at the pump. Carter's standing with Americans as a whole declined virtually throughout the second half of his presidency, the period during which he wore sweaters for some of his televised addresses to the nation on energy policy, encouraging Americans to turn down their thermostats. Every time energy prices rose, it sent further inflationary shocks rippling through the economy. By early 1979, some 45 percent of Americans reported having cut back on food purchases because of rising prices. The takeover of Iran by Muslim fundamentalists in 1979, leading to cuts in the nation's oil production that exacerbated the energy crisis in the U.S. and the subsequent seizure of Americans as hostages at the U.S. Embassy in Teheran, compounded Carter's problems. The president was successful in pushing through a comprehensive energy plan that included deregulation of energy prices, a windfall-profits tax on the oil companies, incentives for development of a variety of alternate energy sources such as synthetic fuels, oil shale and tar sands, solar power, and wind. But the ferocity of Mobil's attacks on Carter's proposals only increased.[16]

A month before the November 1980 election, Mobil launched a series of *Times* op-ed spots that in barely veiled language called for voters to turn Carter out of the White House. On each of the four Thursdays preceding the election, Mobil promised in its op-ed messages that the energy crisis could be ended in the eighties if Americans made the right choice. "We must have strong and wise political leadership if we are to overcome regional biases and the politics of confrontation," Mobil said four weeks before the election. "The present Administration, unfortunately has viewed oil primarily as a source of revenue for progressively greater government spending. . . . The choice between a safe degree of energy security and continued or increased dependence on foreign oil depends on choices made by the American public." A week later, Mobil's spot in the *Times* insisted that "everything needed to meet increasing proportions of higher energy demand with domestic supplies is available to us — everything except appropriate government policy. . . . We may have to endure another energy crisis before the gravity of the situation sinks in."[17]

The week after that, the Mobil op-ed spot blamed the administration for failing to sufficiently develop coal-burning and nuclear power plants, stating that "greater public understanding and support" would be "the only means to assure appropriate government policies and actions." Then on the Thursday before the Tuesday election, Mobil declared: "Our country has reached a point at which fundamental energy decisions must be made — decisions that can alter the course of history. . . . We believe the American people will respond positively to this historic opportunity." Thus, as the interrelated economic and energy dilemmas of the decade mounted in the later seventies, the focus of Mobil's advocacy discourse grew ever more critical in asserting that government was the cause of the problems. If many Americans were worried about what should be done to boost the staggering economy, Mobil was not hesitant to provide unequivocal answers. By the end of the seventies, its message had been honed into a call to replace the government in power in Washington with one that — in Mobil's view — would free big business to solve the crisis. That effort culminated with declarations in the final weeks before the presidential election of 1980 that promised the energy crisis could be ended if Americans made what the oil company offered as the right choice.[18]

CORPORATE FREE-SPEECH MOVEMENT GOES TO COURT

In addition to its editorial-advocacy campaign, Mobil joined other corporate interests that filed amicus curiae (friend-of-the-court) briefs in landmark First Amendment cases on corporate political media spending. "Individuals have the right of free speech; so do groups of individuals," Schmertz declared in 1978. "If these individuals are banded together in a membership corporation and find that they can be more effectively heard when they speak through the corporate voice, then this too is their constitutional right."[19] And in a group of precedent-setting cases decided at the end of the decade, the Supreme Court dramatically redefined the relationship between government and corporation in America, and by extension, the relationship between corporation and society. Those rulings are often referred to as the Court's early "corporate speech" cases.

It is important at this point, however, to re-emphasize what was at issue in those cases. What they specifically granted First Amendment protection to was (and is) *corporate political media spending*. On a literal level, there is no such thing as "corporate speech" since the artificial being that is a corporation cannot of course actually "speak" in the way that human beings can. It can only spend — pay someone to express messages on its behalf (through the spending decisions of corporate management). But in First Amendment jurisprudence, the term "corporate speech" is often used to contrast the type of spending involved from "commercial speech." The relevant bodies of case law are detailed in later chapters. In brief though, many types of spending deemed to be "corporate speech" in law — media efforts that seek to influence political outcomes or social climate — can be restricted by government only by surviving *strict scrutiny*, the most rigorous level of judicial review (detailed in Chapter Five). That is the same test imposed upon government when it seeks to restrict the political speech of individual humans in the United States, and it most often results in the striking down of such regulations as unconstitutional under the First Amendment.

In contrast, spending deemed to be "commercial speech" in law — media efforts that promote products or services — can be regulated by government by surviving a relatively less rigorous level of *intermediate* scrutiny (detailed in Chapter Ten). The significantly greater power of government in relation to commercial speech is manifest in the existence of a massive federal agency (the Federal Trade Commission) and numbers of state agencies whose primary function is protecting consumers from false and deceptive advertising. Thus it is important to keep in mind that all corporate speech is not *commercial*, and neither is all commercial speech *corporate*.

As will be detailed in Chapter Five, the first type of corporate political media spending to which the Supreme Court granted First Amendment rights in 1978 was such spending done to influence the outcome of a referendum (in which voters approve or reject a proposed law, rather than choose a candidate). Mobil did not file a friend-of-the-court brief in that case, *First National Bank of Boston v. Bellotti*, but it enthusiastically applauded the eventual ruling as "heartening" and "much needed," while saluting its own role in the "vanguard" of the corporate free-speech movement of the seventies. The brief for the plaintiffs in the *Bellotti* case (a group of five corporations doing business in Massachusetts) argued that corporate expenditures to influence political decisions were simply another form of free speech. In the same way that Mobil's op-ed messages represented the government regulation of corporations as a looming threat to the wider society, a friend-of-the-court brief filed by Northeastern Legal Foundation and Mid America Legal Foundation (both of which focused on corporate legal issues) warned that "the lessons of history tell us that when a fundamental right is taken from one group in society, that right will not be long enjoyed by others." The U.S. Chamber of Commerce in its brief depicted the political speech of "incorporated enterprise" to be as equally vital to "the free, frank, and robust expression of public opinion" fostered by the First Amendment as was any other source of such speech.[20]

Two years later, in *Consolidated Edison v. Public Service Commission*, the Supreme Court reinforced the *Bellotti* holding with a First Amendment ruling that struck down another state regulation on a different form of corporate political media spending. Mobil submitted a friend-of-the-court brief in support of Consolidated Edison, which prevailed in persuading the Court to overturn a New York ban on sending corporate political messages with electric-bill inserts. In the same style in which it constructed its op-ed messages, Mobil depicted the regulation as an imposition upon American citizens. "The sweeping, governmental ban on speech concerning matters of governing importance at issue in this case constitutes a frontal assault on the core of the First Amendment," it declared. "The issues involve not only the right of expression but the right of citizens to have unfettered access to informed viewpoints on public policy issues currently the subject of intensive debate." The brief cited a number of the company's *New York Times* advocacy messages.

The State of New York argued that the use of utility-bill inserts for corporate political messages was "tantamount to taking advantage of a captive audience, since the consumer cannot avoid receiving the literature with the utility's message" and thus advantaged the corporate voice in the marketplace of ideas. Nothing in the ban prevented corporations from expressing their opinions in a variety of other media forums that were open to contributions from all members of society in general, the government declared. The brief filed by the Consolidated Edison Company countered with an expansive vision of the corporation's role in society, maintaining that it was essential to democratic processes that corporate speech "remain unfettered if the public is to be fully informed." In the way that Consolidated Edison characterized the government regulation at issue as interference with the rights of both corporations and individuals, its brief read much like a Mobil op-ed message. The New York ban on bill inserts was "specifically directed to communications . . . [on which] the need for unfettered discussion is the greatest and governmental interference in the free flow of information and ideas is most harmful," Consolidated Edison said.

A number of other corporate parties in addition to Mobil weighed in on the *Consolidated Edison* case with friend-of-the-court briefs, an indication of the growing strength of the corporate free-speech movement. "As questions of energy supply and distribution have moved to the forefront of national attention, the freedom of utilities to participate in the resulting public debate has gained in significance," said the Edison Electric Institute, a national association of electric-utility companies. Pacific Gas and Electric insisted: "The First Amendment mandates that there be a free flow of information from all sources, including utilities, without governmental invasion of utility bills." Observing that advocacy advertising by corporations had grown substantially in the seventies to become "a commonplace occurrence," the U.S. Chamber of Commerce declared: "This activity is the natural and inevitable result of the evolution of the modern business organization, especially the modern business corporation. . . . It is precisely because modern business organizations have evolved into social institutions which are so intimately interwoven into the American socio-economic-political fabric that they have increased their involvement in recent years in the public affairs arena."[21]

Also in 1980, in *Central Hudson v. Public Service Commission*, the Supreme Court struck down a state energy-conservation regulation that banned advertising that promoted greater consumption of electricity. When utility corporations challenged the law as an infringement of their First Amendment rights, the State of New York contended that it infringed only the utility corporation's desire "to sell more electricity." It said the power company's efforts to use the First Amendment to advance its pursuit of profits reflected complete disregard for society's pressing need to conserve energy. To provide constitutional protection for such expression, the government argued, would work against the interests of a democratic society by diluting First Amendment protection for the political speech of individuals. For its part, Central Hudson Gas and Electric maintained that it was concerned with more than commercial self-interest and was seeking to address "interests of the energy-consuming public." Utilizing rhetoric similar to that of the Mobil corporate-advocacy messages, Central Hudson said New York had banned "speech which conveys information of great importance to the consumer of energy and touches closely on vital societal interests." It was, the utility corporation contended, the sort of expression intended to be protected by the First Amendment in its role of shielding "the free flow of information from the efforts, however well intentioned, of governmental officials to prescribe what is 'good' or 'bad' for the public to know."

A friend-of-the-court brief filed by the Edison Electric Institute also stressed the theme of government regulation of corporate activity depriving society of critically needed information. "This ban imposes a significant restriction on the utilities' freedom of speech as well as on the public's ability to gain information on a subject of vital importance to them," the Institute said. Long Island Lighting Company, another New York State utility company, was even harsher in its brief in representing government as obstructing the democratic interests of Americans. "Instead of respecting the basic notion that, whenever possible, the flow of truthful information should be encouraged in a free society to permit affected individuals to exercise an informed choice among lawful alternatives," it contended, "the [New York Public Service] Commission has chosen to stifle and manipulate the flow of information." Long Island Lighting went so far as to characterize the regulation as less focused on conservation than on social control: "Apparently, the Commission believes that by cutting off the flow of truthful information . . . [it] can affect the behavior pattern of New Yorkers in a manner which the Commission . . . believes is best for them. However, Americans are not rats in a B.F. Skinner experiment."[22]

Thus, as the decade of the seventies ended, the corporate free-speech movement had prevailed in each of the first three landmark Supreme Court First Amendment cases on corporate political media spending. The government had been rejected in its every attempt to protect the marketplace of ideas from corporate domination. In broad terms, the Court embraced the conceptual role of corporate citizenship in democratic processes that discourse by Mobil and other parties had promoted so aggressively over the course of the seventies. A few years later, investigative reporter Robert Sherrill credited Mobil with deciding that "the First Amendment belongs to oil people too" and then playing that gambit to the hilt in its editorial-advocacy campaign.

Warner, the company's former chairman, called the Court's actions on First Amendment rights for corporate media spending "most fortuitous for us. . . . There's no reason a corporation can't speak out." For Schmertz, the father of the Mobil corporate free-speech campaign, the imbalance perceived by big business in the marketplace of ideas early in the seventies had been shifted favorably by the end of the decade. "The imbalance was still there," he said, "but the establishment of the right of corporate speech had improved the situation substantially." Schmertz said his company's editorial-advocacy campaign contributed to establishing that right "in a general sense" by helping make the issue a more prominent one over the course of the decade. "And those [Supreme Court] decisions themselves established that the corporations have First Amendment Rights, and that they are as inviolate as anybody else's. And for Congress to try and make laws that inhibit corporations' free speech is unconstitutional," he said. By any measure, the corporate voice had been more solidly entrenched in American democracy as the decade of the seventies ended.[23]

INCORPORATING A BUSINESS-AS-DEMOCRACY VISION

The impact of the corporate free-speech movement was enhanced by the time and place in which it unfolded. The movement caught the crest of a sociopolitical surge of tsunami proportions, generated by seismic shifts in the American corporate and political landscape during the same period. The unprecedented 1970s effort by big business to assert its interests in the marketplace of ideas drew momentum from interplay with powerful historical currents that influenced the course of the decade politically, socially, and economically. Political scientist Mark A. Smith's analysis of latter twentieth century lawmaking led him to conclude that government policy matches "the collective desires of business only when citizens, through their policy preferences and voting choices, embrace ideas and candidates supportive of what business wants." He wrote in 2000 that "the evidence suggests that in the last two decades, corporate America has helped cause, at least to some extent, changes in public desires regarding what government should and should not do. . . . Its most effective influence arises not through any direct impact upon elected officials but rather through its capacity to shape public opinion."[24]

Indeed, it was particularly over the span of the seventies that big business began to understand that dynamic more clearly than ever. It recognized that its discourse must symbolically mesh its interests with broader popular narratives in order to achieve the greatest political gains. Most broadly of all, that meant actively representing the corporation as synonymous with democracy— rather than a threat to it — redefining the very meaning of freedom in public opinion. The packaging of corporate interests as nothing more than the dearest interests of patriotic citizen-consumers proved a natural extension of marketing trends already well under way.

Recent decades had seen corporations promote themselves more fully than ever in human terms, creating consumer-friendly personas for themselves — Ronald McDonald, Mickey Mouse, the Michelin Man, the Jolly Green Giant, the Pillsbury Doughboy. The use of such genial, appealing figures was not new in the latter twentieth century, just more ubiquitous, more iconographic in the way the technique was employed. The trend had interwined with the rising dominance of "branding" in management theory, the focus on promotion of image over production of goods. As globalization enabled production to be outsourced to the lowest-cost factories, wherever on the planet they might happen to be, it left corporations "free to focus on the real business at hand — creating a corporate mythology powerful enough to infuse real meaning into these objects just by signing its name," Naomi Klein declared in her study of the phenomenon. "Advertising is about hawking product. Branding, in its truest and most advanced incarnations, is about corporate transcendence. . . . The products that will flourish in the future will be the ones presented not as 'commodities' but as concepts: the brand as experience, as lifestyle," she wrote.[25] With marketing already focused upon ever more effective means of humanizing the corporate brand, the evolution toward representing corporate interests as nothing more than the interests of citizens proved a natural one.

The 1970s brought the triumph of the politician who more compellingly than any other would in plain language synthesize the freeing of business interests from government regulation with the protection of regular Americans' liberty. The woes that plagued the nation in the seventies, his campaign promised, could only be righted by making business more dominant in the political equation. The essence of Ronald Reagan's core message was never distilled more purely than the day he was first sworn in as president, when he proclaimed to the nation, "Government is not the solution to our problem: Government is the problem." In the same inaugural address, he declared: "It is time to reawaken this industrial giant, to get government back within its means, and to lighten our punitive tax burden. And these will be our first priorities, and on these principles there will be no compromise." But throughout the speech, the rhetoric was phrased in terms of the way government robbed regular Americans of their freedoms. "Our concern must be for a special interest group that has been too long neglected. . . . It is made up of men and women who raise our food, patrol our streets, man our mines and factories, teach our children, keep our homes, and heal us when we're sick. . . They are, in short, 'We the people,' this breed called Americans," Reagan said. "It is time to check and reverse the growth of government, which shows signs of having grown beyond the consent of the governed. . . . It is no coincidence that our present troubles parallel and are proportionate to the intervention and intrusion in our lives that result from unnecessary and excessive growth of government."[26]

Over decades of making public speeches, first as a popular corporate spokesperson for General Electric in the years leading to his political ascendance, and then in a variety of more direct political messages, Reagan perfected populist phrasing of the business-as-democracy message in terms of the persecuted corporate citizen. "It isn't unfair to say that today the world is divided between those who believe in the free marketplace and those who believe in government control and ownership of the economy," he said, in comments that broadly equated all government regulation with the government-controlled economies of socialist nations. Reagan's calls for lowering corporate taxes were a recurrent cause in his speeches, representing such taxes as impositions upon individual citizens. "Whether it be corporation or corner store, taxes are part of business costs and must be recovered in the price of the product. Meaning that all of us as consumers pay those taxes," he said. "Government can't tax things like business or corporations, it can only tax people." He represented American government as something apart from democratic processes.

"Our problem is a permanent structure of government insulated from the thinking and wishes of the people. . . . Only you and I can change that. We must send congress a mandate to restore government to the people." Government regulation in the interests of citizens was framed as an idealistic notion from the past that had outlived its need. "It was a noble, well intentioned experiment and probably there was some need for it. . . . Most of us have grown up thinking of government regulation as designed to keep big business in its place; to hold it back from becoming an octopus squeezing all of us and robbing us of our earnings. That was the original idea," Reagan would say, before proceeding to dispel such thinking as misguided at best any more. For such regulation was costing Americans tens of billions of dollars annually in "administrative salaries and overhead" and "increased prices — inflation if you will caused by unnecessary regulations," he declared, calling for a system in which "the laws of the marketplace can replace useless regulations and create real savings for consumers."[27]

Just how receptive an audience had developed for anti-government rhetoric in many segments of American life was demonstrated by the stunning late-sixties and early-seventies success — far beyond his Old South roots — of Alabama Governor George Wallace. Reagan offered a more palatable articulation of the anti-government rage that had driven Wallace's third-party presidential candidacy. It carried Wallace to the brink of reaching enough electoral support to throw the 1968 election into the House of Representatives, and it had him dominating the Democratic Party primaries in 1972 when gunshot wounds from an attack while campaigning forced him to withdraw. Wallace correctly "sensed that millions of Americans felt betrayed and victimized by the sinister forces of change" and would respond if given language for their resentment, historian Dan T. Carter has written. "It was clear that George Wallace had been the first politician to sense and then to exploit the changes America had come to know by many names: white backlash, the silent majority, the alienated voters." At his rallies, Wallace drew roaring approval from crowds that he told the nation had come under the control of an elite opposed to the traditional values of patriotic, hardworking Americans. He tapped into fears and fury stirred by race riots in the sixties, court-ordered desegregation of schools and other public facilities, the antiwar movement, the legalization of abortion, rising crime rates, and the spread of counterculture images and ideas through popular media. "His threatening demeanor and fiery personality would limit him to the role of redneck poltergeist," Carter wrote, "but as George Wallace neared the limits of his political popularity, he opened the door for his successors to exploit the politics of anger."[28]

Clearly, purveyors of discourse advancing business interests through anti-government rhetoric were tilling fertile ground in the seventies. It is not surprising that so many sources of such discourse arose and found success during the period. The trend gathered more and more momentum as the evidence demonstrated how well it was suited to the times and how well it worked. Sociologist Walden Bello has written of the complex social process by which "a belief system — a set of theories, beliefs and myths with some internal coherence . . . seeks to universalize the interests of one social sector to the whole community. In market ideology, for instance, freeing market forces from state restraints is said to work to the good not only of business, but also to that of the whole community." Over time, Bello wrote, "an ideology is internalized by large numbers of people, but especially by members of the social groups whose interests it principally expresses. An ideology thus informs the actions of many individuals and groups."[29]

Indeed, instrumental in the dramatic freeing of business interests from regulation since the seventies has been the development of the sort of "sustained, major effort to inform and enlighten the American people" on the part of the business community that future Supreme Court Justice Lewis Powell called for at the beginning of the 1970s. Powell's memo to the United States Chamber of Commerce had advocated much greater coordination and spending "over an indefinite period of years," an effort that he said must include organizing and providing incentives for "staffs of eminent scholars, writers and speakers" to promote the free enterprise system."[30] The years following those recommendations saw what has been characterized as "the creation of a constellation of institutions to support the corporate agenda, including foundations, think tanks, litigation centers, publications, and increasingly sophisticated public relations and lobbying agencies."[31]

Their numbers today are legion, their names often widely recognized, such as the Heritage Foundation, the Cato Institute, the

American Legislative Exchange Council, the Pacific Legal Foundation, the American Enterprise Institute, the Washington Legal Foundation, the Olin Foundation, the Mountain States Legal Foundation, the Manhattan Institute for Policy Research, the Hudson Institute, the Federalist Society, the Project for the New American Century, the Progress and Freedom Foundation, and the Hoover Institution, to name a few. Although the origins of some date farther back, a great many were either founded or expanded in the seventies, with significant funding from corporate sources and from other foundations funded by corporate sources. To be sure, their particular interests vary in many ways, but all have tended to broadly maintain solidarity with a core pro-business, anti-regulatory agenda. Such groups have focused over time on long-term agendas as well as on specific, shorter campaigns targeted at particular legislative initiatives. That has included the form of advocacy advertising that has come to be called "Astroturf" — well-funded efforts to simulate grassroots support on particular issues through media campaigns that appear to be the work of citizens' groups but are in fact industry creations.[32] A related vein of influence on public opinion in recent decades has been the "body of literature known as management theory, a perennially best-selling genre" through which an "army of management theorists" hold forth "the corporation as the ideal vehicle for economic democracy."[33]

Thus, a number of historical forces coalescing with compelling force particularly in the 1970s contributed to the success of broader ideological agendas associated with the corporate free-speech movement. It was in no small part the backlash of "millions of Americans who started getting tired of hippie college kids bad-mouthing America in the sixties, of journalists and Hollywood and professors and liberal judges insulting them and undermining the America they believed in," cultural historian Thomas Frank found, that "made possible the international free-market consensus of recent years." Economic analyst Robert Kuttner wrote in 1997 of how "marketization" began its ascendance when the U.S. economy faltered in the seventies and "a new, radically classical economics gradually gained influence in the academy and in politics" and then "colonized other academic disciplines. Market concepts became widespread in law, political science, and economic history." In time, the marketization movement would be elevated to what has been described by rhetorician

James Arnt Aune as "economic correctness." Historian Kenneth S. Friedman characterized it as "a set of beliefs, comparable to religious beliefs in earlier ages, about the nature of economics and societies. . . . The faithful unquestioningly embrace the credo that the doctrine of non-intervention has generated our most venerated institutions: our democracy, the best possible political system; and our free market economy, the best possible economic system."[34]

In Richard Powers' historical fiction, the CEO who arrives to transform multinational Clare in the eighties frequently evangelizes in a stump speech about how "the market cannot be 'corrected.' It cannot be 'wrong.' The market is just a chalk mark on a wall, a mark of what we want and how much we're willing to do to get it. . . . The consumer's best advocate is her own dollar, a franchise given her over every aspect of her existence. By scrambling to win consumer votes and avoid consumer censure, business becomes the best tool we have for building the world that people want."[35] The conquering gospel of "market populism" and its advancement of an understanding that "real democracy" is "only possible when market forces have been liberated" has been laid out particularly evocatively in nonfiction by Thomas Frank:

> Markets expressed the popular will more articulately and more meaningfully than did mere elections. Markets conferred democratic legitimacy; markets were a friend of the little guy; markets brought down the pompous and the smooth; markets gave us what we wanted; markets looked out for our interests. . . . These ideas became canonical, solidified into a new orthodoxy that anathematized all alternative ways of understanding democracy, history, and the rest of the world. . . . Market populism decries 'elitism' while transforming CEOs as a class into one of the wealthiest elites of all time. It deplores hierarchy while making the corporation the most powerful institution on earth. . . . Once Americans imagined that economic democracy meant a reasonable standard of living for all — that freedom was only meaningful once poverty and powerlessness had been overcome. Today, however, American opinion leaders seem generally convinced that democracy and the free market are simply identical. . . .What is 'new' is this

> idea's triumph over all its rivals; . . . the general belief among opinion-makers that there is something natural, something divine, something inherently democratic about markets."[36]

Near the end of the seventies, Mobil Oil offered a succinct articulation of its own business-as-democracy vision. "Government can become so pervasive that it becomes virtually impossible for the citizenry to turn it around and change its course," it declared in one of its *New York Times* advocacy messages. "But it's doubtful that business could ever get so big or so unresponsive, because it is subject to reaction in the marketplace and to public opinion generally." And in decades to come, Mobil promised, Americans could free themselves and their democracy through greater devotion to the market. "The national orgy of regulation has done vastly more harm than good. The cure for it should be the movement toward a freer market. This will be the radicalism of the '80s."[37]

The rhetoric of Mobil and others in the corporate free-speech movement had the ring of common sense. The promises of a brighter future for America seemed to have a fundamental logic to them. If human citizens would only embrace an understanding of democracy that freed the corporate citizen from the oppression of government regulation, then all citizens would be the better for it. It was a tempting enough message, especially amid the troubles of the seventies, to overlook its contradictions. Clearly, Mobil did not participate in the *Times* op-ed page in the same manner as any other citizen. Very few human citizens could have afforded the cost of publishing hundreds and hundreds of advocacy messages in that prominent forum. And those few who could have done so would have had to choose to expend the required share of their own wealth in order to advance their political views.

Mobil's participation in the particular marketplace of ideas represented by the *Times* op-ed page, however, was not the result of any citizen's choice to make political expenditures of his or her own, but of corporate management spending shareholder profits accumulated through the special wealth-generating advantages of the corporate form. If Mobil had wanted to participate in the *Times* op-ed page just like any other citizen, it would have simply submitted its opinion pieces to be considered through the same selection process as were nonpaid submissions to the page. Buying its way onto the page with much greater frequency than would have been possible in that manner, however, enabled Mobil to wield a heightened power over human individuals in the marketplace of ideas, much as the corporation wields extra power in the economic marketplace.

The decades following the seventies would test such implications, particularly the wisdom of advantaging corporate interests in the marketplace of ideas. But for better or worse, the 1970s represent a historical period that opened up a new era of corporate players more robustly exercising their "citizenship" in the processes of democratic debate and decisionmaking. Over a relatively few years, it led to a dramatic freeing of corporate power from government restraint in American life. The next chapter considers what those changes and the ascendance of the dominant political culture of business as democracy meant for the nation in the years that followed.

[1] See Victor Godinez, "Change in Store for Pizza Hut," *The Dallas Morning News*, 24 December 2003, sec. D, p. 1.

[2] See "Dear Mr. Sulzberger," Advertisement, *The New York Times*, 25 September 1980, sec. 1, p. 27; Robert L. Heath, *Strategic Issues Management: Organizations and Public Policy Challenges* (Thousand Oaks, Calif.: Sage, 1997), 208. For the most detailed discussion of the Mobil campaign in that context, see Robert L. Kerr, *The Rights of Corporate Speech: Mobil Oil and the Legal Development of the Voice of Big Business* (LFB Scholarly: New York, N.Y., 2005). A shorter version of that study can be found at Robert L. Kerr, "Creating the Corporate Citizen: Mobil Oil's Editorial-Advocacy Campaign in *The New York Times* to Advance the Right and Practice of Corporate Political Speech, 1970-80," *American Journalism* 21:4 (Fall 2004) 39-62.

[3] *The New York Times* was the media venue that Mobil chose as the centerpiece of its effort to disseminate messages aimed at influencing the broader marketplace of the ideas. Mobil did publish some of the messages that appeared in the *Times* (as well as additional messages that were similarly themed) in other newspapers and magazines, but it was in the *Times* that Mobil most extensively and prominently disseminated its editorial-advocacy campaign of the 1970s.

[4] See Os Guinness, *The American Hour: A Time of Reckoning and the Once and Future Role of Faith* (New York: Free Press, 1993), 108; Philip Jenkins, *Decade of Nightmares: The End of the Sixties and the Making of Eighties America* (New York: Oxford University Press, 2006); "Learning to Live with the Oil Squeeze," *Fortune*, December 1973, p. 25; Anthony J. Parish, "Oil Company Nets Surge," *The New York Times*, 24 January 1980, sec. 4, p. 1.

[5] See Rawleigh Warner, Jr., and Leonard Silk, *Ideals in Collision: The Relationship Between Business and the News Media* (Pittsburgh: Carnegie Mellon University Press, 1979), 11, 13; Peter Ellis Jones, *Oil: A Practical Guide to the Economics of World Petroleum* (New York: Nichols, 1988), 8; William N. Greene, *Strategies of the Major Oil Companies* (Ann Arbor, Mich.: UMI Research Press, 1985), 126, 140-143, 149; Herbert Schmertz with William Novak, *Goodbye to the Low Profile: The Art of Creative Confrontation* (Boston: Little, Brown and Company, 1986), 23, 134-7, 139; Rawleigh Warner, Jr., telephone interview with author, 10 July 2002. Warner retired from Mobil in 1986. In a transaction completed in 1999 that created the world's largest oil company today, Mobil merged with Exxon.

[6] See "Times Will Offer Daily Forum Page," *The New York Times*, 29 July 1970, sec. 1, p. 39. The editorial page in the *Times* was always on the lefthand, when opened with the following page on the righthand. Thus the following page was "opposite" the editorial page, and hence the term "*op*-ed" for it.

[7] Herbert Schmertz, telephone interview with author, 13 April 2002.

[8] See Oscar H. Gandy, Jr., *Beyond Agenda Setting: Information Subsidies and Public Policy* (Norwood, N.J.: Ablex, 1982), 71; S. Prakash Sethi, *Advocacy Advertising and Large Corporations: Social Conflict, Big Business Image, the News Media, and Public Policy* (Lexington, Mass.: Lexington Books, 1977), 3, 15, 237, 292-3; "Taking a Stand on the Issues Through Advertising," *Association Management*, December 1980, p. 58; John E. O'Toole, "Advocacy Advertising Shows the Flag," *Public Relations Journal* 31, no. 11 (November 1975): 16; "The Backlash Against Business Advocacy," *Fortune*, 28 August 1978, p. 63; "Mobil's Warner Energizes Advocacy Advertising," *Ad Forum*, February 1981, p. 11; "How Good Are Advocacy Ads?" *Dun's Review*, June 1978, p. 76; "Mobil: They Speak Their Mind," *Marketing and Media Decisions*, Spring 1982, p. 87.

[9] See Schmertz, *Goodbye to the Low Profile*, 134, 143, 145; Lars Thorger Christensen and George Cheney, "Self-Absorption and Self-Seduction in the Corporate Identity Game," in Majken Schultz, Mary J. Hatch, and Mogens Holten Larsen, eds., *The Expressive Organization: Linking Identity, Reputation, and the Corporate Brand* (Oxford, England: Oxford University Press, 2000), 250; George Smith and Robert L. Heath, "Moral Appeals in Mobil Oil's Op-Ed Campaign," *Public Relations Review* 16, no. 4 (1990): 48-54; H.W. Simons, "Mobil's System-Oriented Conflict Rhetoric: A Generic Analysis," *Southern Speech Communication Journal* 48 (1983): 243-54; Robert L. Heath and Richard A. Nelson, *Issues Management* (Beverly Hills, Calif.: Sage, 1986), 81; Larry A. Williamson, "Transcendence, Ethics, and Mobil Oil: A Rhetorical Investigation" (Ph.D. diss., Purdue University, 1982); and Gary Kurzbard, "Ethos and Industry: A Critical Study of Oil Industry Advertising from 1974-1984" (Ph.D. diss., Purdue University, 1984); Patricia A. Davis, "Description and Analysis of Mobil Oil Corporation Advertising on the Basis of Content and Context Before, During and After the 1973-74 Oil Crisis" (Ph.D. diss., New York University, 1979), 49, 168-173, 385.

[10] See "An Answer that Raises Questions," Advertisement, *The New York Times*, 8 December 1977, sec. 1, p. 23.

[11] See "Musings of an Oil Person," Advertisement, *The New York Times*, 28 February 1974, sec. 1, p. 37; "Musings of an Oil Person," Advertisement, *The New York Times*, 18 July 1974, sec. 1, p. 35.

[12] See "The Soapbox is a Lonely Place," Advertisement, *The New York Times*, 8 May 1975, sec. 1, p. 39; "How 8 Senators Ignored Overwhelming Evidence," Advertisement, *The New York Times*, 17 June 1976, sec. 1, p. 35; "Oil is Not a Cottage Industry," Advertisement, *The New York Times*, 1 July 1976, sec. 1, p. 29.

[13] See "Response," *The New York Times*, 7 June 1979, sec. 1, p. 23; "Reason, Not Emotion, Should Rule," Advertisement, *The New York Times*, 30

September 1976, sec. 1, p. 41; "An Open Letter to Congressman Rosenthal," Advertisement, *The New York Times*, 14 October 1976, sec. 1, p. 37.

[14] See "Some Energy Options That Haven't Even Been Discussed," Advertisement, *The New York Times*, 2 August 1979, sec. 1, p. 17; Jack Egan, "Mobil Looked at Other Newspapers Besides L.I. Press," *The Washington Post*, 8 April 1977, sec. D, p. 1; "Mobil Won't Buy Paper," *The Washington Post*, 20 April 1977, sec. D, p. 10.

[15] See "Imagine Tomorrow Without Argument," Advertisement, *The New York Times*, 16 August 1979, sec. 1, p. 23.

[16] See Robert Solomon, "What the Oil Shock Is Doing to the World Economy," *Fortune*, 29 December 1980, p. 9; Steven V. Roberts, "Survey Shows Inflation Brings Cutbacks to Many," *The New York Times*, 1 February 1979, p. 14; E.B. Brossard, *Petroleum: Politics and Power* (Tulsa, Okla.: PennWell, 1983), 159; "Energy: Fuels of the Future," *Time*, 11 June 1979, p. 72-76.

[17] See "Embarrassment of Riches?" Advertisement, *The New York Times*, 9 October 1980, sec. 1, p. 35; "To Have or Have Not?" Advertisement, *The New York Times*, 16 October 1980, sec. 1, p. 31.

[18] See "We Still Have Time — Just," Advertisement, *The New York Times*, 23 October 1980, sec. 1, p. 27; "The Fork in the Road," Advertisement, *The New York Times*, 30 October 1980, sec. 1, p. 27.

[19] See Herbert Schmertz, *Corporations and the First Amendment* (New York: American Management Associations, 1978), 6.

[20] See "Bits and Pieces," Advertisement, *The New York Times*, 18 May 1978, sec. 1, p. 23. The briefs highlighted in this passage were all filed in *First National Bank of Boston v. Bellotti*, 435 U.S. 765 (1978).

[21] The briefs highlighted in this passage were all filed in *Consolidated Edison v. Public Service Commission*, 447 U.S. 530 (1980).

[22] The briefs highlighted in this passage were all filed in *Central Hudson v. Public Service Commission*, 447 U.S. 557 (1980). This case is generally considered to be more a part of the commercial-speech case law than the corporate-speech case law. But it straddled the line to some extent, as Justice John Paul Stevens argued in a concurring opinion. He characterized the regulated expression as corporate *political* speech because the banned promotional advertising very well could address crucial questions being considered by political leaders during the energy crises of that time.

[23] See Robert Sherrill, *The Oil Follies of 1970-80* (Garden City, N.Y.: Anchor, 1983), 60; Rawleigh Warner, Jr., telephone interview with author, 10 July 2002; Herbert Schmertz, telephone interview with author, 13 April 2002.

[24] See Mark A. Smith, *American Business and Political Power: Public Opinion, Elections, and Democracy* (Chicago: University of Chicago Press, 2000), 8-11.

[25] See Naomi Klein, *No Logo* (New York: Picador, 1999), 3-30.

[26] See Ronald Reagan, "First Inaugural Address," 20 January 1981, in Kurt Ritter and David Henry, *Ronald Reagan: The Great Communicator* (New York: Greenwood Press, 1992), 156-58.

[27] See "Free Enterprise," radio address, 16 April 1979; "Economics I," radio address, 31 April 1978; "Paperwork and Bureaucrats," radio address, 21 September 1976; "Regulations," radio address, 12 March 1975, all in Kiron K. Skinner, Annelise Anderson, and Martin Anderson, eds., *Reagan in His Own Hand: The Writings of Ronald Reagan That Reveal His Revolutionary Vision for America* (New York: Free Press, 2001), 228, 258-59, 295-7, 294, 295. For a more complete account of the seminal development of Reagan's pro-corporate ideas and rhetoric, see: Thomas W. Evans, *The Education of Ronald Reagan: The General Electric Years* (New York: Columbia University, 2006), 3-30.

[28] See Dan T. Carter, *From George Wallace to Newt Gingrich: Race in the Conservative Counterrevolution*, 1963-1994 (Baton Rouge: Louisiana State University Press, 1996).

[29] See Walden Bello, with Shea Cunningham and Bill Rau, *Dark Victory: The United States, Structural Adjustment, and Global Poverty* (Oakland, Calif.: Institute for Food and Development Policy, 1994), 3.

[30] The U.S. Chamber of Commerce distributed the "Powell Memorandum" to its national membership in its August 23, 1971, *Washington Report* under the headline "Confidential Memorandum: Attack on American Free Enterprise System." It has been widely distributed in recent years, including on the Media Transparency website at: http://www.mediatransparency.org/story.php?story ID=22. Powell joined the Supreme Court bench shortly after authoring that document and went on to vote in favor of corporate interests in all three of the "corporate speech" cases detailed in this chapter.

[31] See Ted Nace, *Gangs of America: The Rise of Corporate Power and the Disabling of Democracy* (San Francisco: Berrett-Koehler, 2003), 143.

[32] For more detailed discussion of the development of such organizations since the 1970s, see Jean Stefancic and Richard Delgado, *No Mercy: How Conservative Think Tanks and Foundations Changed America's Social Agenda* (Philadelphia: Temple University Press, 1996); and Thomas Byrne Edsall, *The New Politics of Inequality* (New York: W.W. Norton, 1984), 117-120.

[33] See Thomas Frank, *One Market Under God: Extreme Capitalism, Market Populism, and the End of Economic Democracy* (New York: Doubleday, 2000), 173-80, 220-21.

[34] See Thomas Frank, *What's the Matter with Kansas? How Conservatives Won the Heart of America* (New York: Metropolitan Books, 2004), 2-6; Robert Kuttner, *Everything for Sale: The Virtues and Limits of Markets* (New York: Alfred A. Knopf, 1997), 3-10; James Arnt Aune, *Selling the Free Market: The Rhetoric of Economic Correctness* (New York: Guilford, 2001), 4; Kenneth S. Friedman, *Myths of the Free Market* (New York: Algora, 2003), 1-7.

[35] See Richard Powers, *Gain* (New York: Picador, 1999), 159.

[36] See Frank, *One Market Under God*, xiv-xv, 15.

[37] See "Liberals, Logical Allies of Business," Advertisement, *The New York Times*, 22 June 1978, sec. 1, p. 23; "The Free Market: Radicalism for the '80s," Advertisement, *The New York Times*, 20 July 1978, sec. 1, p. 21.

CHAPTER FOUR

Pottersville, Inc.

The events and trends documented in the preceding chapters ushered in a significant shift in American political culture, one that would dominate the final decades of the twentieth century and continue into the twenty-first. Mobil Oil and other corporate interests were influential in advancing an ideology that offered patriotic, hard working, middle-class Americans in particular an appealing answer to the complex, socioeconomic crises of the 1970s. That answer, in essence, was an understanding of democracy in which big business would free citizens from the oppressions of government regulation. That message began finding favor among the electorate during the same period when the corporate free-speech movement won First Amendment rights for corporate political media spending from the Supreme Court.

Altogether it represented a dramatic freeing of corporate power from government restraint in a relatively few years. But did it bring forth a new birth of freedom for the citizens whose votes made the sweeping deregulation of business activity possible? Did embracing the dominant political culture of business as democracy transform America into a place more like Bedford Falls — or Pottersville?

This chapter considers the evidence, drawing upon a variety of sources in an attempt to capture a portrait of life in what is asserted here as the age of cognitive feudalism. It suggests that the success of the corporate free-speech movement and related efforts indeed went on to bring sweeping change to America. Advantaging corporate power so sharply, both in the marketplace of ideas and in the halls of government served to institutionalize the profit imperative as quite arguably the most influential force in both. That sort of influence can be seen in a period of American democracy shaped ever more by the few than by the many — to such an extent that a convincing case can be made for characterizing it as more feudal than democratic. The ideological equating of corporate interests with the freedom interests of individual citizens unquestionably advanced the former. But for the interests of the latter, for middle America, a great many measures indicate the outcomes were considerably less favorable.

CORPORATE KINGDOMS RENEWED

After the 1970s and the ascendance of business-as-democracy fervor in so many realms of American political and cultural life, the rhetoric quickly began to translate into action. Within a few years, watershed changes in law and policy loosened decades of antitrust restrictions on corporate merger activity. It unleashed a merging frenzy not seen since the heyday of Standard Oil and U.S. Steel in the late nineteenth century, ultimately making possible such actions as the rejoining together of Exxon and Mobil, the two largest pieces of the old Standard empire before it was broken up by antitrust action in 1911. The process resulted in a landscape where corporate kingdoms on that scale cast longer shadows than ever across the nation's landscape. By any measure, the renewed efforts launched by big business in the seventies to reassert its influence succeeded resoundingly in escalating and consolidating its power over the course of the decades that followed.[1]

The earlier legislative setbacks that business leaders had cited as impetus for those efforts were reversed many times over. Taxes on corporations were slashed so extensively that *The Wall Street Journal* declared in 2004, "It is hard to see how the corporate tax tally could get much smaller." A General Accounting Office report released that year showed that almost two-thirds of corporations operating in the U.S. reported owing *no* federal taxes. Through aggressive lobbying, the nation's largest corporations were able to report soaring profits and plummeting taxes, with corporate taxes as a share of the national economy dropping to their lowest level since World War II and financing only six percent of the cost of the federal government. At the same time, Standard & Poor's reported that the cash reserves of the nation's five hundred largest corporations alone topped $643 billion, a figure an S&P analyst called "out of whack with all historical numbers." Corporate spending on trips for legislators soared, as did the number of lobbyists registered in Washington, quadrupling to 36,000 over the decade preceding 2004. When Congress began work on replacing a tax break for U.S. exporters that had been ruled illegal by the World Trade Organization, "the biggest free-for-all in corporate lobbying that Congress has experienced in nearly 20 years" resulted in a 633-page "perfect storm for pork" with $137 billion in tax giveaways. States and cities joined the giveaway rush as well, competing feverishly to offer the most lucrative tax subsidies to corporate ventures, despite evidence that it often cost the taxpayers more than it brought in and did not even keep many of the recipients around once the money was handed over.[2]

For medieval populations many centuries before, displays of feudal coats of arms provided symbolic reminders of the centers of power of the day. In the latter twentieth century, corporate interests moved into that role more prominently than ever, rivaled as centers of power only by some governmental forces. In many regards, corporate power during the period grew to exceed that of government, commanding vast domains of economic, political, social, and cultural influence. The significant institutions of American life that could any longer exist without corporate sponsorships, for example, grew steadily fewer in number. Across the land, corporate logos came to fly in the manner of latter-day coats of arms over most domains of media, entertainment, education, and other endeavors. Even government itself was increasingly farmed out to corporate contractors. With the turrets of corporate complexes and the institutions they sponsored seldom out of sight for most Americans, could children growing up in this age imagine that *any* activity was truly significant if it did not have a corporate sponsor?

It grew common, for example, for public schools to find themselves so short of government funding that they began auctioning off pieces of themselves off to the highest corporate bidder. A grade school in New Jersey renamed its gym the Shop Rite Center in return for a supermarket sponsorship, while expressing a willingness to make similar deals for virtually anything else on its grounds — or even for the entire school. The principal declared its funding approach would soon be the norm everywhere, and the state chamber of commerce applauded the trend. Philadelphia schools distributed brochures promoting a similar program, dubbing the approach "Leave No Dollar Behind." A Chicago suburb renamed its football venue Rust-Oleum Field, after its new corporate sponsor. A Florida school's facility became Eastern Financial Florida Credit Union Stadium. The Council for Corporate and School Partnerships estimated that by the early

2000s, some 70 percent of U.S. school districts had entered into "some form of business partnership." Across the nation, that meant schools hooking up with sponsors as big as Nike or as small as local tire shops. Organizations such as Commercial Alert and the Commercialism in Education Research Unit at Arizona State University decried the proliferation of advertising as a subversion of the educational mission and taking advantage of impressionable school-age children. But the marketing director for the National Federation of State High School Associations called schools "an unlimited, untapped market" for corporate interests.[3]

Indeed, that sort of marketing almost seemed mild in comparison to many other ways that the presence of corporate influence extended into everyday life during the period. "Stealth strategies" developed over the course of recent decades co-opted the very nooks and crannies of private lives and social relations. In "peer-to-peer" or "viral" marketing, it became common to pay teen-agers to surveil their friends and cultivate profitable trends. Hired actors shilled products in Internet chat rooms and on city streets in order to create "organic" brand awareness. On the blogosphere, commentary that originated in corporate PR offices was posted unattributed by increasing numbers of bloggers as if they were the original source. The story lines of films, comic books, video games, textbooks — seemingly nothing remained off limits — were embedded with corporate logos, slogans, and rhetoric. The friend with the cool new gadget at dinner or the bar last night might well have been paid and coached to show it off, without ever telling you. Such trends represented an unprecedented level of corporate transcendence, moving toward a seamless, ceaseless virtual reality in which no moment and no space would be left unmarketed.[4]

Was it an exaggeration to declare, as activist attorney Joel Balkan put it, that corporations had reached the point that they "determine what we eat, what we watch, what we wear, where we work, and what we do. We are inescapably surrounded by their culture, iconography, and ideology, . . . like the church and the monarchy in other times."[5] Many a community had the stunning reach of corporate power driven home in a variety of ways. In Pennsylvania in 2004, for example, voters elected a new city council member who ran on promises to oppose a quarry proposed for near the township's elementary school, where winds could carry potentially harmful silicates and silicate dust from the quarry. But before he could attend his first meeting on the council, lawyers for the corporation behind the quarry warned him to recuse himself from any issue involving the corporation or face legal action. Unable to afford a legal battle, the new council member complied with the corporation's demand, effectively nullifying the election. In state legislatures around the country, giant corporate Internet service providers successfully lobbied lawmakers to block municipalities from providing low-cost Internet access to their residents — even in areas where the ISPs had refused to offer service. Numbers of communities discovered that cellphone companies had the power to override laws and decisions by local governing bodies in order to build giant cellular transmission towers in their neighborhoods. Fast-food companies won immunity from lawsuits in an increasing number of state legislatures to protect them from the kinds of liability judgments juries have supported against the tobacco companies. In most states, corporate lobbyists helped write the bills and channeled millions of dollars in campaign contributions to politicians who supported the new laws.[6]

And the age of cognitive feudalism saw the rise of one corporate giant with the might to redefine the very nature of American life virtually all by itself. In the hills of Northwest Arkansas, hundreds of smaller companies opened offices and stationed top representatives in order to be as close as possible to the virtually infinite power emanating from the Bentonville headquarters of Wal-Mart, Inc. Among the estimated more than 500 such supplicants were many corporate giants in their own right: Procter and Gamble, Kraft Foods, Walt Disney Co., MGA Entertainment, Levi Strauss, and Nestle USA. For countless vendors of groceries, detergent, clothing, DVDs and much more, it was Wal-Mart that moved more of their product than anyone else. Even players on the scale of Coca-Cola scurried back to the drawing board when Wal-Mart gave a thumbs-down on a new product. In some communities, small businesses could appeal to Wal-Mart for a form of benediction — grant money to enable them to stay afloat when the giant retailer located a Supercenter in their neighborhood.

By the dawn of the twenty-first century, Wal-Mart had become the largest company in the history of the world, with more than a quarter-trillion dollars in annual sales and a hundred-million shoppers in the United States every week of the year. Its computer system had grown more massive than the Pentagon's, and if it were a country, it would have ranked higher than all but seven nations in trade with China. Indeed, many developing countries had begun sending emissaries to Bentonville, so vital was Wal-Mart to their economies. Escalating numbers of American manufacturers were forced to shift their factories to China and other low-wage locations in order to cut labor costs enough to meet Wal-Mart's demands for lower prices. Their sales reps learned they must all venture regularly to Wal-Mart headquarters and negotiate with its buyers, knowing that if they did not meet its price, someone else in the waiting room would. The retail giant delivered bargains to shoppers on such a scale that by some estimates it reduced a full percentage point off U.S. inflation by itself in the latter twentieth century. But its own average wage in the early 2000s was below the federal poverty line, and fewer than half its employees were receiving healthcare coverage. The company's reliance on China grew so great that it de-emphasized the "Made in America" slogan it once promoted. Some studies found that the gains in employment and tax revenue that Wal-Mart brought to a community were zeroed out by the losses experienced by other businesses.[7]

On one level, Wal-Mart came to stand as the ultimate manifestation of subordinating other values to the profit imperative. It represented "the logical end point and the future of the economy in a society whose pre-eminent value is getting the best deal," in the words of former Labor Secretary Robert Reich. In municipalities across the country, the elected officials often wondered if they were directing local affairs or if corporate executives in Bentonville were. Many of them faced referenda sponsored by Wal-Mart to overrule local governments that failed to go along with the company's Superstore-building plans. In other instances, Wal-Mart filed lawsuits in order to pressure local officials to comply with its wishes. The company defended such tactics as necessary in order to advance its plans to build hundreds more of its 200,000-square-foot discount-store/supermarket hybrids, maintaining, "People support and want Wal-Mart Supercenters. We're going to do everything in our power to make certain that Wal-Mart customers are heard." Yet rather than enduring the lengthy local planning debates with officials *elected* by the people in various locales — who might restrict or even block its plans — Wal-Mart often found it more expedient to pay the cost of sponsoring referenda or going to court. Wal-Mart also escalated its lobbying efforts in Washington, and its political-action committee became one of the largest in the United States. Similarly it greatly expanded its public-relations efforts.[8]

IS THIS ANY WAY TO RUN A BUSINESS?

The expanded influence of big business since the seventies can of course be considered from other perspectives. If that influence had also extended to government being run more like a business, would that necessarily be such a bad thing? Certainly much rhetoric accompanying the rise of the dominant political culture of recent years suggested that citizens could expect greater fiscal responsibility in government if they embraced the business-as-democracy approach. It had the ring of common sense — governing the nation according to sound business principles, getting back to basics, abandoning all the elitist nonsense. At a minimum, surely it would seem to have meant a fundamental commitment to ensuring that expenditures did not exceed revenues. That, after all, would be the very first requirement for any viable business, wouldn't it?

And yet, it would be precisely the *opposite* trend that characterized the rise of the dominant political culture over the course of recent decades. Indeed, the evidence indicates that the more dominant that culture, the greater the disproportion of expenditures over revenues. Consider the stunning developments of the first decade of the twenty-first century. With the ascent of the pro-business political culture since the seventies largely complete, having achieved more control over every branch of the federal government than ever before, some $3 trillion in federal debt was added from 2002 to 2005 alone — approaching a 50 percent increase over the total debt on the books until that period. It meant that by itself, just making interest payments on the debt at that point represented more than a twelfth of the federal budget — topping the entire budgets of the departments of Agriculture, Education, Energy, Homeland Security, Health and Human Services, Interior, Justice and Labor combined. Economist Robert Samuelson called it a governing philosophy of "Spend more, tax less."[9]

Conservative commentators were outraged. The American Conservative Union Foundation declared it a period in which "spending has skyrocketed, deficits have ballooned and government has never been bigger." Even with the federal government financing a trillion-dollar war in Iraq, some two-thirds of the spending growth in that period was unrelated to national security, columnist George Will pointed out, noting that "corporate welfare" dwarfed the budget of the Department of Homeland Security. Former Rep. Bob Barr summarized the trends succinctly: "We see bigger deficits. We see more spending. We see more pork." Those in Congress who attempted to restrain the spending found themselves "climbing uphill against a bipartisan pork coalition," political commentator Robert Novak wrote. In 1982, Ronald Reagan had condemned the presence of ten pet spending projects of individual Congressmen (known as "earmarks") in that year's transportation bill as excessive and vetoed the bill. In 2005, a transportation bill with *6,371* earmarks was routinely signed into law. In the decade following 1996, spending on earmarks more than tripled, from $19.5 billion to $64 billion. *The Wall Street Journal* called the 2003 Medicare drug bill "the largest expansion of the entitlement state since LBJ's Great Society." And even more stunning than the specifics of any single enactment was the sheer rate by which they were produced — twenty-four bills to increase spending for every one to cut it, Cato Institute budget analyst Chris Edwards reported on the 2003-04 Congress. Columnist Cal Thomas declared that "conservative" control of the federal government brought spending that far exceeded the "liberal" governments of earlier eras in American history.[10]

What all those massive spending bills for agri-business, education, pharmaceuticals, energy, transportation, etc., were *not* in conflict with, however, was the short-term interest of the profit imperative — filled as they were with one generous tax break after lucrative contract after special perk after another for corporate interests. In the way this book conceptualizes the historic advantaging of the profit imperative in both the marketplace of ideas and in the halls of government, it does not seem surprising that short-sighted financial gain would be advanced over all other interests — even truly conservative interests. Consider how the mind-boggling spending continued to be rolled out almost without pause, despite the fact that the nation was also financing extremely expensive wars in Iraq and Afghanistan. And while doing so, the government promoted a wartime policy that, as characterized in *The Wall Street Journal*, "did not ask America to sacrifice or fight, but to shop."[11]

While telling citizens to shop their way through wartime certainly seemed to suggest a government that had been restructured as a conduit for short-term commercial profit above all else, similarly revealing were U.S. trade regulations that increasingly encouraged American corporations to ship as many of the nation's jobs as possible abroad. Could the millions of citizens who had been won over by the business-as-democracy rhetoric of the seventies have anticipated being told — by the government it brought to power — that it was a *good* thing for billions of dollars in wages once earned by American workers to be shipped to low-wage countries? Certainly, in a world made flat by developments in transportation, communications, and other technologies, cheap labor had to inevitably factor more prominently in a global market. But was it truly in the best interests of voters who made possible the dominant political culture of recent decades for the government to be so aggressively embracing policies that promoted corporate outsourcing abroad?[12]

Such questions grew particularly more urgent for those worried by the potential threat that China's geo-economic juggernaut could represent to the influence of American-style democracy in shaping the world ahead. In a truly free marketplace of ideas, the people of the United States and many other parts of the world could reasonably be expected to choose a model of political freedom something like that idealized in American democratic traditions. But would the profit imperative choose instead the minimal-freedom model that characterized China politically even as it has adopted capitalist methods economically? With one-fifth of humanity, China represents the largest market in history for twenty-first-century multinational corporations. Some economists have projected China's economy not only equaling that of the United States by mid-century but quite possibly dwarfing it. By early in the century China had already taken over solidly as the leader in attracting the world's investment dollars. Almost limitless money poured into Chinese manufacturing, banking, computing, advertising, and engineering, as it maintained through government-enforced discipline a workforce unrivaled in its ability to deliver both skilled labor and obedience to authority for low wages. The world's largest companies demonstrated that they were quite comfortable doing very big business with a nation under the heel of the Chinese Communist Party. For the corporate profit imperative in the twenty-first century, could China represent "the critical mass in the coming order," shaped more by the Chinese authoritarian political culture than by the democratic traditions of American political freedom?[13]

Even if one dismissed as xenophobia warnings by those such as Congressman Dana Rohrabacher of the Chinese government's "megalomaniacal goals", there remained substantial basis for concern. Pulitzer Prize winning columnist Tom Friedman wrote of the great temptation to "cast an envious eye on the authoritarian Chinese political system, where leaders can, and do, just order that problems be solved." Several U.S.-based, multinational Internet and technology corporations, including Google, Microsoft, and Cisco, cooperated with the Chinese government to censor the flow of online information and to conduct surveillance of Internet users. When Chinese President Hu Jintao visited the United States in 2006, he was jeered by human-rights protestors but welcomed warmly by the White House and corporate CEOs representing "nearly every major sector of the U.S. economy," *The Wall Street Journal* reported. American corporate investment in the Chinese police state soared as plans for the most extensive surveillance system of any nation's citizens were implemented.[14]

But one does not need to look to China to find evidence of fundamental American interests being undermined through policies driven by the profit imperative. In the early 2000s, for example, the nation's Environmental Protection Agency administrator deftly reframed ecological science as nothing more than bottom-line economics: "There is no environmental progress without economic prosperity." Otherwise, he said, "our capacity to make environmental gains is gone. There is nothing that promotes pollution like poverty." It demonstrated just how dazzlingly successful had been the journey of Mobil Oil rhetoric from op-ed page to United States government policy. The institutionalization of such an understanding, reducing environmental concerns to mere fiscal policy, has justified a broad transformation in which federal agencies often appeared to be operated more like subsidiaries of corporate campaign donors. The lobbyists for power companies, by many accounts, were bestowed with as much control over environmental policy as EPA officials, if not more. The staggering degree of influence that the energy industry assumed over democratic processes was dramatized in the enactment of the 2005 energy bill, described by Friedman as "the sum of all lobbies." The

1,700-page bill provided special interests with some $85 billion in tax breaks and subsidies.[15]

Massive giveaways to oil companies that were already recording staggering profits represented a capitulation to the short-term demands of the profit imperative that seemed particularly reckless in light of growing evidence of the long-term energy crisis developing due to over reliance on petroleum. Using the same methodology developed by legendary Shell Oil geophysicist M. King Hubbert that correctly predicted the rate of U.S. oil extraction would peak in 1970, a number of geologists in recent years have forecast world extraction to peak out early in the twenty-first century. If those projections prove correct, the ultimate oil crisis would begin when the worldwide peak is reached — not when the oil actually runs out — because global demand in the early 2000s was rising annually by millions of barrels a day. Analysis ranging from insiders at Aramco, the giant Saudi-owned oil company, to a 2005 report by the U.S. Department of Energy's National Energy Technology Laboratory have warned that the age of conventionally produced petroleum as the world's dominant source of energy has begun to peak.[16]

Sadad al-Husseini, Aramco's recently retired top executive declared bluntly that the world is headed for a devastating oil crisis, because demand is rising so sharply that keeping up with it would require the impossible feat of bringing "a whole new Saudi Arabia" into production every couple of years. Of course, the precise quantities of petroleum reserves remaining on earth, and how long they might last, continue to be hotly debated issues. The ultimate truth cannot easily be determined. Oil reservoirs are underground and cannot actually be seen by the geologists who must try to determine how much is really still down there. But by 2005, even some oil companies were beginning to acknowledge the ominous dynamics at work. An advertising spread in *Business Week* by oil giant ChevronTexaco declared: "It took us 125 years to use the first trillion barrels of oil. We'll use the next trillion in 30. . . . One thing is clear: the era of easy oil is over." Another recent ChevronTexaco ad warned: "The fact is, the world has been finding less oil than it's been consuming for twenty years now." At the same time though, ExxonMobil continued to maintain essentially the opposite position. "Oil is a finite resource, but because it is so incredibly large, a peak will not occur this year, next year or for decades to come," the company insisted in a 2006 op-ed spot in *The New York Times.*[17]

The short-sightedness of keeping the nation so dependent on unrestrained consumption of petroleum also played out painfully for the U.S. auto industry in the early 2000s. While record-shattering profits rolled in for the oil industry — ExxonMobil's 2005 revenues alone were greater than any other U.S. corporation and most of the world's nations — American automakers were reeling as a consequence of having focused their business strategies myopically on the short-term. Their balance sheets plummeted into the red, massive layoffs were announced, and the credit-rating agencies dropped the automakers' bond ratings to junk status. As gasoline prices began their sharpest climb since the 1970s, the U.S. automakers found themselves shackled by their years of commitment to relentlessly building and marketing gas-guzzling SUVs and pickup trucks — while Japanese automakers reaped the benefits of years of investment in the development of gas-saving hybrids and other high-mileage vehicles. In the United States, the Detroit automakers had not had the incentive to focus on higher-mileage vehicles that existed in nations where higher gasoline taxes also had helped reduce oil consumption since the seventies. Such taxes would run counter to the fundamental anti-tax tenets of the dominant political culture in America over the same period, even though many analyses make convincing arguments that such a plan could channel revenue away from oil-producing nations that fund terrorism and into efforts to make the United States more energy-independent.[18]

A MARKETPLACE OF ONE IDEA

The degree to which political decisionmaking grew detached from broader considerations of the common good in the latter twentieth and early twenty-first centuries was often startling. But such a trend probably should not be surprising in light of the efforts launched decades before to dominate the marketplace of ideas. Such efforts evolved rapidly and grew deeply entrenched over that time, generating relentless momentum for maintaining the status quo of the dominant political culture in favor of short-term profit interests. Endeavors that advanced any other values were discouraged, often aggressively.

Networks of well-funded advocacy groups wielded their financial clout to advance without compromise the narrow interests of their backers.

Consider for example the way many such groups focused on punishing even solidly conservative politicians who wavered for any reason on tax policy. One group went so far as to tell Pennsylvania Senator Arlen Specter in 2004 that the organization was not interested in the fact that Specter had been rated more conservative than his upcoming opponent or that he had fought hard for such measures as a balanced-budget amendment. What did matter was that Specter had *considered* slightly trimming a 2001 $1.3 trillion tax cut by $250 million (so that the money could be spent on education) — before ultimately casting his final vote for the larger tax cut. So the organization funded his opponent. Other conservative Congressmen routinely had their patriotism attacked in anti-tax coalition advertising when they questioned tax cuts in the face of growing budget deficits. The bottom line was made clear in 2003 to an Alabama governor with a solid conservative record who sought to reform the state's regressive income tax in response to a $675 million budget deficit and education funding problems that he said made the state "last in all the things that are good, first in all the things that are bad." The national anti-tax coalition poured millions of dollars into a campaign not only to block the effort but to make sure the governor would "never be elected to anything again in his life."[19]

As a result, much funding of government shifted from broad-based taxes to sources of revenue that promote the very sort of activities that conservative voters oppose on moral grounds — gambling, alcohol and tobacco, even topless dancing. Politicians fearful to cross the anti-tax coalition have chosen instead to promote the flourishing of vice industries to fund public services. The powerful Americans for Tax Reform, for example, relentlessly pressured politicians nationwide to sign a "pledge" never to raise taxes for any reason. As journalist David Cay Johnston put it, such groups "have worked to make 'tax' a word so vile that many officials would rather make gambling as convenient as buying gasoline and have the state keep count of topless-bar customers than consider fundamental changes in its tax structure." In heartland states such as Oklahoma, so many casinos opened in the 1990s and 2000s (97 as of late 2007) that very few residents any longer lived more than a short drive from one — with a slot machine for every 79 of the state's 3.6 million residents. Lottery tickets could be purchased at even more outlets in the state, and both forms of gambling revenue had grown to fill a crucial role in paying for education and other services. Even the United States military grew to rely on slot machines on its bases to generate millions of dollars in needed funds. Military officials framed it as a matter of maintaining basic freedoms, providing soldiers with "access to the same games and gambling opportunities available to the civilians they are defending."[20]

All that said, the zealous advancement of tax-cutting dogma might still have been worth its excesses to those middle Americans whose support for its influence in the dominant political culture was crucial — if it had at least reduced their tax burden to the degree that it has those of corporations and the most wealthy. Instead, many analyses indicated that an anti-progressive overhaul of the tax code left the middle class paying a larger proportion of taxes than before. Coupled with ongoing reductions in both federal and state services, those citizens were in reality paying more for less — precisely the opposite of what they were promised. Although the wealthy of course continued to pay significant taxes, legislation since the seventies proportionately lightened that burden, while shifting it to the middle class. At the same time, corporate profits grew one third faster than corporate taxes over the latter decades of the twentieth century, with changes in tax policy enabling corporations to pay an ever-dwindling share of the cost of government. And for most Americans, the increased costs and reduced benefits enacted in major programs such as Medicare and Social Security in all likelihood represented only a fraction of changes to come.[21]

The process of dominating the marketplace of ideas evolved through far more institutional influence than simply the anti-tax lobby of course. The sort of efforts that corporate attorney and soon-to-be Supreme Court Justice Lewis F. Powell called for in his 1971 report to the United States Chamber of Commerce were realized on a scale beyond anything he must have imagined. A broad base developed through the funding of foundations and some wealthy individuals devoted to advancing the interests of big business came to fund a network of think tanks and research centers that churned out books, papers, conferences, etc., to provide scholarly justification for advancing those interests. Political strategists converted such material through polling, focus groups, and other marketing/public relations techniques into language with resonance for key segments of the electorate to provide waves of "grassroots" support for politicians who promoted a pro-business policy agenda in the way Powell envisioned. Although certainly many other foundations and think tanks promoted additional views, their policy agendas tended to be less coordinated.[22] Thus, when well-funded, pseudo-research-backed, focus-group-tested phrases like "tax relief," for example, entered the political lexicon in recent years, they had percolated up through that a system that positioned them to successfully engage public opinion. Such terminology was carefully developed so that it did not resonate of the corporate interests that reaped the bulk of the benefits of the legislation it advanced but of the suffering of the working man — who certainly needed "relief" and understandably was likely to sense affinity with those who offered it. From "tort reform" to "death tax" to "the ownership society," one campaign after another advanced corporate interests as those of hard-working, ordinary citizens, opposed only by unpatriotic cultural elites sneering down at the concerns of real Americans.[23]

Beyond that, both major corporations and government agencies mastered the technique of feeding public-relations messages cloaked as news reports into the marketplace of ideas so effectively that they increasingly grew impossible to distinguish from reports produced by independent news organizations. And large numbers of such news organizations quite willingly participated in the deception, running the segments with their own anchors and reporters reading scripted "lead-ins" so that they fit seamlessly into newscasts. Thus, "video news releases" featuring actors playing reporters and promoting everything from prescription drugs to war policy routinely came to reach television viewers disguised as journalism. And the gaming of the marketplace of ideas by government on behalf of corporate business interests went well beyond VNRs. Ostensibly independent academics and other commentators, for example, increasingly professed views publicly in return for payment. In many cases, they simply were paid to put their name on articles or opinion pieces written by corporate public-relations representatives.[24]

Efforts to manipulate public information went so far as to repackage scientific findings in a variety of ways in order to render them more compatible with the agendas of big business. The sweeping extent of such practices was made clear when the Union of Concerned Scientists issued a thirty-seven-page report in 2004 detailing the censoring and suppression of government scientists, the stacking of advisory committees with unqualified political appointees, and the disbanding of government panels that provided undesired recommendations. A statement endorsing the report was signed by more than six thousand scientists, including forty-eight Nobel laureates, sixty-two National Medal of Science recipients, and one-hundred thirty-five members of the National Academy of Sciences. Reporter Ross Gelbspan spent years documenting how the petroleum, automotive, coal, and other industries formed organizations such as the Global Climate Coalition and the Information Council on the Environment to develop a campaign to reposition global warming as theory rather than fact.[25]

Additionally, government documents were edited to play down links between automobile and energy-industry emissions and global warming. In 2002 and 2003, a former lobbyist for the American Petroleum Institute, the largest trade group representing the interests of the oil industry, working as chief of staff for the White House Council on Environmental Quality, made dozens of changes in reports on climate research that government scientists and their supervisors had already approved. After the editing was made public, the official immediately left the White House and joined ExxonMobil, which had long financed extensive advertising and lobbying efforts to question the science on global warming. Similar alteration and suppression of scientists' findings by government officials was also reported by researchers concerning their reports related to policy on land management, water quality, wildlife preservation, and other matters. Such efforts to doctor evidence grew so sophisticated as to include the manipulation of legislative histories. Such records are intended to provide documentation of the legislative intent behind laws when courts are called upon in later years to assess legal challenges that may arise involving the laws. But much evidence suggests an increased likelihood that courts will find themselves relying upon legislative histories virtually drafted by corporate interests.[26]

WHAT MATTERS WITH BIG MEDIA

At the same time that corporate interests developed such extensive influence over messages that government generated in the marketplace of ideas, it grew relatively less likely that Americans would learn about what government and big business were really doing from a free press either. News media increasingly were operated as the subsidiaries of business conglomerates that too often recognized little distinction between their news operations and the rest of their divisions. As detailed in Chapter Nine, great numbers of the nation's media organizations over the course of recent decades were gathered under the control of a very small number of corporate parents. It created an environment in which, more than ever, journalism could be neglected, but profit margins could not. Thus, the power of the press — a gateway to the marketplace of ideas so crucial that its legal independence from government was specified by the drafters of the Constitution — found itself subjugated instead by the heightened pressures of the profit imperative.

That is, recent decades brought considerably less thorough news and analysis on government, business, and serious problems facing society. Increasingly more time and attention were devoted to the proclivities and perversities of Paris Hilton, Michael Jackson, and other celebrities of the moment. More and more often, good investigative reporting was deemed simply too expensive in comparison to sound-bite hodgepodges of entertainment, gossip, and punditry. Further, with media conglomerates aggressively lobbying government for regulatory advantage, tax breaks, and giveaways, hard-hitting reports on the workings of government grew less welcome at corporate headquarters. As media scholar Robert McChesney observed, for example, media organizations that were the most aggressive in their broadcast support for going to war in Iraq were at the same time pressing the federal government to further revise media-ownership rules so that they could control larger numbers of media outlets in each market. McChesney has written extensively on the dizzying consolidation of great numbers of media outlets under the ownership of a handful of corporate parents. He emphasizes that the situation is not driven by a corporate "conspiracy" but by a focus on profit so singleminded that the media conglomerates "could not care less about their critics — on the left or right. . . . It is never about values, just money."[27]

Steve Barkin's research in political communication led him to identify the mid nineties as the time when it became clear that "the center of gravity in TV news had shifted. Neither the stern, unyielding predominance of the profit motive nor the blithe . . . rejection of the goals of public service and civic responsibility was new, but, it seemed to me, they had finally carried the day in an unquestioning, and disturbing, spirit." Barkin concluded that the Telecommunications Act of 1996 gave so much private control to such a small number of commercial interests that public ownership of the broadcast airwaves existed afterward "in theory only." In the wake of the FCC's 1999 revision of local television- and radio-ownership rules, permitting one owner to acquire larger numbers of stations in each market than ever before, analysis of program listings of television stations in the fifty largest markets indicated that large numbers of stations had virtually gone silent on local news and public affairs.[28]

Examining changes in the evening news on the major broadcast networks from 1969 to 1998, James Hamilton documented the way emphasis on profits over public service rose sharply, which translated into more coverage of celebrities and less coverage of Congress. It meant a marketplace of ideas no longer free enough to give audiences many things they wanted — such as quality journalism, less commercial pandering, etc. — "because it can only address what makes the most short-term profit for the media giants." That relentless dynamic steadily made media a significant anti-democratic force in American society, McChesney contended, in that they increasingly tended to promote a system that "works best when elites make most fundamental decisions and the bulk of the population is depoliticized." Other research found that, indeed, though there were more media outlets than ever, they were actually covering less news, so "more coverage . . . does not always mean greater diversity of voices." The popular notion of the Internet opening up access to a cornucopia of news was dispelled through analysis determining, for example, that although Google News offered access to 14,000 stories on a day chosen at random in 2005, they represented accounts of just 24 news events.[29]

A 2005 study by the Center for Creative Voices in Media and Fordham University found that the four radio companies that had grown largest through relaxed ownership rules were responsible for 96 percent of FCC fines for indecency from 2000 to 2003. The findings reflected management's tendencies to replace much of their local programming with shock jocks, such as Howard Stern and "Bubba the Love Sponge," who attracted the large audiences of young listeners that advertisers seek most. During that period, indecency complaints soared, with the FCC issuing twice as many indecency fines as it had through the entire decade of the 1990s. A 2006 study by the Parents Television Council concluded that even more violent incidents were featured on children's programming than on adult-oriented television — 7.96 per hour during after-school and Saturday morning programming for children, compared to 4.71 during prime-time programming. The same year, the journal *Archives of Pediatrics and Adolescent Medicine* published a thick issue devoted to a series of studies on the impact of recent media fare on children and declared: "Media need to be recognized as a major public health issue." A 2004 Rand Corporation study found that teens who viewed the most sexual content on television were more than twice as likely to become sexually active as those who viewed the least.[30]

The same year, a public furor ensued after singer Janet Jackson's breast was exposed briefly during the Super Bowl halftime show. One wonders why anyone was shocked, given the way that very NFL season had begun a few months before with a "Kickoff Live from the National Mall Presented by Pepsi Vanilla." It featured pop star Britney Spears having her pants torn off in what would have been considered a striptease routine in a more modest era. Yet that extravaganza was followed by a message to the nation from the president declaring that the event celebrated "the values that make our country strong." How could anyone have been surprised that the commercial impulse to keep pushing the envelope further would soon test the acceptability of ripping off Janet Jackson's boustier on national television? As sportswriter Sally Jenkins observed afterward, "For years NFL marketers have . . . appropriated sex, patriotism, war and even the tragedy of Sept. 11 as commercial vehicles, and used them all to peddle more Coors and cars." Indeed, it was the dominant political culture of recent years, with its priority on freeing the profit impulse from all restraint, that had brushed aside middle America's moral concerns rather than addressing them. "The assaults on its values, the insults, and the Hollywood sneers," cultural historian Thomas Frank wrote, "are products of capitalism as surely as are McDonald's hamburgers and Boeing 737s."[31]

MIDDLE-CLASS MELTDOWN

For citizens concerned more with what the dominant political culture delivered materially than morally in recent years, there was better news — at least for some. A few Americans even grew so wealthy they began taking over communities like Nantucket, the Massachusetts island off the Cape Cod coast where the Vanderbilts, Mellons, duPonts and other wealthy families had once built Gilded Age mansions and established it as one of the nation's most exclusive enclaves of privilege. Yet over the latter twentieth and early twenty-first centuries an even wealthier class developed. Many of its representatives set themselves up in a manner beyond the means of most of Nantucket's already affluent, dividing residents into what one called "the haves and the have-mores." They built bigger mansions, sailed pricier yachts, formed their own country clubs. They bought up established, multi-million-dollar estates simply to improve their view or house the help. They represented that fraction of a fraction of Americans — the top one-thousandth — that had pulled far away from all other Americans in income since 1980. Over the period, that group of some 145,000 citizens saw their average individual incomes, adjusted for inflation, multiply by two and a half times — from $1.2 million to $3 million. No other segment of the population experienced anything close to that during the same period.[32]

Certainly not the great mass of middle-class Americans who were told they were voting for change that would advance *their* interests as their support made possible the seismic political shift of recent decades. Of all the recent historical trends examined in this chapter, it is the accumulation of evidence on how the well-being of the nation's middle class deteriorated over the course of recent decades that offers the most compelling manifestation of what the age has meant. After an historic expansion through the first three quarters of the twentieth century that represented an unmatched fulfillment of the American Dream, the middle class thereafter saw its share of the pie steadily downsized and its opportunities for upward mobility diminished. Corporate profits soared, but very little trickled down to most of the population.

In 1979, the wealthiest one percent of Americans, as a group, had roughly half as much money left after taxes as did the bottom forty percent. Two decades later, the wealthiest one percent had *twice* as much. Adjusted for inflation, median family income doubled between 1947 and 1973. But then over the next thirty years, families' income improved by a total of only twenty-two percent — and much of that resulted not from rising wages but from the sharp upsurge in wives who once stayed home entering the paid labor force. Real wages (after inflation) stagnated for most people in recent decades. Since 1966, only the top ten percent of Americans enjoyed a growth rate of real wage and salary income equal to or above the average rate of productivity growth. And over the first half of the 2000s, median income saw its longest continued decline since the 1960s. (Median income is the meaningful measure for assessing the matter, because it represents the statistical midpoint for all incomes. The mean — or mathematical average — income figure distorts the picture, because the few exceptionally large incomes clustered at the top raise the mean to levels that do not accurately reflect overall income levels.) On the whole, expansion of upward mobility basically ground to a halt during the period examined in these pages, and income inequality reached extremes not seen since just before the Great Depression.[33]

While some costs of living in recent decades, such as food and clothing, rose more slowly than median family incomes, or even fell significantly for such products as electronics, the vital costs of education, health care, and housing skyrocketed in the latter twentieth and early twenty-first centuries. No longer was it only the poor who were unable to meet such expenses. Increasingly it was the middle class as well. When Barbara Ehrenreich wrote about the middle class in 1989, she titled her book *Fear of Falling.* Just a little over a decade later, it was not the fear but the actual fall that increasing numbers of middle Americans were dealing with firsthand. In 2001, Ehrenreich wrote about how millions had found it was possible to "work hard — harder than you ever thought possible — and still find yourself sinking ever deeper into poverty and debt." Exacerbating the crunch were the changes in tax policy resulting in the middle class paying both a greater share of overall taxes and more for government services lost or made more costly by budget cutbacks. And as baby boomers moved closer to traditional retirement age, the reality of shrinking health and pension benefits began to redefine sharply downward what their golden years would actually mean.[34]

In their struggle to keep up, more and more Americans found themselves borrowing record amounts. The nation's total consumer debt reached a trillion dollars for the first time in 1994. Only a decade later, that total had doubled, and American credit cardholders held an average of ten cards each. After being deregulated in the seventies, the credit-card industry brought forth what consumer-finance scholar Robert Manning called "one of the most costly, creative, and enormous mass marketing campaigns ever unleashed by corporate America." Such efforts focused most of all on middle-class households, inundating each with mailings of thirty-five to seventy-five preapproved card offers annually. Elizabeth Warren's extensive research on bankruptcy led her to conclude that two-income families had less money to spend, in inflation-adjusted dollars, than one-income families did three decades before. That was because they were forced to spend almost seventy percent more on their home mortgage and more than sixty percent more on health insurance. As a result, bankruptcy grew more common than divorce, heart disease, or cancer, and home-mortgage foreclosures and auto repossessions reached record levels. More than ninety percent of the bankruptcies came from the middle class.[35]

Warren's research indicated that the epidemic in family bankruptcies derived above all from parents trying to meet the skyrocketing expenses of maintaining a middle-class lifestyle for their children. On top of trying to meet the steep costs of a home in a decent neighborhood and adequate health care, Americans faced a similar uphill challenge in financing their children's college education. As legislative funding for higher education was slashed — with state appropriations accounting for only a little over a third of costs nationally by the early 2000s — public colleges and universities were forced to raise tuition and fees by staggering amounts and to allow even greater influence by commercial interests on campus in return for corporate funding.[36]

The age of American higher education as a gateway of opportunity had given way to "a defacto privatization of the institutions that played a crucial role in the creation of the American middle class," and a return to a system in which opportunity tended too often to be available only to those able to pay the ever higher costs themselves. For many students, it meant being forced to scale back their ambitions, to attend community colleges or not to attend college at all. For others it required taking on crushing levels of debt before they even completed their degrees and often working so many hours while in school that precious little time was left to devote to their studies. Making higher education less affordable promised only to flatten middle-class opportunities for upward mobility still further.[37]

THE WORST YET TO COME?

The pages of this chapter paint a depressing picture of what trends in recent decades have meant for most Americans. Much evidence was provided on the preceding pages in an effort to support the broad assertions. But decisions of selection and emphasis are inevitably a part of assembling any historical account. Especially when one attempts to ascertain the direction in which relatively recent history may be pointing a society, one must acknowledge that the passing of time can alter the perspective that current interpretations of available data may present. So perhaps the appraisal offered in this chapter will in the course of events prove overly pessimistic. Perhaps.

Or perhaps it will turn out that things at this writing are actually even worse, and we will discover that the trends of recent decades indeed were steering the nation into a crisis of devastating proportions for most Americans. For at the same time that the American middle class found itself sinking into unprecedented levels of debt, so too has its government. As this is written, the latest figures are much worse than has been widely reported. The official budget deficit for fiscal year 2005 was announced at $319 billion. But the Treasury Department's Financial Report of the United States Government (issued late in the year without even a press release) revealed that the actual deficit for that one year alone — that is, the real difference between the money the government received and the obligations it added for the year — was *$760 billion*. In the spring of 2006, the Congress raised the federal debt limit to $9 trillion, the fourth time it was raised in five years. Whatever else may be debatable about what the dominant political culture has wrought since the seventies, it now seems clear that responsible fiscal management of government was not part of the outcome.[38]

And just how much does that matter in the greater scheme of things? Consider the pronouncements of some of the most pro-business voices in America. The United States is "a country in the beginning stages of what can best be described as hegemonic decay," declared William Gross, director of PIMCO, one of the most successful investment companies in the world. He called the U.S.'s debt-dominated economic policy "nonsense [that] belongs in Mad magazine." In a recent annual letter to shareholders of his Berkshire Hathaway fund, multi-billionaire Warren Buffett said that by increasingly financing massive debt through foreign investors, the United States has become "like a family that consistently overspends its income . . . [and] finds that it is working more and more for the 'finance company' and less for itself."

Pete Peterson, chairman of the Blackstone Group investment firm and a former Commerce Secretary and chairman of the Federal Reserve Bank of New York, condemned recent economic policy as "a new level of fiscal irresponsibility . . . and virtually endless policy of debt creation," relentlessly choosing tax cuts over providing genuine financing for Social Security, paying for the war in Iraq, or even getting serious about homeland security. Former Treasury Secretary Robert Rubin, who in the late nineties presided over the only period of federal deficit reduction in recent decades, has called the need to redress fiscal imbalances "an immediate and critical imperative." Former Federal Reserve chairman Paul Volcker, surveying the mounting debt, dependence on foreign financiers, and ongoing lack of fiscal discipline in Washington, put it even more bluntly: "Altogether the circumstances seem to me as dangerous and intractable as any I can remember, and I can remember quite a lot."[39]

It is this book's thesis that democratic decisionmaking in the United States was greatly altered over the course of recent decades by the rise of a dominant political culture that advantaged a single-minded overemphasis on short-term profit over other interests in the marketplace of ideas. Central to that process was the legal success of the corporate free-speech movement. The next three chapters connect those legal developments to the trends outlined in this chapter. Detailing the Supreme Court's historical development of First

Amendment protection for corporate political media spending provides a framework for articulating the constructs of the unified theory that forms the heart of this analysis. It is through First Amendment law that the dominating force of government-advantaged corporate power in the economic marketplace has been transferred directly to the marketplace of ideas, contributing to a similar domination there.

That theory is grounded deeply in mainstream economic, legal, and philosophical schools of thought. It represents the connective tissue between the representation of reality put forth in this chapter and the degree of confidence we can have in the validity of that representation. Specifically, it provides a comprehensive theoretical basis to justify the assertion that First Amendment protection for corporate political media spending has undermined the political marketplace of ideas and significantly distorted American democratic processes as a result. Understanding the issue of First Amendment protection for corporate political media spending in American society today requires examining not only the relevant legal questions but also a number of broader assumptions that have been forcefully promoted in political discourse and have taken root both in the courtroom and far beyond.

[1] For a particularly thorough account of the changes in federal law, jurisprudence, and regulatory philosophy in antitrust policy since 1980, see Keith Conrad, "Media Mergers: First Step in a New Shift of Antitrust Analysis?" 49 *Federal Communication Law Journal* 675 (1997).

[2] See Justin Lahart, "Corporate Tax Burden Shows Sharp Decline," *The Wall Street Journal*, 13 April 2004, sec. C, p. 3; Lynnley Browning, "In Study, Most Companies Reported No Taxes," *The New York Times*, 6 April 2004, sec. C, p. 9; Lynnley Browning, "Study Finds Accelerating Decline in Corporate Taxes," *The New York Times*, 23 September 2004, sec. C, p. 3; Joe Bel Bruno, Associated Press, "Corporate America Has Record Cash Stockpiles on Hand," *The Oklahoman*, 28 May 2006, sec. C, p. 8; Brody Mullins, "More Lawmakers Take Trips Funded by Corporations: Businesses Find New Ways to Sway Congress Members After Finance Reform," *The Wall Street Journal*, 15 April 2005, sec. A, p. 1; "The Long Goodbye," *The Economist*, 8 April 2006, p. 31-32; Edmund L. Andrews, "How Tax Bill Gave Business More and More," *The New York Times*, 13 October 2004, sec. C, p. 1; Louis Uchitelle, "States Pay for Jobs, but It Doesn't Always Pay Off," *The New York Times*, 10 November 2003, sec. A, p. 1.

[3] See Geoff Mulvihill, Associated Press, "Cash-Strapped School Reaps Profits from Corporate Naming Rights," *The Norman Transcript*, 19 April 2004, sec. A, p. 7; Tamara Lewin, "In Public Schools, the Name Game as Donor Lure," *The New York Times*, 26 January 2006, sec. A, p. 1; Murray Evans and Bobby Anderson, "Corporate Aid for Schools Could Ease Budget Pains," *The Oklahoman*, 30 November 2002, sec. A, p. 4; Bill Pennington, "Reading, Writing and Corporate Sponsorships," *The New York Times*, 18 October 2004, sec. D, p. 1.

[4] For more on the extent of corporate efforts to "outsource the influencer," to make brands "living, breathing entities that have DNA," and to engineer the "commercialization of chitchat," see Gina Piccalo, "The Pitch That You Won't See Coming," *Los Angeles Times*, 22 August 2004, sec. E, p. 1; Rob Walker, "The Hidden (in Plain Sight) Persuaders," *The New York Times Magazine*, 5 December 2004; Brian Steinberg, "Look – Up in the Sky! Product Placement!" *The Wall Street Journal*, 18 April 2006, sec. B, p. 1; Michael Barbaro, "Wal-Mart Enlists Bloggers in its Public Relations Campaign," *The New York Times*, 7 March 2006, sec. C, p. 1; Louise Story, "Anywhere the Eye Can See, It's Likely to See an Ad," *The New York Times*, 15 January 2007, sec. A, p. 1; Naomi Klein, *No Logo* (New York: Picador, 1999). Klein documents at length how corporate branding has evolved into a concept of cultural pervasiveness.

[5] See Joel Balkan, *The Corporation: The Pathological Pursuit of Profit and Power* (New York: Free Press, 2004), 5.

[6] See Transcript, *NOW*, 18 February 2005. Accessed 22 July 2005 at: http://www.pbs.org/now/transcript/transcriptNOW107_full.html; Transcript, *NOW*, 25 February 2005. Accessed 22 July 2005 at: http://www.pbs.org/now/transcript/transcriptNOW108_full.html; Katie Hafner, "First Come Cellphone Towers, Then the Babel," *The New York Times*, 1 May 2005, sec. A, p. 1; Paul Krugman, "Free to Choose Obesity?" *The New York Times*, 8 July 2005, sec. A, p. 23; Melanie Warner, "The Food Industry Empire Strikes Back," *The New York Times*, 7 July 2005, sec. C, p. 1; Ira Dreyfuss, Associated Press, "State 'Cheeseburger Bills' Aim to Melt Fat Lawsuits," *The Norman Transcript*, 5 September 2004, sec. B, p. 4.

[7] See Anne d'Innocenzio, Associated Press, "Wal-Mart Becomes New Address for U.S.," *The Norman Transcript*, 21 September 2003, sec. B, p. 6; Melanie Warner, "When Wal-Mart Shops for Groceries, It Gets Whatever It Wants," *The New York Times*, 3 March 2006, sec. C, p. 1; Michael Barbaro, "Wal-Mart Offers Aid to Rivals," *The New York Times*, 5 April 2006, sec. C, p. 1; Paul Krugman, "Always Low Wages. Always," *The New York Times*, 13 May 2005, sec. A, p. 23; Paul Solman, "Global Giant," Transcript, *The NewsHour*, 23 August 2004. Accessed 25 August 2004 at: http://www.pbs.org/newshour/bb/business/july-dec04/walmart_8-23.html; Steven Greenhouse, "Wal-Mart, a Nation Unto Itself," *The New York Times*, 17 April 2004, sec. B, p. 7; Steve Lohr, "Is Wal-Mart Good for America?" *The New York Times*, 7 December 2003, sec. 4, p. 1; Abigail Goldman and Nancy Cleeland, "An Empire Built on Bargains Remakes the Working World," *Los Angeles Times*, 23 November 2003, sec. A, p. 1, 30; Anthony Bianco and Wendy Zellner, "Is Wal-Mart Too Powerful?" *Business Week*, 6 October 2003, p. 102-10; "The Wal-Marting of America," *The Week*, 15 August 2003, p. 13.

[8] See Steve Lohr, "Is Wal-Mart Good for America?" *The New York Times*, 7 December 2003, sec. 4, p. 1; Kemba J. Dunham and Kortney Stringer, "Wal-Mart's Region Enjoys Rapid Rise, but Not All Benefit," *The Wall Street Journal*, 10 February 2005, sec. A, p. 1; Anne d'Innocenzio, Associated Press, "Wal-Mart Employees Campaign-Style Tactics to Promote its Expansion," *The Norman Transcript*, 2 May 2004, sec. B, p. 5; John M. Broder, "Voters in Los Angeles Suburb Say No to a Big Wal-Mart," *The New York Times*, 7 April 2004, sec. A, p. 20; Jeanne Cummings, "Wal-Mart Opens for Business in a Tough Market: Washington," *The Wall Street Journal*, 24 March 2004, sec. A, p. 1; Steven Greenhouse, "Wal-Mart Driving Workers and Supermarkets Crazy," *The New York Times*, 19 October 2003, sec. WK, p. 3; Steve Lohr, "Is Wal-Mart Good for America?" *The New York Times*, 7 December 2003, sec. 4, p. 1; Charles Fishman, *The Wal-Mart Effect: How the World's Most Powerful Company Really Works — And How It's Transforming the American Economy* (New York: Penguin, 2006); Paul Solman, "Wal-Mart Works to Counteract

Negative Image," Transcript, *The NewsHour with Jim Lehrer*, 14 December 2005, accessed 15 December 2005 at: http://www.pbs.org/newshour/bb/busines s/july-dec05/walmart_12-14.html; Michael Barbaro, "A New Weapon for Wal-Mart: A War Room," *The New York Times*, 1 November 2005, sec. A, p. 1; Jeffrey Goldberg, "Selling Wal-Mart: Can the Company Co-opt Liberals?" *The New Yorker*, 2 April 2007, p. 32-38.

[9] See David Broder, "A Price to be Paid for Folly," *The Washington Post*, 11 September 2005, sec. B, p. 7; Jackie Calmes, "Expanding Bush Budgets Irk Conservatives," *The Wall Street Journal*, 24 January 2006, sec. A, p. 4; Robert J. Samuelson, "Cynical Conservatism," *The Washington Post*, 5 October 2005, sec. A, p. 23.

[10] See Michael D. Tanner, *Leviathan on the Right: How Big-Government Conservatism Brought Down the Republican Revolution* (Washington, D.C.: Cato Institute, 2007); Richard A. Viguerie, *Conservatives Betrayed: How George W. Bush and Other Big Government Republicans Hijacked the Conservative Cause* (Los Angeles: Bonus Books, 2006); Jeff Crouere, "GOP Addicted to Big Government," *American Conservative Union Foundation*, 31 August 2005, accessed 5 Sept. 2005 at: http://acuf.org/issues/issue42/050828po l.asp; Linda Bilmes and Joseph E. Stiglitz, "The Economic Costs of the Iraq War: An Appraisal Three Years after the Beginning of the Conflict," KSG Working Paper No. 06-002, Social Science Research Network, January 2006, accessed 22 April 2006 at: http://ssrn.com/abstract=832646; George F. Will, "Grand Old Spenders," *The Washington Post*, 17 November 2005, sec. A, p. 31; Steve Chapman, "Supersizing the Federal Government," *Chicago Tribune*, 15 December 2005, sec. A, p. 27; Robert Novak, "Earmark Foes May Force Roll Calls," *The Chicago Sun-Times*, 30 January 2006, sec. A, p. 39; "Cold Shoulder: Sadly, Coburn's Pork-Busting is Rebuked," Editorial, *The Oklahoman*, 23 October 2005, sec. A, p. 18; Transcript, *NOW*, 6 May 2005, sec, accessed 22 July 2005 at: http://www.pbs.org/now/transcript/transcriptNO W118_full.html; "Pet Projects Make Roads Bill a Real Lulu — of Excess," *USA Today*, 10 August 2005, sec. A, p. 10; "Republicans DeLayed," Editorial, *The Wall Street Journal*, 1 October 2005, sec. A, p. 18; Chris Edwards, *Downsizing the Federal Government* (Washington, D.C.: Cato Institute, 2005), 16; Cal Thomas, "Our Spending Obscenities," *The Oklahoman*, 22 March 2006, sec. A, p. 13.

[11] See Mark Helprin, "Failing the Test of September 11," *The Wall Street Journal*, 16 September 2002, sec. A, p. 14.

[12] For a discussion of these trends, see, for example, Pete Engardio, Aaron Bernstein, and Manjeet Kripalani, "Is Your Job Next?" *Business Week*, 3 February 2003, 50; Balkan, *The Corporation*, 111-38; Lou Dobbs, *Exporting America: Why Corporate Greed is Shipping American Jobs Overseas* (New York: Warner Books, 2004); Thomas L Friedman, *The World is Flat: A Brief*

History of the Twenty-first Century (New York: Farrar, Straus and Giroux, 2005); Louis Uchitelle, *The Disposable American: Layoffs and Their Consequences* (New York: Alfred A. Knopf, 2006); Jeff Faux, *The Global Class War: How America's Bipartisan Elite Lost Our Future — And What It Will Take to Win it Back* (New York: John Wiley & Sons, 2006).

[13] For analysis of the pivotal role that China is already playing in the world economy, see, for example, Ted C. Fishman, *China, Inc.: How the Rise of the Next Superpower Challenges America and the World* (New York: Scribner, 2005); C. Fred Bergsten, Bates Gill, Nicholas R. Lardy, and Derek Mitchell, *China: The Balance Sheet* (Hoboken, N.J.: Public Affairs, 2006)); Peter Navarro, *The Coming China Wars: Where They Will Be Fought and How They Can Be Won* (Upper Saddle River, N.J.: Financial Times Press, 2007).

[14] See Transcript, House Subcommittee on Oversight and Investigations, *Chinese Influence on U.S. Foreign Policy through U.S. Educational Institutions, Multilateral Organizations and Corporate America: Hearing before the Committee on International Relations*, 109th Congress, 2d sess. 14 Feb. 2006, accessed 15 February 2006 at: http://wwwc.house.gov/international_relations/oihear.htm; Thomas L. Friedman, "Thou Shalt Not Destroy the Center," *The New York Times*, 11 November 2005, sec. A, p. 25; Tom Zeller Jr., "Critics Press Companies on Internet Rights Issues," *The New York Times*, 8 November 2005, sec. C, p. 6; David Barboza, "Google Cuts Two Features for China," *The New York Times*, 25 January 2006, sec. C, p. 1; Joseph Kahn, "China's Leader, in Seattle, Tells U.S. Not to Dwell on Divisive Issues," *The New York Times*, 20 April 2006, sec. A, p. 6; Neil King, Jr., Jay Solomon, and Jason Dean, "Hu Yields Little on Major Issues in Bush Summit: Business Ties Underscored at CEO-Heavy Luncheon," *The New York Times*, 21 April 2006, sec. A, p. 1; Keith Bradsher, "Wall St. Sees an Opportunity in China's Surveillance Boom," *The New York Times*, 11 September 2007, sec. A, p. 1.

[15] See Felicity Barringer, "New Priorities in Environment," *The New York Times*, 14 September 2004, sec. A, p. 1; Christopher Drew and Richard A. Oppel, Jr., "How Power Lobby Won the Battle of Pollution Control at E.P.A.," *The New York Times*, 6 March 2004, sec. A, p. 1; Bruce Barcott, "Changing All the Rules," *The New York Times*, 4 April 2004, sec. 6, p. 38; Thomas L. Friedman, "Too Much Pork and Too Little Sugar," *The New York Times*, 5 August 2005, sec. A, p. 15; Michael Grunwald and Juliet Eilperin, "Energy Bill Raises Fears About Pollution, Fraud: Critics Point to Perks for Industry," *The New York Times*, 30 July 2005, sec. A, p. 1.

[16] Petroleum geologists define the concept of peaking as the critical point at which oil fields can no longer produce increasing amounts of oil, generally when the field is about half-empty. Once that point is reached, production from the field begins an inevitable decline, no matter how many more wells are drilled in it.

[17] See David Goodstein, *Out of Gas: The End of the Age of Oil* (New York: W.W. Norton & Company, 2004); Kenneth S. Deffeyes, *Hubbert's Peak: The Impending World Oil Shortage* (Princeton, N.J.: Princeton University Press, 2001); Peter Maass, "The Breaking Point," *The New York Times Magazine*, 21 August 2005, p. 30; Chip Cummings, Bhushan Bahree, and Jeffrey Bell, "Why the World is One Storm Away from Energy Crisis," *The Wall Street Journal*, 24-25 September 2005, sec. A, p. 1; Christopher Palmeri and Peter Coy, "Is There Plenty of Oil?" *Business Week*, 11 July 2005, p. 28; "So Why Should You Care?" Advertisement, *Business Week*, 11 July 2005, p. 4-5; "The World Consumes Two Barrels of Oil for Every Barrel Discovered," Advertisement, *The New Yorker*, 5 September 2005, p. 8-9; "Peak Oil? Contrary to Theory, Oil Production Shows No Sign of a Peak," Advertisement, *The New York Times*, 2 Marcy 2006, sec. A, p. 29.

[18] See Edwin Black, *Internal Combustion: How Corporations and Governments Addicted the World to Oil and Derailed the Alternatives* (New York: St. Martin's Press, 2006); Thomas L. Friedman, "Et Tu, Toyota?" *The New York Times*, 3 October 2007, sec. A, p. 25; Simon Romero and Edmund L. Andrews, "At ExxonMobil, a Record Profit But No Fanfare," *The New York Times*, 31 January 2006, sec. A, p. 1; Micheline Maynard, "Detroit Grapples With a New Era: The Not-So-Big 3," *The New York Times*, 11 May 2006, sec. A, p. 1; Martin Fackler, "With $12 Billion in Profit, Toyota Has G.M. in Sight," *The New York Times*, 11 May 2006, sec. C, p. 4; Gina Chon, "GM and Ford Miss Out on Gain in U.S. Car Sales; Detroit Duo Lose Share To Asian, European Rivals And Plan to Cut Production," *The Wall Street Journal*, 2 March 2006, sec. A, p. 3; Jeffrey McCracken and Joseph P. White, "Detroit Stuck in Neutral; As Gas Prices Rise Again, Big Three's Current Products Don't Match High-MPG Talk," *The Wall Street Journal*, 26 January 2006, sec. A, p. 1; Jeremy W. Peters, "U.S. Makers Facing Glut of S.U.V.'s as Gas Rises," *The New York Times*, 3 May 2006, sec. C, p. 3; Micheline Maynard and Vikas Bajaj, "G.M. Reports Big Losses as Its Woes Grow," *The New York Times*, 27 January 2006, sec. C, p. 1; Jeffrey McCracken and Joseph P. White, "Ford Will Shed 28% of Workers In North America; Car Maker to Close 14 Plants As It Joins GM in Overhaul Of Detroit's Business Model," *The Wall Street Journal*, 24 January 2006, sec. A, p. 1; Vikas Bajaj, "Ford Eliminating Up to 30,000 Jobs and 14 Factories," *The New York Times*, 23 January 2006, sec. C, p. 1; Victor Davis Hanson, "Oil Gluttons in Need of an Intervention," *Chicago Tribune*, 13 January 2006, sec. A, p. 21; Jeffrey Bull, John J. Fialka, and Russell Gold, "Backlash Spreads as Profits Surge at Oil Companies," *The Wall Street Journal*, 28 October 2005, sec. A, p. 1; Jad Mouawad and Simon Romero, "Big Rise in Profit Puts Oil Giants on Defensive," *The New York Times*, 28 October 2005, sec. C, p. 1; Jad Mouawad, "Senators Grill Oil Executives on Prices and Profits," *The New York Times*, 10 November 2005,

sec. C, p. 1; Danny Hakim, "G.M. Will Reduce Hourly Workers in U.S. by 25," *The New York Times*, 8 June 2005, sec. C, p. 1; Gina Chon, "Sales of SUVs Fall Sharply," *The Wall Street Journal*, 4 October 2005, sec. D, p. 1; Lee Hawkins Jr., Neal E. Boudette, and Kris Maher, "GM, Amid Industry Overhaul, Cuts Health Benefits for Retirees," *The Wall Street Journal*, 18 October 2005, sec. A, p. 1; Gina Chon, "Car Makers Forced to Pile on More Discounts," *The Wall Street Journal*, 25 October 2005, sec. D, p. 1; Neal Boudette and Joseph P. White, "How Slumping Market for SUVs is Hurting Detroit's Bottom Line," *The Wall Street Journal*, 13 May 2005, sec. A, p. 1; Danny Hakim, "G.M. and Ford Stuck in Reverse as Buyers Look Beyond Detroit," *The New York Times*, 15 April 2005, sec. C, p. 1; Paul Roberts, "Power Outage: The U.S. is Falling Behind its Rivals in Developing Alternative Energy Sources," *Los Angeles Times*, 23 May 2004, sec. M, p. 1; Danny Hakim, "A Fuel-Saving Proposal From Your Automaker: Tax the Gas," *The New York Times*, 18 April 2004, sec. 3, p. 5; Thomas L. Friedman, "Fly Me to the Moon," *The New York Times*, 5 December 2004, sec. 4, p. 13.

[19] See Matt Bai, "Fight Club," *The New York Times Magazine*, 31 August 2003, p. 25-26; Jeffrey Gettleman, "A Tax Increase? $1.2 Billion? Alabamians, It Seems, Say No," *The New York Times*, 6 September 2003, sec. A, p. 1.

[20] See William M. Bulkeley, "To Boost Revenues, State Lotteries Wager on Slots," *The Wall Street Journal*, 30 March 2006, sec. A, p. 1; David Cay Johnston, "A Texas Bid to Shift School Finances to 'Sin Taxes,'" *The New York Times*, 21 April 2004, sec. A, p. 14; Nicholas Confessore, "Breaking the Code," *The New York Times Magazine*, 16 January 2005, p. 35; Linda Miller, "Going for the Jackpot," *The Oklahoman*, 9 September 2007, sec. F, p. 1; Tony Thornton, "State to Get Rolling on Pick 3," *The Oklahoman*, 9 November 2005, sec. A, p. 1; Tony Thornton, "State to Roll Out its Latest Game," *The Oklahoman*, 7 November 2005, sec. A, p. 1; "Playing the Numbers: Gaming, Tobacco Issues Loom Large," Editorial, *The Oklahoman*, 10 November 2005, sec. A, p. 10; Judy Gibbs Robinson, "State, Indian Tribes Bolster Partnership," *The Oklahoman*, 13 October 2005, sec. A, p. 1; Associated Press, "Tribes Become Gaming Leaders," *The Oklahoman*, 16 February 2005, sec. A, p. 11; Tony Thornton, "Casino Overload? Experts Doubt It," *The Oklahoman*, 8 January 2005, sec. A, p. 1; Tony Thornton, "Casinos' Growth No. 2 in Nation," *The Oklahoman*, 25 June 2006, sec. A, p. 1; Tony Thornton, "Gaming Sees Big Growth," *The Oklahoman*, 13 October 2007, sec. A, p. 1; Diana B. Henriques, "Temptation Near for Military's Problem Gamblers," *The New York Times*, 19 October 2005, sec. A, p. 1.

[21] See "Getting Real About Taxes," Editorial, *Business Week*, 5 May 2003, p. 110; Matt Bai, "Drip, Drip, Drip," *The New York Times Magazine*, 8 June 2003, p. 78; Alan B. Krueger, "Connecting the Dots from Tax Cuts for the Wealthy to Loss of Benefits" *The New York Times*, 16 October 2004, sec. C, p.

2; David Cay Johnston, *Perfectly Legal: The Covert System to Rig Our Tax System to Benefit the Super Rich — and Cheat Everybody Else* (New York: Portfolio, 2003); Dana Milbank and Jonathan Weisman, "Middle Class Tax Share Set to Rise," *The Washington Post*, 4 June 2003, sec. A, p. 1; Michael Zweig, ed., *What's Class Got to Do With It? American Society in the Twenty-First Century* (Ithaca, N.Y.: Cornell University Press, 2004); Kevin Phillips, *Boiling Point: Republicans, Democrats, and the Decline of Middle-Class Prosperity* (New York: Random House, 1993).

[22] See Bill Bradley, "A Party Inverted," *The New York Times*, 30 March 2005, sec. A, p. 17; Philip Shenon, "On Opinion Page, A Lobby's Hand is Often Unseen," *The New York Times*, 23 December 2005, sec. A, p. 1; Eamon Javers, "Op-Eds for Sale," *Business Week Online*, 16 December 2005, accessed 19 December 2005 at: http://www.businessweek.com/bwdaily/dnflash/dec2005/nf20051216_1037_db016.htm; John J. Miller, "The Very Foundation of Conservatism," *The New York Times*, 28 November 2005, sec. A, p. 23; Jason DeParle, "Goals Reached, Donor on Right Closes Up Shop," *The New York Times*, 29 May 2005, sec. 1, p. 1; Paul Krugman, "Design for Confusion," *The New York Times*, 5 August 2005, sec. A, p. 15; Jason DeParle, "Goals Reached, Donor on Right Closes Up Shop," *The New York Times*, 29 May 2005, sec. 1, p. 1; Nicholas Confessore, "Meet the Press: How James Glassman Reinvented Journalism — As Lobbying," *Washington Monthly*, December 2003, accessed 5 October 2005 at: http://www.washingtonmonthly.com/features/2003/0312.confessore.html; Benjamin Wallace-Wells, "In the Tank: The Intellectual Decline of AEI," *Washington Monthly*, December 2003, accessed 5 October 2005 at: http://www.washingtonmonthly.com/features/2003/0312.wallacewells.html; Jean Stefancic and Richard Delgado, *No Mercy: How Conservative Think Tanks and Foundations Changed America's Social Agenda* (Philadelphia: Temple University Press, 1996); James Arnt Aune, *Selling the Free Market: The Rhetoric of Economic Correctness* (New York: Guilford, 2001), 5-6.

[23] For examples of this phenomenon at work, see Frank Luntz, *Words That Work: It's Not What You Say, It's What People Hear* (New York: Hyperion, 2007); George Lakoff, "Framing the Dems," *The American Prospect*, 1 September 2003, p. 32; Jodi Wilgoren, "Politicized Scholars Put Evolution on the Defensive," *The New York Times*, 21 August 2005, sec. A, p. 1; Frank Rich, "A High-Tech Lynching in Prime Time," *The New York Times*, 24 April 2005, sec. 4, p. 13; Roger Lowenstein, "A Question of Numbers," *The New York Times*, 16 January 2005, sec. 6, p. 10; Maureen Dowd, "Rove's Revenge," *The New York Times*, 7 November 2004, sec. 4, p. 11; Paul Krugman, "Bush's Own Goal," *The New York Times*, 13 August 2004, sec. A, p. 21.

[24] See David Barstow and Robin Stein, "The Message Machine: How the Government Makes News," *The New York Times*, 13 March 2005, sec. 1, p. 1; General Accounting Office, "Media Contracts: Activities and Financial

Obligations for Seven Federal Departments," 13 February 2006 (GAO-06-305), accessed 16 February 2006 at: http://www.gao.gov/htext/d06305.html; Richard Williamson, "Bush Spent $1.6 Bil. on 'Spin'," *Adweek Online*, 13 February 2006, accessed 15 February 2006 at: http://www.adweek.com/aw/national/article_display.jsp?vnu_content_id=1001996193. In April 2005, the Federal Communications Commission warned broadcasters that it could take action against stations that failed to disclose the sponsors of such messages. See Federal Communications Commission, "FCC Public Notice to Remind Broadcasters and Cable Operators of Video News Release (VNR) Requirements and Seeking Comment on VNR Use," 13 April 2005 (FCC 05-84, MB Docket No.05-171). A few months later, the Government Accountability Office ruled that VNRs promoting federal education policy in the early 2000s violated a statutory ban on the dissemination of "covert propaganda." See Robert Pear, "Buying of News by Bush's Aides is Ruled Illegal," *The New York Times*, 1 October 2005, sec. 1, p. 1. A year later, studies found the use of VNRs remained widespread, with many broadcasters doing no more than paying "lip service to the rules." See Joe Flint, "TV Stations Still Can't Resist Pre-Packaged Video News," *The Wall Street Journal*, 26 April 2006, accessed 29 May 2006 at: http://online.wsj.com/public/article/SB114591 2173664344589KT2kVeFjbRby2Jm5lTAV_rlaU0_20060525.html?mod=tff_main_tff_top; Stations during that period were found to routinely air the VNRs during their news shows without disclosure to viewers, disguising the sponsored content to make it appear to be their own reporting, but almost never actually balancing the sponsor's message with independent footage or reporting. See Diane Farsetta and Daniel Price, "Fake TV News: Widespread and Undisclosed," Center for Media and Democracy, 6 April 2006, accessed 1 May 2006 at: http://www.prwatch.org/fakenews/execsummary; Michael Schroeder, "Some Professors Take Payments to Express Views," *The Wall Street Journal*, 10 December 2004, sec. B, p. 1.

[25] See James Glanz, "Scientists Say Administration Distorts Facts," *The New York Times*, 19 February 2004, sec. A, p. 18; "Scientific Integrity in Policymaking," Union of Concerned Scientists, 18 February 2004, accessed 1 May 2006 at: http://www.ucsusa.org/scientific_integrity/interference/reports-scientific-integrity-in-policy-making.html; Ross Gelbspan, *Boiling Point: How Politicians, Big Oil and Coal, Journalists, and Activists are Fueling the Climate Crisis* (New York, N.Y.: Basic Books, 2004); Transcript, *NOW*, 22 April 2005, accessed 22 July 2005 at: http://www.pbs.org/now/transcript/transcriptNOW116_full.html.

[26] See Andrew C. Revkin, "Bush Aide Edited Climate Reports," *The New York Times*, 8 June 2005, sec. A, p. 1; Andrew C. Revkin, "Former Bush Aide Who Edited Reports Is Hired by Exxon," *The New York Times*, 15 June 2005, sec. A, p. 21; Heather Timmons, "British Science Group Says Exxon

Misrepresents Climate Issues," *The New York Times*, 21 September 2006, sec. C, p. 2; "Scientists' Report Documents ExxonMobil's Tobacco-like Disinformation Campaign on Global Warming Science," Union of Concerned Scientists, 3 January 2007, accessed 21 April 2007 at: http://www.ucsusa.org/news/press_release/ExxonMobil-GlobalWarming-tobacco.html; Transcript, *NOW*, 22 July 2005, accessed 28 July 2005 at: http://www.pbs.org/now/transcript/transcriptNOW129_full.html. Various aspects of the trend to manipulate legislative history are examined in Cassandra Imfeld and Victoria Smith Ekstrand, "The Music Industry and the Legislative Development of the Digital Millennium Copyright Act's Online Service Provider Provision," 10 *Communication Law and Policy* 291 (2005); David Nimmer, "Appreciating Legislative History. The Sweet and Sour Spots of the DMCA's Commentary," 23 *Cardozo Law Review* 909 (2002); William T. Mayton, "Law Among the Pleonasms: The Futility and Aconstitutionality of Legislative History in Statutory Interpretation," 41 *Emory Law Journal* 113 (1992); Jane S. Schacter, "The Confounding Common Law Originalism in Recent Supreme Court Statutory Interpretation: Implications for the Legislative History Debate and Beyond," 51 *Stanford Law Review* 1 (1998); Allison C. Giles, "The Value of Nonlegislators' Contributions to Legislative History," 79 *Georgetown Law Journal* 359 (1990); Jessica Litman, "Copyright Legislation and Technological Change," 68 *Oregon Law Review* 275 (1989).

[27] See Transcript, *NOW*, 5 August 2005, accessed 19 August 2005 at: http://www.pbs.org/now/transcript/transcriptNOW131_full.html; Robert W. McChesney and John Nichols, *Our Media, Not Theirs: The Democratic Struggle Against Corporate Media* (New York: Seven Stories Press, 2002), 31-45.

[28] Steve M. Barkin, *American Television News: The Media Marketplace and the Public Interest* (Armonk, N.Y.: M.E. Sharpe, 2003), xi-xiii, 173-74; Loy A. Singleton and Steven C. Rockwell, "Silent Voices: Analyzing the FCC 'Media Voices' Criteria Limiting Local Radio-Television Cross-Ownership," 8 *Communication Law and Policy* 385 (2003).

[29] James T. Hamilton, *All the News That's Fit to Sell: How the Market Transforms Information into News* (Princeton, N.J.: Princeton University Press, 2004), 161-89; Robert W. McChesney, *Rich Media, Poor Democracy: Communication Politics in Dubious Times* (Urbana, Ill.: University of Illinois Press, 1999), 2-3; Katharine Q. Seelye, "Study Finds More News Media Outlets, Covering Less News," *The New York Times*, 13 March 2006, sec. C, p. 3; "The State of the News Media 2006," Project for Excellence in Journalism, March 2006, accessed 1 May 2006 at: http://www.stateofthemedia.org/2006/.

[30] Jonathan Rintels. "Ownership Concentration and Indecency in Broadcasting: Is There a Link?", *Center for Creative Voices in Media*, 6 May 2005, accessed 9 September 2005 at: http://www.creativevoices.us/php-

bin/news/showArticle.php?id=135&PHPSESSID=29cfd8aac436b84abce7939cd8846b3d; Kristen Fyfe, "Wolves in Sheep's Clothing: A Content Analysis of Children's Television," Parents Television Council, 2 March 2006, accessed 12 May 2006 at: http://www.parentstv.org/PTC/publications/reports/childrensstudy/childrensstudy.pdf; *Archives of Pediatrics & Adolescent Medicine*, 160:4 (April 2006): 335-453; Rebecca Collins et al., "Watching Sex on Television Predicts Adolescent Initiation of Sexual Behavior," *Pediatrics*, 114:3 (September 2004), e280-89, accessed 12 May 2006 at: http://pediatrics.aappublications.org/cgi/content/full/114/3/e280.

[31] Christopher Knight, "Public Trust, Private Gain," *Los Angeles Times*, 15 February 2004, sec. E, p. 42; Sally Jenkins, "NFL Exposed For What It Is," *The New York Times*, 3 February 2004, sec. D, p. 1; Thomas Frank, *What's the Matter with Kansas? How Conservatives Won the Heart of America* (New York: Metropolitan Books, 2004), 241-42.

[32] Geraldine Fabrikant, "Old Nantucket Warily Meets the New," *The New York Times*, 5 June 2005, sec. A, p. 1; David Cay Johnston, "Richest Are Leaving Even the Rich Far Behind," *The New York Times*, 5 June 2005, sec. A, p. 1.

[33] This discussion was developed from a number of sources, including reports from the U.S. Census Bureau (http://www.census.gov/); Internal Revenue Service (http://www.irs.gov/); Congressional Budget Office (http://www.cbo.gov/); Economic Report of the President (http://www.gpoaccess.gov/eop/); National Bureau of Economic Research (http://www.nber.org). Also drawn upon were a variety of analyses of relevant statistical trends, including: Thomas Piketty and Emmanuel Saez, "Income Inequality in the United States, 1913-1998," NBER Working Paper 8467, National Bureau of Economic Research, September 2001, accessed 2 May 2006 at: http://www.nber.org/papers/w8467; Paul Krugman, "Letter to the Secretary," *The New York Times*, 24 March 2006, sec. A, p. 21; Brendan M. Case and Angela Shah, "Worst Inflation in Years Pokes Holes in Spending Power," *The Dallas Morning News*, 15 October 2005, sec. A, p. 1; Lynnley Browning, "U.S. Income Gap Widening, Study Says," *The New York Times*, 25 September 2003, sec. C, p. 2; Paul Krugman, *The Age of Diminished Expectations: U.S. Economic Policy in the 1990s*, 3d ed. (Cambridge, Mass.: MIT Press, 1998); Ian Dew-Becker, Robert J. Gordon, "Where Did the Productivity Growth Go? Inflation Dynamics and the Distribution of Income, " NBER Working Paper No. 11842, National Bureau of Economic Research, December 2005, accessed 2 May 2006 at: http://www.nber.org/papers/w11842; Simon Head, *The New Ruthless Economy: Work and Power in the Digital Age* (New York: Oxford University Press, 2003); Miles Corak, ed., *Generational Income Mobility in North America and Europe* (Cambridge, U.K.: Cambridge University Press, 2004); Clive Crook, "The Height of Inequality: America's Productivity Gains

Have Gone to Giant Salaries for Just a Few," *The Atlantic Monthly*, September 2006, p. 36; David Cay Johnston, "Income Gap is Widening, Data Shows," *The New York Times*, 29 March 2007, sec. C, p. 1.

[34] Milt Freudenheim, "Employees Paying Ever-Bigger Share for Health Care," *The New York Times*, 10 September 2003, sec. A, p. 1; Robert Pear, "Big Increase Seen in People Lacking Health Insurance," *The New York Times*, 30 September 2003, sec. A, p. 1; Jeff Madrick, "The No-Frills Middle Class," *The New York Times*, 4 September 2003, sec. C, p. 1; Stephanie Strom, "For Middle Class, Health Insurance Becomes a Luxury," *The New York Times*, 16 November 2003, sec. 33, p. A; Barbara Ehrenreich, *Fear of Falling: The Inner Life of the Middle Class* (New York: Pantheon, 1989); Barbara Ehrenreich, *Nickel and Dimed: On (Not) Getting By in America* (New York: Metropolitan Books, 2001); Robert Berner, "Driving the SUV to the Food Pantry: More Displaced Executives are Having to Rely on Handouts," *Business Week*, 28 April 2003, 68; Danielle DiMartino, "Even Rich are Losing Homes," *The Dallas Morning News*, March 19 2004, sec. D, p. 4; Gene Koretz, "Land of Less Opportunity," *Business Week*, 30 June 2003, 28; David Wessel, "As Rich-Poor Gap Widens in the U.S., Class Mobility Stalls," *The Wall Street Journal*, 13 May 2005, sec. A, p. 1; Micheline Maynard, "United Air Wins Right to Default on Its Pensions," *The New York Times*, 11 May 2005, sec. C, p. 1; Robert Pear, "Retirees Are Paying More for Health Benefits, Study Says," *The New York Times*, 15 December 2004, sec. A, p. 27; David Henry, "The New Pinch from Pensions," *Business Week*, 5 August 2002, p. 44; Mary Williams Walsh, "Once Safe, Public Pensions Are Now Facing Cuts," *The New York Times*, 6 November 2006, sec. A, p. 1.

[35] Patrice Hill, "The New Debt," *The Washington Times*, 10 February 2006, sec. A, p. 1; Bob Davis, "Lagging Behind the Wealth, Many Use Debt to Catch Up," *The Wall Street Journal*, 17 May 2005, sec. A, p. 1; Robert D. Manning, *Credit Card Nation: The Consequences of America's Addiction to Credit* (New York: Basic Books, 2000); Elizabeth Warren and Amelia Warren Tyagi, *The Two-Income Trap: Why Middle-Class Mothers and Fathers are Going Broke* (New York: Basic Books, 2003); Allison B. Cohen, "The Middle-Class Housing Squeeze," *Los Angeles Times*, 7 March 2004, sec. K, p. 1; Randall Turk, "Home a Distant Dream for Growing Numbers of Americans," *The Norman Transcript*, 11 April 2004, sec. B, p. 4; Stephanie Stoughton, Associated Press, "The Revolving Door: Payday Lenders Keep Borrowers Returning," *The Oklahoman*, 23 May 2006, sec. B, p. 6.

[36] For a fuller discussion of the "relentless growth of commercial-ization" in America's colleges and universities, see Derek Bok, *Universities in the Marketplace: The Commercialization of Higher Education* (Princeton, N.J.: Princeton University Press, 2003).

[37] Sam Dillon, "At Public Universities, Warnings of Privatization," *The New York Times*, 16 October 2005, sec. A, p. 12; John Merrow, "Academic Squeeze," *The NewsHour with Jim Lehrer*, 22 June 2005, accessed 24 June 2005 at: http://www.pbs.org/newshour/bb/education/jan-june05/commcollege_6-22.html; Kevin Starr, "The Dream in Transition," *The Los Angeles Times*, 20 June 2004, sec. M, p. 1; June Kronholz, "Tuition Rises 11% at Public Colleges," *The Wall Street Journal*, 20 October 2004, sec. D, p. 1; John Hechinger, "College Tuition Costs Increase at Twice the Rate of Inflation," *The Wall Street Journal*, 19 October 2005, sec. D, p. 3; Greg Winter, "Public University Tuition Rises Sharply Again for '04," *The New York Times*, 20 October 2004, sec. A, p. 16; David Leonhardt, "As Wealthy Fill Top Colleges, Concerns Grow Over Fairness," *The New York Times*, 22 April 2004, sec. A, p. 1; Angela Shah, "Between Horns and a Hard Place: UT System Tries to Balance Flagship Status While Competing for Diminishing Dollars," *The Wall Street Journal*, 13 June 2004, sec. E, p. 1; Loretta Chao, "Working on the Double: More Grads are Moonlighting to Make Ends Meet as They Begin Careers in Many Fields," *The Wall Street Journal*, 1 November 2005, sec. B, p. 1; Pamela Yip, "High Degree of Debt: More College Graduates are Facing Bigger Student Loan Burdens," *The Dallas Morning News*, 19 June 2006, sec. D, p. 1; Jonathan D. Glater, "As Support from States Lags, Colleges Tack on Student Fees," *The New York Times*, 9 September 2007, sec. A, p. 1.

[38] David Broder, "Red Ink Run Amok," *The Washington Post*, 13 April 2006, sec. A, p. 21; "2005 Financial Report of the U.S. Government," U.S. Treasury Department, p. 6, accessed 2 May 2006 at: http://www.fms.treas.gov/fr/05frusg/05frusg.pdf.

[39] William H. Gross, "What, We Worry? Yes," *The Washington Post*, 13 January 2004, sec. A, p. 17; Warren E. Buffett, "Chairman's Letter," Berkshire Hathaway Inc., 28 February 2005, p. 20, accessed 2 May 2006 at: http://www.berkshirehathaway.com/letters/2004ltr.pdf; Peter G. Peterson, "Deficits and Dysfunction," *The New York Times Magazine*, 8 June 2003, p.78; George Will, "Conservatism, Um, Evolving" *Newsweek*, 8 December 2003, p. 110; Robert E. Rubin, "Attention: Deficit Disorder," *The New York Times*, 13 May 2005, sec. A, p. 23; Paul A. Volcker, "An Economy on Thin Ice," *The Washington Post*, 10 April 2005, sec. B, p. 7.

CHAPTER FIVE

Adam Smith in the Marketplace of Ideas

If this book has a patron saint, it would have to be Adam Smith. At this point, in a work critical of recent corporate ideology, it may seem out of place to draw so centrally upon the eighteenth-century thinker best known for writing *The Wealth of Nations*. That book's enduring influence for more than two centuries makes him hands-down the consensus choice to be called the father of the economic system now known as capitalism. But Smith's life stands in cautionary testament to the stunning way that time reduces even the greatest historical figures to convenient bits of shorthand. Today, what comes to mind most often when Smith is mentioned is the "invisible hand." And that phrase has been endlessly parroted out of context and out of proportion to render Smith in popular imagery as something of a supernatural chamber-of-commerce publicist. In that role, Smith serves as the ultimate talisman, wielded as the ultimate philosophical defense to bat away any restrictions of any kind on business interests as unjustifiable interference. Consider though that Smith mentioned his "invisible hand" concept only one time in all of *The Wealth of Nations*, and in quite qualified and nuanced language in that instance. That's because in his most famous book, as in his life, his concerns encompassed so much more than that widely misinterpreted and misused phrase on the way that pursuit of self-interest *can* contribute to the public good. Smith believed in free markets, without question. But the understanding of a free market that he articulated at great length was not by any means one in which the profit imperative should trump all other societal interests.

In this chapter and the two that follow, the Supreme Court's series of First Amendment cases since 1978 dealing with corporate political media spending are laid out in a historical narrative. That narrative also provides the framework for articulating this book's theoretical core for placing recent trends in American political culture in context — that First Amendment protection for such spending by corporations represents a fundamental threat to democratic decisionmaking because it structurally advantages the few over the many in the marketplace of ideas. This chapter focuses on the Supreme Court's landmark ruling that gave the corporate free-speech movement its first big First Amendment victory. More broadly, that ruling represents a cornerstone in the construction of an ideology of corporate citizenship by big business in America since the seventies. As detailed in the preceding chapters, that broader effort has significantly contributed to development of a dominant political culture with functional qualities more feudal than democratic.

That historical narrative and this book's theoretical understanding of it both begin with the Supreme Court's *First National Bank of Boston v. Bellotti* decision in 1978. In that case, the spending of company profits by corporate management on political media messages was for the first time ruled to be a First Amendment right. That is, such spending was held to be a form of expression constitutionally protected from government regulation. As it has in so many other First Amendment cases, the Court grounded its reasoning in the marketplace-of-ideas concept — the guiding principle that the best means available for assessing the truth of an idea is to see how it fares in a marketplace of free competition. It was not only that concept that Justice Holmes put forth in the course of his historic assertion that "the best test of truth is the power of the thought to get itself accepted in the competition of the market." He also made clear how important it is to understand law in that sort of theoretical context. "That at any rate is the theory of our Constitution," he said of his marketplace-of-ideas concept. "It is an experiment, as all life is an experiment. Every year if not every day we have to wager our salvation upon some prophecy based upon imperfect knowledge."[1]

The linkage between application of theory and constitutional jurisprudence was clear. Ideas have consequences. And so also does the misunderstanding of ideas. As this chapter will make clear, the Supreme Court's history-changing holding in *Bellotti* represents a case of the latter. And we can best see that by going back to the seminal marketplace economics of Adam Smith. By considering his basic principles for maintaining free economic markets we can better determine the dynamics vital to a truly free marketplace of ideas. That is, Smith's concept of *individuals* competing equally in a free market toward the greatest good for society can be applied to the concept of *ideas* competing in a free market. His principles consistently demonstrate how restrictions on corporate political media spending do not reduce ideas in the marketplace of ideas but instead enable more ideas to flourish in a true competition.

Justice Holmes articulated his concept of the marketplace of ideas in metaphorical terms. But Smith's fundamental principles enable us to consider the workings of that market in more practical terms beyond the metaphor. The econometric data and models used in analysis of financial markets are difficult to adapt to the amorphous dynamics involved when considering trade in ideas rather than in tangible commodities. Even in terms of *media* markets — a related but still very different animal from the marketplace of *ideas* — economics is limited in its ability to provide criteria for assessment, as the work of economist James Hamilton shows. Yet Smith's basic principles can not only be successfully translated from the economic marketplace to the marketplace of ideas, they provide compelling language for communicating their relevance in terms of law and public policy. However useful the complex, abstract mathematical models of modern economics may be in making accurate predictions based on narrow, technical questions, they are less helpful in understanding life beyond the spreadsheet. But time has shown that the basic concepts Smith laid out remain fundamentally sound more than two centuries later. Over that time, Ronald Coase said in his acceptance speech for the Nobel Prize in economics in 1991, it seemed to him "the main activity of economists" had been simply to build upon the foundation that Smith had erected."[2]

ADAM SMITH IN HIS OWN TIME

Though he is known today almost exclusively as the founder of classical economics, Smith's work in that field was done in a much broader context. As a professor of moral philosophy at Glasgow University in the second half of the eighteenth century, Adam Smith lectured in theology, ethics, and jurisprudence. He became part of a circle of scholars at the Scottish universities at Glasgow and Edinburgh whose concerns particularly focused upon historical changes in concepts of property and the effects of such changes on society. Smith became famous with the 1759 publication of *The Theory of Moral Sentiments*, in which he focused on ethical theory. In *An Inquiry Into the Nature and Causes of the Wealth of Nations*, published in 1776, Smith advanced his economic theories. After his death in 1790, students' notes from his lectures at Glasgow were published as *Lectures on Jurisprudence*, which focused on his theories of justice.[3]

Smith's work centered on investigating the effects of market commercial society on individuals and government and reflected a deep normative interest in how to improve both. The whole of his analysis comprises inquiries not only into the economic wealth of the nation, but also into both the well-being of society and the freedom of individuals within society.[4] In most basic terms, Smith called for limiting government in order to allow the motivation of self-interest to flourish and generate material benefits for society — because that advanced the utilitarian value of the common good, Smith's ultimate concern. However, he also emphasized that a system of justice was essential to protect all members of society as well as possible — including protecting free markets from domination by the most powerful business interests. Rather than providing justification for the untrammeled pursuit of self-interest, Smith's work in fact justifies the regulation of self-interest — but only to the extent that such pursuit clearly endangers the common good.

Yet the popular image of Smith remains that of an economist who advocated the pursuit of profits governed by nothing but the invisible hand. Even taking that famous reference on its face though, Smith phrased the matter in far less absolute terms than most references to it suggest. In the first place, in his sole use of the term in *The Wealth of Nations*, Smith employed it not in the course of developing an invisible-hand concept as such, but simply as a part of a discussion of domestic versus foreign investment of capital. "As every individual, therefore, endeavours as much as he can to both employ his capital in the support of domestic industry, and so to direct that industry that its produce may be of the greatest value; every individual necessarily labours to render the annual revenue of the society as great as he can," Smith wrote in the passage. And then: "He generally, indeed, neither intends to promote the public interest, nor knows how much he is promoting it. . . . He intends only his own security. . . . He intends only his own gain, and he is in this, as in many other cases, led by an invisible hand to promote an end which was no part of his intention."

That's the source of that famous line. But in the very next sentence, Smith qualified his assertion: "Nor is it *always* the worse for the society that it was no part of it." And he qualified it once again in the sentence after that: "By pursuing his own interest he *frequently* promotes that of the society more effectually than when he really intends to promote it." The italics are added here to emphasize the key elements of the language Smith used — and how greatly different the meaning of those lines would be if he had omitted those qualifying adverbs. On the question of domestic versus foreign investment of capital, Smith recommends leaving the decision to individuals rather than government. But by no means does he advocate leaving *all* governing of society to whatever the pursuit of profits dictates, and he makes that clear in many other parts of *The Wealth of Nations*.[5]

Over time, however, Smith's legacy would not be characterized by such nuanced readings of his work. After his death, the interpretation of his ideas was taken up by many who were interested only in his work on political economy. Many Americans in later years learned economics from texts that tended to "distort both Smith's moral theory and his economics," as Smith scholar J. Ralph Lindgren expressed it. "These texts emphasized laissez-faire, a word Smith did not use — it never appears even once in *Wealth of Nations* — and competitive individualism, at the cost of the benevolence and justice which Smith emphasized." Thus, far too much of the impact of *Wealth of Nations* has derived from incorrectly utilizing it to justify unrestrained pursuit of economic self-interest.[6]

Smith based his economic theories upon his theories of jurisprudence, and those in turn were based upon his moral theories. So his work reflected a much broader, more humane subject than economics as generally taught in universities today. "Smith's modern followers tend to be economists without a strong sense of civic life, and so that is how his admirers and detractors see Smith himself," in the assessment of economist Athol Fitzgibbons. As a result, "Even in its traditional, run-of-the-classroom versions, the prevailing view of Adam Smith's philosophy renders him far more like Boesky and Gekko than even the most rabid reading allows," concludes Robert C. Solomon, holder of a distinguished chair in business and philosophy at the University of Texas." In reality, the "greed is good" philosophy espoused by 1980s Wall Street icons Ivan Boesky (whose deals made him a multimillionaire before he was sent to prison for insider trading) and Gordon Gekko (the fictional character with a similar story in Oliver Stone's 1987 film *Wall Street*) bears little resemblance to the actual work of Adam Smith. "There is nothing in Smith's work that would even for a moment suggest that 'greed is good,' " Solomon points out.[7]

SMITH'S FREE-MARKET PRINCIPLES

The tendency to misinterpret free-market principles played out with great consequence in First Amendment jurisprudence in 1978 when the Supreme Court declared corporate political media spending in referenda a First Amendment right. Justice Lewis Powell's majority opinion grounded the Court's rationale in a laissez-faire interpretation of government's role in the marketplace of ideas. In essence, his reasoning went, opening up the marketplace of ideas to corporate political media spending would advance the First Amendment role of making that market freer and providing more ideas and information to political debate on public issues. Smith's work on the fundamentals of free markets, however, ring with conceptual insights as to why considering the marketplace of ideas in laissez-faire terms is unlikely to produce the sort of robust debate the Court has championed in *Bellotti* and other cases — with information flowing freely so that all ideas can compete fairly.

Over the course of almost a century, the Supreme Court has deeply established the guiding principle of government neutrality in the marketplace of ideas in its First Amendment cases.[8] Smith's essential principles provide a convincing case for understanding how that neutrality cannot be successfully achieved through the sort of jurisprudence reflected in the *Bellotti* ruling. Instead, First Amendment protection for corporate media spending serves as a conduit for the transfer of the corporation's government-provided advantages from the economic market directly to the marketplace of ideas. Smith's concepts do emphasize openness and similar opportunities for all competitors in the economic marketplace. Yet rather than laissez-faire economics, he stressed that the efforts of the most powerful competitors can be expected to work against maintaining freedom of competition in the marketplace. "The interest of the dealers ... in any particular branch of trade or manufactures, is always in some respects different from, and even opposite to, that of the public," he wrote. "To widen the market and to narrow the competition, is always the interest of the dealers. To widen the market may frequently be agreeable enough to the interest of the public; but to narrow the competition must always be against it." Further, he declared, "People of the same trade seldom meet together, even for merriment and diversion, but the conversation ends in a conspiracy against the public, or in some contrivance to raise prices."[9]

Adam Smith believed that concentrated economic resources could easily be translated into political influence, something he considered similar to other commodities for which supply and demand exist. He condemned the process by which powerful business interests were able to exert excessive influence on legislation. "The proposal of any new law or regulation of commerce which comes from this order ought always to be listened to with great precaution, and ought never to be adopted . . . but with the most suspicious attention," Smith wrote. "It comes from an order of men, whose interest is never exactly the same with that of the public, who have generally an interest to deceive and even to oppress the public, and who accordingly have, upon many occasions, both deceived and oppressed it."[10] Smith indisputably saw government as a potential instrument for suppressing the beneficial competitive forces of a free market. But just as indisputably, he saw dominant business interests in similar terms.

Smith maintained that keeping markets free actually involved making sure that neither government nor powerful business interests used their influence to overwhelm the freedom of the market. And in his view, the free market could similarly be overwhelmed through allowing business interests to manipulate the political arena. Smith called not for rejecting *all* government regulation but more precisely for rejecting the sort that was dominant at the time he was writing *The Wealth of Nations* in mid eighteenth-century England. That regulation was characterized by mercantilist policies of sanctioning monopolies, putting quotas on imports, heavily regulating activities of individual tradesmen, and restricting other such aspects of economic behavior. Smith called for abandoning such regulation because it privileged the few at the expense of the many and prevented most from competing fairly in a free market.[11]

"It cannot be very difficult to determine who have been the contrivers of this whole mercantile system; not the consumers, we may believe, whose interest has been entirely neglected; but the producers whose interest has been so carefully attended to," Smith wrote. He supported regulation that served to resist the narrowing of the marketplace, particularly a system of justice that emphasized liberty, competition, and fair play. In *Wealth of Nations*, he wrote that government is responsible for "protecting, as far as possible, every member of the society from the injustice or oppression of every other member of it." Indeed, when considered in this broader context of Smith's work, his invisible-hand concept is more accurately understood not as an independent force but as a *dependent* variable — one that must be protected by government in order for it to function effectively. All participants cannot be free to compete in a market when the many are dominated by the few, particularly by competitors with government-provided advantages. The Smithian market works closest to the way that he conceptualized it when all parties have similar opportunities to compete in it. In Smith's ideal economic market, the freedom of the many to participate tends to produce better results than a market in which the few make decisions for the many. The parallel with freedom from dominance by the few in marketplace-of-ideas theory could hardly be stronger.[12]

THE *BELLOTTI* BLUNDER

In the developments that culminated in the *First National Bank of Boston v. Bellotti* ruling, we see the basic dynamics of Smith's central thesis at work. With a one-vote victory at the Supreme Court, the powerful interests of the corporate free-speech movement succeeded in blocking legislative and judicial efforts to prevent domination of political processes through corporate influence. Corporate political corruption had been well established as legitimately subject to regulation by Congress and the courts since early in the twentieth century. But in the 1970s, the regulation of corporate political spending grew so intertwined with First Amendment law that it allowed the former to be constitutionally barred by the latter for the first time. The process of sorting out the specifics on such First Amendment questions began to reach the courts more and more often thereafter.

Corporations have been prohibited from direct financial involvement in federal elections since the 1907 enactment of the Tillman Act, which was replaced by the stronger Federal Corrupt Practices Act in 1925. The general concern over corporate power around the turn of the century was catalyzed into the first major reform efforts by a series of scandals, such as the huge contributions wealthy financier Marcus A. Hanna raised from Standard Oil and other large corporations for William McKinley's victorious presidential campaign of 1896. The legislation of that era was aimed at protecting the political process from the reality or appearance of undue influence by powerful economic interests and preventing corporate shareholders from having their investments used for political purposes that they might not support. It established a regulatory framework that held firm for several decades.

Momentum for sweeping new campaign finance reform next reached critical mass in the 1970s, first in response to concerns about sharply increasing demands for campaign funds to meet spiraling media costs. The Federal Campaign Act (FECA) of 1971 replaced the Corrupt Practices Act and sought to reduce campaign expenses through a detailed series of disclosure requirements and limitations related to media expenditures in political campaigns. Even more comprehensive campaign-finance legislation was enacted after revelations of numerous illegal contributions made by corporations and wealthy individuals during Richard Nixon's 1972 presidential campaign. Congress added a series of amendments to FECA in 1974, which became law the next year and tightened the reporting rules on disclosure requirements, placed limits on contributions to candidates and independent expenditures on behalf of candidates, and established the Federal Election Commission as a watchdog of campaign fund-raising.[13]

A crucial prelude to the eventual outcome in *Bellotti* was the challenging of those new campaign-finance regulations on First Amendment grounds. The plaintiffs basically argued that the government did not have the right to dictate how much citizens could spend to make their voices heard, even in political campaigns. When the case, *Buckley v. Valeo*, reached the Supreme Court, the majority concluded that money was tantamount to speech "because virtually every means of communicating ideas in today's mass society requires the expenditure of money." Concerning the specific campaign-finance regulations in question, the Court upheld limits on contributions made directly to candidates, while striking down as unconstitutional limits on expenditures made in support of candidates. The majority reasoned that direct contributions represented a potentially corrupting influence on democratic processes but that independent expenditures did not.[14] That reasoning was grounded in a narrow definition of political corruption as strictly the quid-pro-quo exchange of favors provided in return for direct contributions. Conversely, the Court embraced a very broad understanding of the relationship between political spending and free speech.

Thus Buckley provided the profit imperative a crucial opening to wedge itself even more substantially into First Amendment law through the *Bellotti* case. Vital to the unfolding of that process was the Court's landmark equating of dollars with political speech in terms so as to place the spending of money squarely within the powerful protections of the First Amendment. *Buckley* altered the long established basis in law for regulating the power of big money to influence electoral processes. By protecting political media expenditures as a form of expression protected by the First Amendment, an array of such spending activities were placed off limits to regulation. The *Buckley* case focused only on the rights of *individuals* to spend for political purposes though. It did not involve challenges to campaign-finance regulations on corporations, and the Court made no pronouncements in that regard in the case.

But now the door was open to a First Amendment challenge to regulation of *corporate* political spending. And just two years after the *Buckley* decision was handed down, the *First National Bank of Boston v. Bellotti* case arrived at the Supreme Court. For some sixteen years before then, the legislature and corporate interests in Massachusetts had battled over whether the state could ban corporate spending on referendum questions that did not materially affect corporate interests. At the time of the *Bellotti* decision, thirty-one states had similar regulations, with many having been on the books for decades. The Massachusetts regulation went through much revision and litigation over the years, reaching the state's Supreme Court three times before going on to the U.S. Supreme Court in 1978. In addition to First

National Bank of Boston, the corporate plaintiffs were New England Merchants National Bank, Gillette, Digital Equipment, and Wyman-Gordon.[15]

The State of Massachusetts argued that the regulation was crucial in maintaining public confidence in the integrity of government and elections by preventing the potential corruption of corporate wealth drowning out the voices of individual citizens and undermining democratic processes. The Supreme Court affirmed that preventing corruption and sustaining individual citizens' involvement in political processes were indeed "interests of the highest importance." But the five-to-four majority declared that referenda posed no danger of corruption of political processes because only referendum *issues* were voted upon, with no *candidates* involved who could be vulnerable to quid-pro-quo corruption. Further, the Court said, media spending concerning the issues in a referendum is the type of speech "indispensable to decisionmaking in a democracy" and thus necessary to maintain the free flow of information protected by the First Amendment.

Most significantly in *Bellotti*, the majority declared that a form of expression that is otherwise protected by the First Amendment does not lose that protection when its source is a corporation. With sharp dissent from the four justices in the minority, the Court grounded its reasoning in terms of a First Amendment right of the public to receive information that contributes to democratic decisionmaking. Thus, the Court said its decision barred government from limiting the marketplace of ideas' range of information — by restricting corporate political media spending — to which the public is exposed. Reasoning that protecting corporate political media spending in the marketplace of ideas would make it a freer market, the Court said "the direct participation of the people in a referendum, if anything, increases the need for 'the widest possible dissemination of information from diverse and antagonistic sources.' " That assertion was constructed in such a manner as to recognize no distinction between individual citizens and corporate management wielding special access to wealth generated through the government-advantaged corporate form. Thus, the Court accepted a marketplace of ideas in which government provides some participants — and *their* viewpoints — with significantly greater advantages over others.

The *Bellotti* Court's most critical misinterpretation of free-market principles is reflected in its assertion that if corporate speech were restricted, "much valuable information which a corporation might be able to provide would remain unpublished because corporate management would not be willing to risk the substantial criminal penalties" contained in the Massachusetts regulation. Corporate management actually would only risk penalties under such regulation if it spent corporate revenues to influence referenda. Managers of such business corporations would risk no such penalties if they simply participated in referenda campaigns themselves as citizens, with no advantages bestowed upon them by government. By participating through deployment of their corporate treasuries, however, the managers then wield the special, wealth-generating advantages (perpetual life, limited liability, and tax treatment) that are granted by government to the corporate form — but not to individuals. In that manner, managers are permitted to transfer those advantages from the economic marketplace directly over to the political marketplace, diminishing true free trade in ideas because other participants are not provided with such significant advantages.

Of course, the *Bellotti* majority certainly had the right to ground its conceptualization of the marketplace of ideas in laissez-faire terms. But given the fact that Adam Smith's central free-market concepts rejected laissez-faire reasoning and remain widely recognized as the foundation of market economics today, his principles represent a sounder basis for understanding the marketplace of ideas. Recent analysis has asserted convincingly that rather than maximizing opportunity for all by maintaining economic equilibrium, a laissez-fair approach is more likely to reinforce economic disparities. Crucial to democratic processes, that process manifests itself in the way that concentrations of economic power can consistently outbid other interests for political influence in a process that left unrestrained tends to perpetuate itself.[16] Indeed, writing in dissent in the *Bellotti* case, Justice William Rehnquist declared that it was most reasonable to "fear that the corporation would use its economic power to obtain further benefits beyond those already bestowed."

Thus, First Amendment protection for corporate political media spending transfers the structural, government-provided corporate advantage in the economic marketplace to the political marketplace.

What that means in practice is that the interests of a few do not compete similarly with the interests of the many in a free marketplace of ideas. It means instead that corporate managers wield a structural funding advantage in American political debate. Therefore, in terms of the basic free-market principles of Adam Smith, First Amendment protection for corporate political media spending does not allow more ideas to compete in the marketplace. Instead, it provides the structural advantage for a relatively few ideas to flood the political marketplace, funded by unrelated activity in the economic marketplace.

SMITH AND THE GREATER GOOD

In his time, such dominance of government and society by the few were precisely the focus of Adam Smith's work. That focus was integral to the economic realities of the historical context in which he lived and wrote. Smith's economic theories emphasized market forces and consumer autonomy as an alternative to the political economy of mercantilism. His system, which later would be referred to as capitalism, has been characterized to have been "as revolutionary a concept with respect to the dominant mercantilism of its day as Marx's communism was to the capitalism of the mid-nineteenth century." The greatest priority of the economic system of mercantilism was enriching the nation-state, basically by maximizing exports and minimizing imports. Thus, mercantilism enriched producers and other advantaged interests at the expense of consumers and the growing middle class, who were forced to pay inflated prices for domestic goods shielded from foreign competition by protectionist mechanisms. As Smith characterized mercantilism's structural advantaging of the few over the many, the interests of the system's "contrivers" were "carefully attended to," while the interests of others were "entirely neglected."[17]

Smith envisioned as ideal a sort of society that would open up wider opportunities to all. The driving force behind Smith's vigorous critique of the status quo was his desire to improve the harsh living conditions he saw in Scotland and England. Rather than blaming the poor for their misfortunes, as mercantilist theory did, Smith blamed the economic system. To that end he called for abandoning government policies that sanctioned monopolies, imposed quotas on imports, regulated tradesmen, and restricted many other aspects of economic behavior. Smith opposed that sort of government regulation because it privileged the few at the expense of the many and prevented most from competing fairly in a free market. Thus we find "the thread that runs through all his works," Smith scholar Jerry Muller has written, is "how the market can be structured to make the pursuit of self-interest benefit consumers."[18]

While Smith called for dismantling the mercantilist system, he did not by any means advocate eliminating the role of government. Although he firmly believed freer markets would be preferable to mercantilism, he did not expect that markets would solve all problems or could be relied upon to provide all that society needed in order to function best. He in fact specified five particularly significant problems that would be fostered by market economies: Impoverishing the spirit of the workers and the work ethic more generally, creating cities in which anonymity facilitated price-fixing, expanding the ranks of the idle rich, inducing government to foster monopolies and selective privileges, and separating ownership and control as the scale and capital requirements of business firms increased.[19]

Smith advocated strong roles for government in maintaining national defense, law enforcement, and a judicial system; protecting copyrights and patents; enforcing contracts; regulating mortgages; controlling paper money and the banking system; administering taxation necessary to fund required services, enforcing limits on interest rates to protect consumers, overriding free trade when foreign-policy measures necessitated it, funding public-works projects such as roads, canals, bridges and harbors; and providing broad public education.[20] Certainly such expansive involvement of government in so many areas of life is at odds with a laissez-faire approach to social organization. But community-oriented concerns are prominent in Smith's work. In his *The Theory of Moral Sentiments* he articulated at length his concept of the "impartial spectator." That was the name Smith gave to the instinct that "whenever we are about to act so as to affect the happiness of others, calls to us, with a voice capable of astonishing the most presumptuous of our passions, that we are but one of the multitude, in no respect better than any other in it." It is the impartial spectator who "shows us the propriety of generosity and the deformity of injustice; the propriety of resigning the greatest interests of our own for the yet greater interests of others."[21]

This concept is crucial to Smith's concept of justice advancing the common good, which is equally central to both *The Theory of Moral Sentiments* and *The Wealth of Nations*. Indeed, the two works treat essentially the same topics in different realms — the former's examination of the basis for morals and legislation extended to form the ethical foundation for the latter's focus on political and economic spheres. In *The Theory of Moral Sentiments*, for example, Smith called the pursuit of wealth illusory but useful. "If we consider the real satisfaction which all these things are capable of affording, . . . it will always appear in the highest degree contemptible and trifling," he said. "The pleasures of wealth and greatness . . . strike the imagination as something grand, and beautiful, and noble, of which the attainment is well worth all the toil and anxiety which we are so apt to bestow on it. And it is well that nature imposes upon us in this manner. It is this deception which rouses and keeps in continual motion the industry of mankind." Then in *The Wealth of Nations*, he similarly grounded his concept of limited government encouraging individual self-interest to flourish in the relentless passion of humans for "bettering our condition, a desire which, though generally calm and dispassionate, comes with us from the womb, and never leaves us till we go in the grave. . . . In the whole interval which separates those two moments, there is scarce perhaps a single instant in which any man is so perfectly and completely satisfied with his situation, as to be without any wish of alteration or improvement of any kind."[22]

In *The Theory of Moral Sentiments*, Smith wrote that a competitor "may run as hard as he can, and strain every nerve and every muscle, in order to outstrip all his competitors. But if he should jostle, or throw down any of them, the indulgence of the spectators is entirely at an end. It is a violation of fair play, which they cannot admit of." And in *The Wealth of Nations*, he emphasized that government is responsible for "protecting, as far as possible, every member of the society from the injustice or oppression of every other member of it."[23] Thus it distorts Smith's work to focus only on the self-interest concepts while ignoring the emphasis he placed on their context within a system of social justice.

Smith was a champion of individualism, but not to the extent that its excesses destroyed community. When we consider the marketplace of ideas in terms of Smith's free market, it is clear that openness for all competitors and consumers is the priority. As Smith scholar Patricia Werhane has emphasized, his emphasis on equality of economic and political opportunity does not "imply that Smith favored equality of outcomes. Clearly he did not, nor did he think that such equality would be a result of a free-market economy. But the market is most efficient and most fair when there is competition among similarly matched parties."[24] Similarly, the marketplace of ideas will operate more efficiently and fairly when competing parties have similar opportunities to communicate ideas.

As Smith made clear, however, the interests of the most powerful competitors may work against the freedom of markets for other competitors. "To narrow the competition, is always the interest of the dealers," he wrote, as noted earlier. In terms of the marketplace of ideas, regulation of corporate political media spending works to resist such narrowing by preventing domination by structurally advantaged competitors. That sort of regulation serves Smith's "impartial spectator" function and enables more ideas to flourish, expanding the freedom of the marketplace and working in the long-term interests of society at large.

Broadly, that sort of reasoning is reflected in the federal legislation dating back to the earliest efforts in the twentieth century to prohibit corporate financial influence from dominating democratic processes. The Court's action in *First National Bank of Bellotti* fundamentally contradicted Smith's essential conceptualization of free markets and promoted a structural advantaging of the few over the many in the marketplace of ideas. The effect was to institutionalize in First Amendment law a powerful dynamic that is much closer to feudalism as a governing principle than it is to the sort of truly free market that was central to Smith's reasoning. And the Court continued to advance that reasoning in other First Amendment cases on corporate political media spending that followed *Bellotti*. That line of case law remains firm. Over time, however, another doctrine developed support on the Court, one which has served thus far to hold the line against a full victory by the corporate free-speech movement. The cases that followed *Bellotti* and the driving force on the Court in shaping that doctrine and in First Amendment law are the focus of Chapter Six.

[1] See *Abrams v. U.S.*, 250 U.S. 616, 630 (1919) (Holmes, J., dissenting).

[2] See James T. Hamilton, *All the News That's Fit to Sell: How the Market Transforms Information into News* (Princeton, N.J.: Princeton University Press, 2004), 1-36, 262-63; Ronald H. Coase, "The Institutional Structure of Production," Nobel Prize Lecture, 9 December 1991, accessed 5 May 2006 at: http://www.nobel.se/economics/laureates/1991/coase-lecture.html#not1.

[3] See John D. Bishop, "Adam Smith's Invisible Hand Argument," *Journal of Business Ethics* 14, no. 3 (March 1995): 165; Roy Pascal, "Property and Society — The Scottish Historical School of the Eighteenth Century," *Modern Quarterly* 61, no. 1 (1938): 167-78.

[4] See Robert Boyden Lamb, *Property Markets and the State in Adam Smith's System* (New York: Garland, 1987), 431, 433; Robert Falkner, *A Conservative Economist? The Political Liberalism of Adam Smith Revisited* (London: Mill Institute, 1997), 5.

[5] See Adam Smith, *An Inquiry into the Nature and Causes of the Wealth of Nations,* vol. 2 (1776, reprint, London: Penguin, 1999), 32.

[6] See J. Ralph Lindgren, *The Social Philosophy of Adam Smith* (The Hague, Netherlands: Martinus Nijhoff, 1973), ix. See also John E. Hill, *Revolutionary Values for a New Millennium: John Adams, Adam Smith and Social Virtue* (Lanham, MD: Lexington, 2000), 140; Albert O. Hirschman, *The Passions and the Interests: Political Arguments for Capitalism before Its Triumph*, 20th anniv. ed. (Princeton: Princeton University Press, 1997), 100.

[7] See Athol Fitzgibbons, *Adam Smith's System of Liberty, Wealth, and Virtue: The Moral and Political Foundations of "The Wealth of Nations"* (New York: Oxford University Press, 1995), 22; Robert C. Solomon, *Ethics and Excellence: Cooperation and Integrity* (New York: Oxford University Press, 1992), 85.

[8] See W. Wat Hopkins, "The Supreme Court Defines the Marketplace of Ideas," 73 *Journalism & Mass Communication Quarterly* 40 (1996), for analysis of how the marketplace of ideas as a specific term or obvious reference appeared in at least 125 opinions in 97 cases between 1919 and 1995 and was used to advance free speech in virtually every area of First Amendment jurisprudence. Twenty-four of the forty-nine justices who served on the Court for at least one year during that period made at least one such reference.

[9] See Smith, *Wealth of Nations,* vol. 1, 358, 232.

[10] See Smith, *Wealth of Nations,* vol. 1, 358-59. See also G.R. Bassiry and Marc Jones, "Adam Smith and the Ethics of Contemporary Capitalism," *Journal of Business Ethics* 12, no. 8 (August 1993).

[11] See Bishop, "Adam Smith's Invisible Hand Argument;" Denis Collins, "Adam Smith's Social Contract: The Proper Role of Individual Liberty and

Government Intervention in Eighteenth Century Society," *Business and Professional Ethics Journal* 7, no. 3-4 (fall-winter 1988).

[12] See Smith, *Wealth of Nations,* vol. 2, 247, 297; Patricia H. Werhane, *Adam Smith and His Legacy for Modern Capitalism* (New York: Oxford University Press, 1991), 109-10.

[13] For a more detailed historical discussion of campaign-finance legislation, see Melvin I. Urofsky, *Money and Free Speech: Campaign Finance Reform and the Courts* (Lawrence, Kan.: University Press of Kansas, 2005); Ann B. Matasar, *Corporate PACs and Federal Campaign Financing Laws: Use or Abuse of Power* (New York: Quorum, 1986); Nancy Lammers, ed., *Dollar Politics*, 3d ed. (Washington, D.C.: Congressional Quarterly, 1982).

[14] See *Buckley v. Valeo*, 424 U.S. 1 (1976). The case has been and continues to be the subject of much scholarly discourse. See, for example, several recent analyses by leading legal scholars in E. Joshua Rosenkranz, ed., *If Buckley Fell: A First Amendment Blueprint for Regulating Money in Politics* (New York: The Century Foundation Press, 1999).

[15] See *First National Bank of Boston v. Bellotti*, 435 U.S. 765 (1978).

[16] For a comprehensive analysis of laissez-faire economics in practice, see Kenneth S. Friedman, *Myths of the Free Market* (New York: Algora, 2003). Through historical evidence and principles of nonlinear thermodynamics Friedman demonstrates that — without some intervening force — a system in which equilibrium is displaced is more likely to grow further out of balance than to be rebalanced through laissez-faire non-intervention.

[17] See Bassiry and Jones, "Adam Smith and the Ethics of Contemporary Capitalism," 623; Eli Ginzberg, *The House of Adam Smith* (New York: Octagon, 1964); Smith, *Wealth of Nations,* vol. 2, 247.

[18] See Collins, "Adam Smith's Social Contract;" Jerry Z. Muller, *Adam Smith in His Time and Ours: Designing the Decent Society* (New York: Free Press, 1993).

[19] For a fuller discussion of Smith's articulation of such concerns, see James Wilson, "Adam Smith on Business Ethics," California Management Review 32, no. 1 (Fall 1989).

[20] See Smith, *Wealth of Nations,* vol. 2, 279-406.

[21] See Adam Smith, *The Theory of Moral Sentiments* (1759; reprint, Amherst, N.Y.: Prometheus, 2000), 194.

[22] See Smith, *Theory of Moral Sentiments*, 263; *Wealth of Nations,* vol. 1, 441.

[23] See Smith, *Theory of Moral Sentiments*, 120; *Wealth of Nations,* vol. 2, 297.

[24] See Werhane, *Adam Smith and His Legacy for Modern Capitalism*, 105.

CHAPTER SIX

The Rationale of the Rehnquist Doctrine

The narrow majority on the Supreme Court that determined the outcome in *First National Bank of Boston v. Bellotti* held serve for some time. Its development of First Amendment rights for corporate political media spending moved forward in a number of cases that will be discussed in this chapter. But as the process continued, a different line of reasoning gradually began to take root on the Court. In time, it attracted its own majority of justices and they aligned behind a doctrine focused on restraining some aspects of corporate political media spending. The cases in which that majority prevailed now represent the body of case law that stands between the corporate free-speech movement and total victory at the Supreme Court.

Given the way the dominant political rhetoric of recent decades has tended to frame the big-business agenda as synonymous with the "conservative" agenda, one might guess that the majority in those cases was led by a "liberal" justice. It was not. The justice who most fully and consistently articulated a constitutional rationale for protecting democratic processes from corporate domination in those First Amendment cases is widely considered to be one of the most conservative minds to serve on the High Court in recent history. When William H. Rehnquist died in 2005 at the age of 80, the first sentence of his obituary noted that he "helped lead a conservative revolution on the Supreme Court during 19 years as chief justice of the United States."[1] Although Rehnquist's arguments were made in dissent in the early First Amendment cases on corporate political media spending, in time they garnered sufficient support in enough rulings to establish a doctrine justifying regulation of such spending. That doctrine is grounded in protecting democratic processes from corruption deriving from the special economic advantages bestowed by government upon the corporate form of business.

Rehnquist voiced his advocacy for that doctrine in bedrock terms of democracy requiring an understanding that "the economic is subordinate to the political"[2] — which stands in sharp contrast to the business-as-democracy rationale of the corporate free-speech movement. As noted in Chapter Three, the use of the term "corporate speech" is for the most part a disingenuous turn of phrase. It is itself an act of rhetorical framing, creating the impression that something that does not in fact actually exist is an everyday reality. It can be compared, for example, to rhetoric popularizing the term "death tax." It does not actually refer to a tax on dying, but to taxes imposed in certain circumstances on recipients of extremely large inheritances. However the term "tax on receiving an extremely large inheritance" does not have the widespread political resonance that "death tax" does.[3] And neither does "corporate political media spending" push the same buttons as "corporate speech." The latter term sounds like the very act of human expression that the First Amendment is intended to protect from government interference. And yet, a corporation cannot of course "speak." Corporate management can, however, *spend* — pay someone to express messages on behalf of the corporation.

Rehnquist's jurisprudence clearly focused on the reality of corporate political media spending, rather than the rhetoric of corporate "speech." He once wrote that to treat the institutional messages of corporations the same in First Amendment law as those of natural persons "is to confuse metaphor with reality."[4] In case after case, he championed a judicial doctrine that firmly maintained that distinction. It reflected his broader understanding of corporate rights as limited to those necessary for its participation in the legal system — basically property and contract rights. For Rehnquist, the fundamental political rights protecting the people and their sovereign role in American democracy were not bestowed upon the artificial corporate entity when it was created by government as a legal format for more effectively organizing business activity.

Before considering Rehnquist's specific efforts in corporate political media spending cases further, it is important to emphasize how central his understanding of the corporation was in shaping those efforts. Over the course of the development of the business corporation, various theories have been put forth for considering the nature of corporate personhood in law.[5] In the First Amendment cases on corporate political media spending, Rehnquist drew upon what is most commonly referred to as the "state-creation" or "fictional-entity" theory of the corporation. Basically, that school of jurisprudence considers the corporation a legal fiction or artificial being existing only as a legal creation of government. Thus it is subject to regulatory oversight by government as deemed necessary to serve the public interest — in exchange for the economic advantages provided the corporate form, particularly limited liability, perpetual life and tax advantages for enhancing accumulation of capital. The roots of that concept run deep in U.S. law, as evidenced by Chief Justice John Marshall's oft-cited declaration from the seminal 1819 corporate-law case, *Dartmouth College v. Woodward.* The corporation, Marshall wrote, "is an artificial being, invisible, intangible, and existing only in contemplation of law. Being the mere creature of law, it possesses only those properties which the charter of its creation confers upon it, either expressly, or as incidental to its very existence."[6] Crucially, in state-creation theory, corporations do not possess the same constitutional rights as human individuals and therefore can be regulated more extensively.

That concept stands in contrast to theoretical perspectives of the corporation that generally argue against government regulation of corporate activity. The most prominent of those is referred to as "aggregate" theory, which considers the corporation to be a collection of individual owners rather than a collective entity. In that school of thought, there should be no distinction made between the constitutional rights of individuals and those of corporations. The related "contractual" or "nexus-of-contracts" theory asserts that the corporation should be treated in law as nothing more than a set of contracts among those who participate in the business – particularly shareholders, managers, creditors, employees. In that line of reasoning, full constitutional protection of "freedom of contract" is due the corporation through the Constitution's contract clause, which bars states from interfering with contractual agreements. A related approach, referred to as the "real entity" or "natural entity" theory, broadly conceptualizes the corporation as an organism or system that exists as more than a creation of the state and therefore not as absolutely subject to regulation as the state-creation theory holds.

Although aggregate theories and contract theories of the corporation have been prominent in scholarly legal debate in recent years, the courts have not definitively embraced any single theoretical characterization of the corporation. The opinions of Supreme Court justices in relevant cases have drawn on various theories of the corporation, sometimes overtly, sometimes only by implication.[7] Clearly, adherence to one of these theoretical perspectives of the corporation over others will significantly influence interpretation of First Amendment law in relation to corporate political media spending. Viewing the corporation as a legal fiction created by government, without the constitutional protections of human individuals, justifies more substantial regulation of corporate speech than do views that a corporation represents nothing more than either a group of such individuals exerting fundamental rights protected by the First Amendment or a set of contracts protected from government interference.

At the very dawn of the age of the corporate-political-media-spending cases, in the landmark *Bellotti* case, Rehnquist began asserting a countervailing line of thinking driven by a state-creation understanding of the corporation more vigorously and consistently than any other put forth in that body of case law. In *Bellotti*, for example, the majority did not clearly rely upon a specific theory of the corporation in articulating its decision, focusing instead on the right of the public to receive information — rather than the corporation's right to disseminate it. Rehnquist's dissent, however, forcefully argued a state-creation theory as the primary basis for why the Massachusetts regulation should have been upheld. He focused on the "broad consensus of governmental bodies expressed over a period of many decades" that "restrictions upon the political activity of business corporations are both politically desirable and constitutionally permissible." Rehnquist argued that previous Courts had granted "considerable deference" to that consensus and that future Courts should as well. He drew on the Court's *Dartmouth College* decision on the nature of the corporation being defined by its state-chartered creation, "either expressly, or as incidental to its very existence." He also focused upon the more recent *United States v. White* ruling that corporations do not necessarily enjoy the liberties of natural persons, declaring that "it cannot be disputed that the mere creation of a corporation does not invest it with all the liberties enjoyed by natural persons."[8]

Rehnquist emphasized: "A State grants to a business corporation the blessings of potentially perpetual life and limited liability to enhance its efficiency as an economic entity. It might reasonably be concluded that those properties, so beneficial in the economic sphere, pose special dangers in the political sphere." He argued that political-spending rights are not necessary for business corporations to carry out the functions for which they were created in law, insisting that the First Amendment protects the public interest in a free flow of information by and among human – not corporate – beings. Therefore, he wrote, whatever regulations might be placed on corporate political spending, "all natural persons, who owe their existence to a higher sovereign than the Commonwealth, [will] remain as free as before to engage in political activity."[9] And in the most telling passage of Rehnquist's dissent, we find what would prove to be an outline of the central theory that he would advance in the later cases on corporate political media spending:

> It might be argued that liberties of political expression are not at all necessary to effectuate the purposes for which States permit commercial corporations to exist. So long as the Judicial Branches of the State and Federal Governments remain open to protect the corporation's interest in its property, it has no need, though it may have the desire, to petition the political branches for similar protection. Indeed, the States might reasonably fear that the corporation would use its economic power to obtain further benefits beyond those already bestowed. I would think that any particular form of organization upon which the State confers special privileges or immunities different from those of natural persons would be subject to like regulation, whether the organization is a labor union, a partnership, a trade association, or a corporation."[10]

CORPORATE FREE-SPEECH MOVEMENT MARCHES ON

Two years after *Bellotti*, the Court struck down another regulation on corporate media spending in *Central Hudson Gas & Electric Corp. v. Public Service Commission*, though the justices disagreed on whether it was purely a commercial advertising case or something more. *Central Hudson* involved a First Amendment challenge of a New York State energy-conservation regulation that banned ads by utility corporations promoting consumption of electricity. Justice John Paul Stevens argued for considering it as a regulation on corporate political media spending, because the sort of advertising banned could address questions under debate by political leaders (in that case, the energy crisis of the 1970s). However, Justice Lewis Powell declared in the majority opinion that although *Central Hudson* reinforced protection for "direct comments on public issues" by corporations, similar protection for expression "made only in the context of commercial transactions" would dilute the force of First Amendment protection for political speech. So the Court used the case to distinguish commercial from political advertising by creating a special test for courts to use in challenges concerning "expression related solely to the economic interests of the speaker and its audience."[11] (First Amendment issues related to corporate commercial advertising are examined in greater detail in Chapter Ten.)

The Court focused more directly on corporate political media spending the same year in *Consolidated Edison Co. of New York v. Public Service Commission.* In that case, another New York State measure, this one ordering utility corporations to stop including political-message inserts with their customers' utility bills, was ruled unconstitutional. The Court applied the same sort of First Amendment analysis to the regulation that it would have to a restriction on the political speech of human citizens, and concluded that the regulation could not be justified. Similarly, in *Pacific Gas & Electric Co. v. Public Utilities Commission* in 1986, the Court struck down a California law that required utility corporations to allow other views to be included with corporate utility-bill political messages. To do so could unconstitutionally force a corporation to associate with messages with which it disagreed — something that the First Amendment protects human citizens against — the ruling said.[12] As a group, the *Central Hudson*, *Consolidated Edison*, and *Pacific Gas* decisions served to expand the scope of First Amendment rights established in the *Bellotti* case for corporate political media spending.

Rehnquist joined Justice Harry Blackmun's dissent in *Consolidated Edison* and authored a lengthy dissent of his own in *Central Hudson*, continuing his argument that the First Amendment does not grant the same rights to non-human entities — such as state-created monopoly utilities and other corporations — that it does to human citizens. To do so, he said, dangerously undermines the way the marketplace of ideas is intended to function. "In a democracy," Rehnquist wrote, "the economic is subordinate to the political, a lesson that our ancestors learned long ago, and that our descendants will undoubtedly have to relearn many years hence." He also dissented in *Pacific Gas*, writing a few months before being confirmed as chief justice. In that case, Rehnquist pointed out that a corporation would be "speaking" in an institutional capacity in the political messages in question — not expressing the views of the actual individuals who comprised the corporation as employees and investors. Therefore, the expression involved had nothing to do with the liberty of a natural person. Rehnquist declared that extending First Amendment protection to corporations based on "individual freedom of conscience ... strains the rationale ... beyond the breaking point. To ascribe to such artificial entities an 'intellect' or 'mind' . . . is to confuse metaphor with reality."[13]

In those cases, Rehnquist was laying out a foundation for the future. His reasoning did not win majority support in those cases, but that would change over time. Even before the ruling in the *Pacific Gas* case, there were signs that a shift was developing on the Court. It would never go so far as to reverse any of the early rulings on corporate political media spending. All remain firmly in place as precedents in the case law that have been applied by American courts ever since. But over the course of the 1980s, a majority on the Court coalesced around the line of reasoning put forth by Rehnquist time and again. The decisions rendered in the group of cases in which that reasoning prevailed now form a counterweight of sorts to the earlier cases, holding back a full victory by the corporate free-speech movement for the time being.

THE BUILDING BLOCKS OF A DOCTRINAL SHIFT

The ascendancy of Rehnquist's reasoning on corporate political media spending began to form in *Federal Election Commission v. National Right to Work Committee*. In that 1982 decision, the Court upheld a section of the Federal Election Campaign Act of 1971 limiting the sources from which corporations and labor unions could legally solicit contributions for their political action committees. The FEC maintained that the regulation preventing corporations from using their general treasury funds to influence federal election campaigns was necessary to ensure that "substantial aggregations of wealth" accumulated through the economic advantages provided by government to the corporate form not be converted into political "war chests." The Supreme Court had ruled twenty-five years before that deployment of such war chests could lead to the incurring of political debts by candidates campaigning for election.[14]

Further, the FEC argued, Congress had enacted the law "only after it became aware of widespread abuses that were thought to present imminent danger of corruption to the federal election process, resulting in a decline of public confidence in the integrity of elected officials and the fair operation of government." Even in the *Buckley v. Valeo* and *First National Bank of Boston v. Bellotti* rulings, that sort of corruption had been recognized by the Court as "a governmental interest of the highest order." The FEC also contended that individuals who had invested in corporate stock for financial reasons should be protected from having that money used to support political candidates to whom they might be opposed. The Supreme Court had also embraced that principle thirty-four years before.[15]

Writing for the majority, Rehnquist described the regulation as the culmination of a "careful legislative adjustment of the federal electoral laws . . . to prevent both actual and apparent corruption . . . [reflecting] a legislative judgment that the special characteristics of the corporate structure require particularly careful regulation." The majority ruled that the interests Congress had sought to protect in that legislation were compelling enough to outweigh the First Amendment rights asserted by the NRWC. "The governmental interest in preventing both actual corruption and the appearance of corruption of elected representatives has long been recognized and there is no reason why it may not in this case be accomplished by treating unions, corporations and similar organizations differently from individuals," Rehnquist wrote.[16]

The Court took another crucial step three years later in *Federal Election Commission v. National Conservative Political Action Committee*. In a decision striking down federal limits on campaign expenditures by political action committees, the Court declared that group entities *other than* business corporations do not represent the same threat of real or apparent corruption. By emphasizing that distinction, the court highlighted the specific nature of its concerns over corporate political spending. The Court specified that the speech interests of individuals joined together to express political viewpoints were fully protected by the First Amendment – in contrast to the economic interests advanced by corporate managers spending from company treasuries accumulated through the special advantages of the corporate form. Rehnquist again delivered the opinion of the Court. "The groups and associations in question, designed expressly to participate in political debate, are quite different from the traditional corporations organized for economic gain," he wrote. "While in *NRWC* we held that the compelling governmental interest in preventing corruption supported the restriction of the influence of political war chests funneled through the corporate form, in the present cases we do not believe that a similar finding is supportable."[17]

Then in *Federal Election Commission v. Massachusetts Citizens for Life, Inc.*, the next year, the Court even more unequivocally distinguished the specific threat that political spending by business corporations represented in the marketplace of ideas. Government-created advantages enable corporations to use "resources amassed in the economic marketplace" to obtain "an unfair advantage in the political marketplace," Justice William Brennan wrote for the majority. "The resources in the treasury of a business corporation . . . are not an indication of popular support for the corporation's political ideas. They reflect instead the economically motivated decisions of investors and customers. . . . These resources may make a corporation a formidable political presence, even though the power of the corporation may be no reflection of the power of its ideas." However, the Court said, citizens who join together specifically for the purpose of supporting political ideas — as had the members of Massachusetts Citizens for Life, an anti-abortion group — represent a different type of incorporated body. And those types of corporations *do* have First Amendment rights to make expenditures in support of political candidates — because they were formed to disseminate political ideas rather than to amass capital, and thus should not be subject to the concerns underlying regulation of political activity by business corporations. Based on that reasoning, the Court in its ruling established a special test that defines the characteristics that separate *ideological* corporations from business corporations — with one critical element being no funding of the former by the latter.[18]

The Court's articulation of such a definitive distinction between ideological corporations and business corporations — specifically in terms of the potential threat of corruption to the political marketplace — represented a powerful signal of the shift in the Court's majority doctrine regarding corporate political media spending. It can be tracked in those three mid-eighties First Amendment cases involving Federal Election Commission regulations on corporate political spending — known by their acronyms as the *NRWC*, *NCPAC* and *MCFL* decisions. In those cases, the key elements of Rehnquist's fundamental reasoning on corporate First Amendment rights had coalesced. It formed the basis for a doctrine embracing the long-established legislative judgment that government-created advantages of the business corporation in the economic marketplace represent a force that undermines democracy when deployed in the political marketplace of ideas.

That doctrine provides solid constitutional justification for regulating business corporations in special ways to prevent both actual and apparent corruption of elected representatives in candidate campaigns. It asserts the interest in preventing corruption of democratic processes as compelling enough to outweigh the First Amendment rights granted to the types of corporate political spending in the other cases. The doctrine holds that the interests of citizens joined together even to advance the political interests of business corporations are still protected because they can be expressed through political action committees — funded not by corporate treasuries but by contributions from human members of the PAC who wish to express their political support for its ideas. All those critical elements would come together even more dramatically a few years later in the Court's most significant corporate political media spending case since *Bellotti*.

A CORROSIVE THREAT TO THE MARKETPLACE OF IDEAS

In 1990's *Austin v. Michigan State Chamber of Commerce*,[19] the Court found constitutional a Michigan campaign-finance regulation that prohibited business corporations from using general treasury funds for independent expenditures in support of candidates in state elections. In its decision, the Court clearly relied upon the holdings and reasoning from the *NRWC*, *NCPAC* and *MCFL* cases, aligning *Austin* with the doctrine of corporate political-spending regulation that had been asserted most fully and consistently by Justice Rehnquist ever since *Bellotti*. The *Austin* majority embraced a linking of the state's interest in preventing corruption of democratic processes with a regulatory effort aimed at preventing the exercise of political influence by corporate economic power that did not possess corresponding political support from human individuals. In doing so, it affirmed the centrality in First Amendment law of protecting the political marketplace of ideas from undue influence via the economic marketplace.

Although Justice Antonin Scalia denounced the majority decision in *Austin* as accepting a form of "New Corruption" that was "hitherto unrecognized" by the Court, the majority in fact grounded its decision in interests already accepted in the *NRWC* and *MCFL* cases. As the State of Michigan asserted in defending its regulation, it served the two interests that the Court had held compelling in *NRWC*: (1) Ensuring that aggregations of money amassed by the special advantages of the corporate form not be converted to potentially corrupting political war chests and (2) protecting individuals who pay money into a corporation for purposes other than political activity from having their money used in support of candidates whom they may not support. Michigan also argued that the regulation served a third interest for limitations on corporate expenditures that had been deemed compelling by the Court in *MCFL*: To prevent organizations that accept contributions from business corporations from serving as conduits for corporate spending that threatens the political marketplace of ideas.[20]

The state also carefully distinguished its regulation from others that had been held unconstitutional by the Court in earlier campaign-finance cases. Although *Buckley* struck down a limit on independent expenditures by individuals and political committees, the Court in that case did not consider the constitutionality of a ban on such expenditures by corporations. And while *Bellotti* struck down a complete prohibition against corporate expenditures in referenda, the Court in that ruling did not consider the validity of regulations like Michigan's that banned such expenditures in candidate elections.[21]

Justice Thurgood Marshall wrote in the *Austin* majority opinion that "Michigan identified as a serious danger the significant possibility that corporate political expenditures will undermine the integrity of the political process, and it has implemented a narrowly tailored solution to that problem." Requiring corporations to make campaign expenditures through separate funds solicited expressly for political purposes, Marshall wrote, reduced the threat that "huge corporate treasuries amassed with the aid of favorable state laws will be used to influence unfairly the outcome of elections." The regulation, he said, was "precisely targeted to eliminate the distortion caused by corporate spending while also allowing corporations to express their political views" through PACs, whose speech accurately reflects contributors' support for the corporation's political views" because such contributions are made for political purposes.[22]

The *Austin* majority's emphasis on denying protection to corporate political spending lacking the popular support of human individuals embodied Chief Justice Rehnquist's long-argued assertion that non-human forms of specially advantaged economic entities must be subordinate to human citizens politically. The Court maintained that corporate treasuries represent a "corrosive" threat in candidate elections — not because of the amount of wealth corporations wield, but because that wealth derives from special advantages not possessed by human individuals and not reflecting the popular support of human individuals. The power of corporate treasuries is only a measure of "economically motivated decisions of investors and customers," Marshall wrote, accumulated through the "special advantages" bestowed by government upon the corporate form. It is those advantages, he stressed, particularly "limited liability, perpetual life, and favorable treatment of the accumulation and distribution of assets — that enhance their ability to attract capital and to deploy their resources in ways that maximize the return on their shareholders' investments."[23]

The majority emphasized that, as the Court had held in earlier cases, the "legislative judgment that the special characteristics of the corporate structure require particularly careful regulation." All business corporations, regardless their size, "receive from the State the special benefits conferred by the corporate structure and present the potential for distorting the political process," the Court said.[24] It highlighted the significance of those benefits: "Whereas unincorporated unions, and indeed individuals, may be able to amass large treasuries, they do so without the significant state-conferred advantages of the corporate structure" for accumulating wealth.[25] Thus, the *Austin* Court did not accept Michigan's regulation on political spending "simply because its source is a corporation that cannot prove, to the satisfaction of a court, a material effect on its business or property" – the basis that *Bellotti* had rejected.[26] Rather, *Austin* did so because the state sought to prevent potential corruption of the political marketplace of ideas through wealth that had been generated via the special advantages provided the corporate form in the economic marketplace.

Further, the Court declared that the quid-pro-quo corruption that had been focused upon in the *Buckley v. Valeo* case a decade and a half earlier was not the only form of corruption that could threaten democratic processes. The Michigan regulation, Justice Marshall wrote, "aims at a different type of corruption in the political arena: the corrosive and distorting effects of immense aggregations of wealth that are accumulated with the help of the corporate form and that have little or no correlation to the public's support for the corporation's political ideas." Therefore, he said, "corporate wealth can unfairly influence elections when it is deployed in the form of independent expenditures, just as it can when it assumes the guise of political contributions."[27]

Chief Justice Rehnquist did not author a separate opinion in *Austin*, but there was no reason for him to do so. The key tenets that he had long argued concerning First Amendment law and corporate political spending were soundly addressed in Marshall's majority opinion, which Rehnquist joined. That opinion is grounded solidly in the premise that it is a compelling interest of government to protect democratic processes from the use of "state created advantages" by corporations to deploy " 'resources amassed in the economic marketplace' to obtain 'an unfair advantage in the political marketplace.' "[28] As Chief Justice Rehnquist had asserted repeatedly, corporate political media spending represents no individual speech interests but only the interests of a form of business organization created and advantaged in law by government specifically for economic purposes.

Thus, a series of the Supreme Court's First Amendment decisions on corporate political media spending, beginning in the decade of the 1980s, represents efforts to construct a doctrinal firewall between the economic marketplace and the marketplace of ideas. The process advanced Rehnquist's dictum that "the economic is subordinate to the political" in democratic processes. To that end, those decisions affirmed the legislative judgment, first rendered early in the twentieth century and restated on multiple occasions since then, that corporate treasuries represent a threat of corruption when deployed directly in candidate elections. As noted above though, the *Bellotti*-era corporate First Amendment cases and the rights they established remain intact and powerful as precedents. And substantial efforts to revive the ideological momentum of the corporate free-speech movement and override the *Austin* line of cases continue. The reasoning that drives such efforts, and a comprehensive discussion of how it fundamentally undermines American democracy, are the focus of Chapter Seven.

[1] See Linda Greenhouse, "William H. Rehnquist, Architect of Conservative Court, Is Dead at 80," *The New York Times*, 4 September 2005, sec. A, p. 38.

[2] See *Central Hudson Gas & Electric Corp. v. Public Service Commission*, 447 U.S. 557, 599 (1980) (Rehnquist, J., dissenting).

[3] "Change the name and you change the fortunes," wrote political consultant Frank Luntz of his central role in promoting use of the term "death tax" as a political strategy. See Frank Luntz, *Words That Work: It's Not What You Say, It's What People Hear* (New York: Hyperion, 2007), 166.

[4] See *Pacific Gas & Electric Co. v. Public Utilities Commission of California*, 475 U.S. 1, 33 (1986) (Rehnquist, J., dissenting).

[5] For fuller examination of the various theoretical perspectives of the corporation and the course of debate on them in U.S. legal history, see Henry N. Butler and Larry E. Ribstein, *The Corporation and the Constitution* (Washington, D.C.: AEI Press, 1995); Frank H. Easterbrook and Daniel R. Fischel, *The Economic Structure of Corporate Law* (Cambridge, Mass: Harvard University Press, 1991); James Willard Hurst, *The Legitimacy of the Business Corporation in the Law of the United States, 1780-1970* (Charlottesville: University of Virginia Press, 1970); William W. Bratton, Jr., "The New Economic Theory of the Firm: Critical Perspectives from History," 41 *Stanford Law Review* 1471 (1989); R.H. Coase, "The Nature of the Firm," in Kenneth E. Boulding and George J. Stigler, eds., *Readings in Price Theory* (Chicago: R.D. Irwin, 1952); John C. Coates IV, "State Takeover Statutes and Corporate Theory: The Revival of an Old Debate," 64 *New York University Law Review* 806 (1989); Morton J. Horwitz, "Santa Clara Revisited: The Development of Corporate Theory," 88 *West Virginia Law Review* 173 (1985); David Millon, "Theories of the Corporation," 1990 *Duke Law Journal* 201 (1990); Michael J. Phillips, "Reappraising the Real Entity Theory of the Corporation," 21 *Florida State University Law Review* 1061 (1994).

[6] See *Dartmouth College v. Woodward*, 17 U.S. 518, 636 (1819).

[7] See Charles D. Watts, Jr., "Corporate Legal Theory Under the First Amendment: *Bellotti* and *Austin*," 46 *University of Miami Law Review* 317 (1991).

[8] See *First National Bank of Boston v. Bellotti*, 435 U.S. 765, 823 (1978) (Rehnquist, J., dissenting); *Dartmouth College v. Woodward*, 636 (1819); *United States v. White*, 322 U.S. 694, 698-701 (1944).

[9] See *First National Bank of Boston v. Bellotti*, 435 U.S. 765, 825-28 (1978) (Rehnquist, J., dissenting).

[10] See *First National Bank of Boston v. Bellotti*, 826-27 (Rehnquist, J., dissenting).

[11] See *Central Hudson Gas & Electric Corp. v. Public Service Commission*, 447 U.S. 557, 561, 566, 580-81 (1980).

[12] See *Consolidated Edison Co. of New York v. Public Service Commission*, 447 U.S. 530 (1980); *Pacific Gas & Electric Co. v. Public Utilities Commission*, 475 U.S. 1 (1986).

[13] See *Consolidated Edison Co. of New York v. Public Service Commission*, 548-57 (Blackmun, J., dissenting); *Central Hudson Gas & Electric Corp. v. Public Service Commission*, 588-89, 596-97, 599 (Rehnquist, J., dissenting); *Pacific Gas & Electric Co. v. Public Utilities Commission*, 33 (Rehnquist, J., dissenting).

[14] See Brief for Appellant, *Federal Election Commission v. National Right to Work Committee*, 459 U.S. 197 (1982); *United States v. United Auto Workers*, 352 U.S. 567, 579 (1957).

[15] See Brief for Appellant, *Federal Election Commission v. National Right to Work Committee*, 17-18; *Buckley v. Valeo*, 424 U.S. 1, 27, 47 (1976); *First National Bank of Boston v. Bellotti*, 788-89; *United States v. Congress of Industrial Organizations*, 335 U.S. 106, 113 (1948).

[16] See *Federal Election Commission v. National Right to Work Committee*, 208-09, 210-11.

[17] See *Federal Election Commission v. National Conservative Political Action Committee*, 470 U.S. 480, 500-01 (1985). Specifically, the Court held unconstitutional a section of the Presidential Election Campaign Fund Act that made it illegal for an independent political committee to expend more than $1,000 to further the election of a presidential candidate who had elected to accept public financing.

[18] See *Federal Election Commission v. Massachusetts Citizens for Life, Inc.*, 479 U.S. 238, 257-64 (1986). The Court found a section of the Federal Election Campaign Act, prohibiting corporations from using treasury funds to make expenditures in connection with elections, unconstitutional when applied to the class of ideological corporations that it defined in the decision. Detailing the category of ideological corporations it created in this case, the Court said: "In particular, MCFL has three features essential to our holding that it may not constitutionally be bound by [this] restriction on independent spending. First, it was formed for the express purpose of promoting political ideas, and cannot engage in business activities. If political fundraising events are expressly denominated as requests for contributions that will be used for political purposes, including direct expenditures, these events cannot be considered business activities. This ensures that political resources reflect political support. Second, it has no shareholders or other persons affiliated so as to have a claim on its assets or earnings. This ensures that persons connected with the organization will have no economic disincentive for disassociating with it if

they disagree with its political activity. Third, MCFL was not established by a business corporation or a labor union, and it is its policy not to accept contributions from such entities. This prevents such corporations from serving as conduits for the type of direct spending that creates a threat to the political marketplace."

[19] See *Austin v. Michigan State Chamber of Commerce*, 494 U.S. 652 (1990).

[20] See *Austin v. Michigan State Chamber of Commerce*, 684 (Scalia, J., dissenting) and Brief for Appellant, 19-24, 28-34, filed in the same case.

[21] See Brief for Appellant, 36, and Reply Brief for Appellant, 1-2, *Austin v. Michigan State Chamber of Commerce*.

[22] See *Austin v. Michigan State Chamber of Commerce*, 668-69, 660-61.

[23] See *Austin v. Michigan State Chamber of Commerce*, 658-60.

[24] See *Austin v. Michigan State Chamber of Commerce*, 661 (quoting *Federal Election Commission v. National Right to Work Committee*, 209-10).

[25] See *Austin v. Michigan State Chamber of Commerce*, 665.

[26] See *First National Bank of Boston v. Bellotti*, 784.

[27] See *Austin v. Michigan State Chamber of Commerce*, 660.

[28] See *Austin v. Michigan State Chamber of Commerce*, 659 (quoting *Federal Election Commission v. Massachusetts Citizens for Life*, 257).

CHAPTER SEVEN

Incorporating Meiklejohn's Model More Faithfully

The preceding two chapters have laid out the arguments that First Amendment rights for corporate political media spending contradict both Adam Smith's free-market economics and a compelling body of case law shaped by the late Chief Justice William Rehnquist. This chapter considers ongoing arguments on the other side of the issue. It does so in terms of one of the most influential understandings of the First Amendment and its central role in defining the meaning of political freedom — because it remains a core contention of the corporate free-speech movement that it diminishes that freedom to restrict corporate political spending. That assertion is reflected in scholarly and legal discourse, and the debate over it is far from academic. As will also be discussed in this chapter, in 2004 the Supreme Court's five-to-four vote in the biggest case on the subject in a decade and a half showed how closely divided the justices remain on the subject.

This chapter brings the theoretical constructs from the two previous chapters into harmony with the "town meeting" model for promoting freedom of speech that Alexander Meiklejohn famously and successfully introduced in mid twentieth century. When the Supreme Court originally established First Amendment rights for corporate political media spending in the *First National Bank of Boston v. Bellotti* case, it invoked Meiklejohn's ideas as significant in its reasoning. The *Bellotti* majority also cited substantially the *New York Times v. Sullivan* case, a 1964 decision powerfully shaped by Meiklejohn's First Amendment concepts. The Supreme Court has cited Meiklejohn on a great many occasions, and his most enduring contribution to First Amendment thinking — his town-meeting model — provides vital insights for maintaining a truly free marketplace of ideas. Its primary tenet, this chapter argues, can be understood as stipulating a neutral role for government in that marketplace — specifically, neither advantaging nor disadvantaging speakers so as to diminish discussion of public affairs. Further, as the following pages will detail, bestowing First Amendment rights upon corporate political media spending represents exactly the sort of advantaging in the marketplace of ideas that government must avoid.[1]

Essentially, Meiklejohn's First Amendment principles call for government to act as a neutral town-meeting moderator, serving a parliamentary role in promoting democratic debate and self government by the people. The town-meeting understanding of the marketplace of ideas presented in this chapter is consistent with Adam Smith's seminal economics principles for keeping a marketplace truly free. Similarly, it meshes with the line of First Amendment cases in which Rehnquist's reasoning shaped a doctrine focused on preventing the transfer of government-provided corporate advantages from the economic marketplace to the political marketplace.

THE SOVEREIGNTY OF THE PEOPLE

Meiklejohn was a well-known philosophy professor and university administrator who wrote extensively in the 1940s and 1950s to urge that courts foster free discussion of all points of view, rather than to suppress unpopular or unconventional ones.[2] He based his thinking on the First Amendment above all on the people's constitutionally guaranteed sovereignty. "Under the compact upon which the Constitution rests, it is agreed that men shall not be governed by others, that they shall govern themselves," Meiklejohn wrote. As constitutional drafter James Madison explained, whereas in a monarchy, sovereignty lay with the king, "In the United States the case is altogether different. The People, not the Government, possess the absolute sovereignty." In the *Sullivan* case, the Supreme Court emphasized: "The people, not the government, possess absolute sovereignty." For Meiklejohn, the First Amendment above all meant that the government could not encroach upon the people's right to engage in political discourse so as to make informed decisions on how the nation will be governed. Because denying the people this right would undermine their ability to govern themselves, Meiklejohn declared that expression involving political matters should receive the fullest protection of the First Amendment.[3]

But that did not mean a passive, laissez-faire role for government. "The government itself must limit the government," Meiklejohn said. He contended that the constitutional protection provided to the political speech of legislators must be provided just as fully to all citizens' political speech. Otherwise, government would empower elected officials with advantages undermining the sovereignty of the people. Meiklejohn made it clear that the objective is not the elimination of government in deference to private interests but the maintaining of the people's sovereignty in government. "Political freedom does not mean freedom from control. It means self control," he wrote. "If We, the People are to be controlled, then We, the People must do the controlling."[4]

Meiklejohn expressed agreement — to a point — with Justice Oliver Wendell Holmes' influential 1919 assertion that "the best test of truth is the power of the thought to get itself accepted in the competition of the market." Holmes' dictum, Meiklejohn wrote, "rightly tells us that the only truth which we self-governing men can rely on is that which we win for ourselves in the give and take of public discussion and decision." Indeed, Meiklejohn declared, "no other" test of truth exists. The problem that he did have with Holmes' articulation of marketplace-of-ideas theory lay in the extent to which Meiklejohn believed it contributed to an "intellectual laissez-faire" in which "truth is what a man or an interest or a nation can get away with." He contended that fostered a tendency for many people to believe they had no responsibility for testing the truth of their own thinking. All that said, in terms of barring government from viewpoint discrimination, Meiklejohn's dictate that "no idea, no opinion, no doubt, no belief, no counterbelief, no relevant information, may be kept from [citizens]" reflects an essential compatibility with Justice Holmes' assertion that "the ultimate good desired is better reached by free trade in ideas."[5]

Meiklejohn's work has been the subject of much scholarly assessment, and his influence widely recognized. Cass Sunstein called him "the greatest philosopher of the First Amendment." Lee Bollinger declared Meiklejohnian thought to have become "a major part of the idiom of the modern First Amendment," though he contended the rhetorical power of Meiklejohn's ideas was more responsible for his enduring influence than was the legal reasoning involved. Indeed, Meiklejohnian thought is argued here as providing not legal reasoning so much as a compelling philosophical framework for expressing the substantial legal basis underlying the Supreme Court's prevailing doctrine of corporate-political-media-spending regulation. His theoretical concepts offer a nuanced but plain-language understanding of the First Amendment's paradox of forbidding not the abridgement of *speech*, but rather the abridgement of *freedom of speech*.[6] Scholarship that has found difficulties with Meiklejohn's First Amendment interpretation has tended to focus on its lack of attention to questions related to expression that could be considered outside Meiklejohn's political realm.[7] However, this book's assessment of Meiklejohn's town-meeting model does not require engaging those problems with his work. For it is not the *substance* of any expression that is the concern here, but whether government has advantaged some speakers over others to a degree so as to significantly diminish public discussion.

THE CORE PRINCIPLE OF THE TOWN MEETING MODEL

The concept of Meiklejohn's town meeting represents self-governance theory in metaphorical terms. It puts forth "a model by which free political procedures may be measured," he said. "It is self-government in its simplest, most obvious form." The model suggests that rather than a laissez-faire marketplace — in which government would play no role in preventing domination of the process by some participants — a democratically conducted town-hall meeting provides the most effective manner for "protecting the common needs of all the members of the body politic."[8] This passage presents Meiklejohn's description of his model, with italics added to highlight the critical dynamics through which neutral, procedural abridgment of *speech* promotes greater *freedom of speech*:

> In the town meeting the people of a community assemble to discuss and to act upon matters of public interest. . . . Every man is free to come. They meet as political equals. Each has a right and a duty to think his own thoughts, to express them, and to listen to the arguments of others. The basic principle is that the freedom of speech shall be unabridged. *And yet the meeting cannot even be opened unless, by common consent, speech is abridged.* A chairman or moderator is, or has been,

> chosen. He "calls the meeting to order." And the hush which follows that call is a clear indication that restrictions upon speech have been set up. The moderator assumes, or arranges, that in the conduct of the business, certain rules of order will be observed. Except as he is overruled by the meeting as a whole, he will enforce those rules. . . . The meeting has assembled, not primarily to talk, but primarily by means of talking to get business done. And the talking must be regulated and abridged as the doing of the business under actual conditions may require. . . . *The town meeting, as it seeks for freedom of public discussion of public problems, would be wholly ineffectual unless speech were thus abridged.* . . . It is not a dialectical free-for-all. It is self-government.[9]

Beyond metaphor, however, how should the town-meeting concept translate into law and policy in practical terms? Like the marketplace of ideas, the town-meeting model cannot be manifest literally. It is not possible for a democratic society with millions of citizens to conduct any sort of tangible town-hall meeting where all interested participants can actually gather together to make and hear all arguments relevant to any particular public issue. Yet Meiklejohn's town-meeting concept can be translated into a core principle in First Amendment jurisprudence, one that specifies government must *neither advantage nor disadvantage* any participant in a way so significant as to diminish the range of ideas available to the theoretical town meeting. The government's role must be strictly limited to that of a town-meeting moderator committed to fairness and opportunity for all participants, providing no more and no less than the *procedural* structure that any deliberative body requires in order to function.

This interpretation of Meiklejohn's town-meeting model is grounded squarely in his emphasis on the forms of abridgement that the First Amendment denies to government. He said citizens "may not be barred from speaking . . . because their views are believed to be false or dangerous, . . . because someone in control thinks [them] unwise, unfair, or un-American, . . . because we disagree with what [they intend] to say." By taking such action, the government would be significantly disadvantaging those speakers in a manner that diminished the range of ideas available to public discussion. When the government disfavors some speakers based on viewpoint discrimination, the decisionmaking process of the town meeting "must be ill-considered, ill-balanced planning for the general good. *It is that mutilation of the thinking process of the community against which the First Amendment to the Constitution is directed*." Just as the government disadvantaging speakers in that manner mutilates democratic decisionmaking, it follows that government's advantaging of speakers will similarly damage the process and thus must also be prohibited by the First Amendment. In Justice Holmes' articulation of marketplace-of-ideas theory can be seen the same emphasis on the social value of barring viewpoint discrimination by government. "The *ultimate good desired* is better reached by free trade in ideas," Justice Holmes declared. "The best test of truth is the power of the thought to get itself accepted in the competition of the market."[10] For the government to favor or disfavor speakers so as to reduce the range of ideas available to public discussion would be to diminish the free trade and competition in the marketplace of ideas that Justice Holmes held forth as essential to the process of serving the greater good. No market is truly free or truly competitive when some participants are significantly advantaged or disadvantaged by government. Similarly, that is the essence of the town-moderator element in Meiklejohnian thinking.

Thus, we arrive not at a laissez-faire town meeting in which government's role is reduced to one of nonexistence, but one in which government has a "heavy and basic responsibility to promote the freedom of speech." For Meiklejohn that means that government "is not debarred from all action upon freedom of speech. Legislation which abridges that freedom is forbidden, but not legislation to enlarge and enrich it." Any regulation implemented to that end must be designed not to suppress speech but to allow for a full airing in an orderly fashion of all relevant viewpoints. Government may prevent some participants from dominating the deliberation — as does a fair and impartial town-meeting moderator — but it may not decide which ideas are acceptable or unacceptable. As an example of the moderator's role in guarding against such domination, Meiklejohn noted the case in which "twenty like-minded citizens have become a 'party,' and if one of them has read to the meeting an argument which they all have approved, it would be ludicrously out of order for each of the others to insist on reading it again." He emphasized that the rationale for preventing efforts to dominate the meeting unfairly is the same as that for preventing government from favoring or disfavoring speakers based on viewpoint — maximizing the effectiveness of democratic decisionmaking by allowing citizens access to the full *range* of ideas in public discussion. "The point of ultimate interest is not the words of the speakers, but the minds of the hearers. The final aim of the meeting is the voting of wise decisions," Meiklejohn maintained.[11]

It is the emphasis on the "minds of the hearers," however, that has been taken out of context to the rest of Meiklejohn's town-meeting model. It has been asserted in defense of a laissez-faire right to receive information that would deny the constitutionality of any regulation of corporate political media spending. Meiklejohn does assert that the substance of political speech must be constitutionally protected from government interference, but it must be within the procedural context of an ordered structure that brings the greatest benefit to the audience — rather than to speakers advantaged by government. No speakers are bestowed with more time, volume, or repetition for their messages in Meiklejohn's town meeting. Yet all speakers choose which ideas and information to present and how to fashion their rhetoric. Government is not rendered nonexistent by the First Amendment, but rather is barred by it from significantly advantaging or disadvantaging speakers in a manner that diminishes public discussion and thus the quality of democratic decisionmaking. It was upon that model of free speech that the Supreme Court developed its decision in *New York Times v. Sullivan*.

MEIKLEJOHN AND THE MOMENTOUS *SULLIVAN* RULING

Though Meiklejohn had been cited in many Supreme Court cases before then, it was in the landmark *Sullivan* case that his understanding of the meaning of the First Amendment was most fully embraced. In that case, Alabama courts had awarded a Montgomery city commissioner a $500,000 libel judgment against *The New York Times* and individual civil-rights activists responsible for an advertisement critical of local governments' treatment of black students who were protesting segregation in Alabama and other southern states. In a unanimous decision, the Supreme Court reversed the Alabama ruling. Close to half a century after being handed down, *Sullivan* remains one of the most discussed First Amendment rulings ever, arguably the most important in modern free-speech law. The Court held that a public official could not succeed in a libel suit without showing "actual malice" — proof that the defamation was produced with knowledge of its falsity or reckless disregard for its potential falsity. In the same vein in which Meiklejohn wrote that the government may not discourage citizens from speaking "because their views are believed to be false or dangerous," the Court held that criticism of public officials must not be so easily punished that it discourages citizens from engaging in such expression.[12]

It is important to understand precisely how the Court's reasoning was shaped in *Sullivan*, because of its continued influence on First Amendment law. Justice William Brennan acknowledged the significance of Meiklejohnian theory to the case at length, writing not long after the decision. In the *Sullivan* majority opinion, Brennan wrote that the rule of law applied by the Alabama courts unconstitutionally punished political speech, disadvantaging citizens' speech rights to criticize government in discussion of public issues. Such discussion represents the essential sort of deliberation intended to be most protected through Meiklejohn's town-meeting concept. In order to further the "profound national commitment" to full debate on political matters, Brennan said, the Constitution requires protecting citizens for honest misstatements of fact in discussion of the activities of government officials. After *Sullivan*, that would be achieved by requiring government officials to prove the higher standard of fault represented by actual malice in libel cases — thus protecting citizens' public deliberation in the same way that constitutional privilege protects that of officials in their governing duties. "Compelling the critic of official conduct to guarantee the truth of all his factual assertions — and to do so on pain of libel judgments virtually unlimited in amount" — served to disadvantage citizens by intimidating them into self-censorship, Brennan declared.[13]

As Sunstein has written of *Sullivan*, it established a Meiklejohnian "ideal toward which the right of free speech is meant to pave the way." That ideal represents an understanding of the Constitution that "the political process is a forum for broad deliberation on public issues and that rights of speech and the press have a distinctive role to play in the deliberative process," and therefore, "to the extent that libel law can be invoked against popular discussion of public issues, there will be much less discussion." The Court's majority opinion in *Sullivan*, wrote Harry Kalven, another legal scholar, "almost literally incorporated Alexander Meiklejohn's thesis that in a democracy the citizen as ruler is our most important public official." Brennan declared that *Sullivan* presented "a classic example of an activity that Dr. Meiklejohn called an activity of 'governing importance' within the powers reserved to the people and made invulnerable to sanctions imposed by their agency-governments."[14]

In *Sullivan*, the Court stressed its purpose of preventing government from disadvantaging some citizens in a manner so as to diminish the range of ideas in public discussion. Throughout the opinion, that overriding purpose is clear. "A privilege for criticism of official conduct is appropriately analogous to the protection accorded a public official when he is sued for libel by a private citizen," the Court declared. It characterized this principle as grounded in the most fundamental principles that drove the founders' efforts to ensure that the "structure of the government dispersed power in reflection of the people's distrust of concentrated power, and of power itself at all levels." Nothing is more consistent in the language of *Sullivan* than its priority on how the decision is intended, *above all*, to help maintain the sovereignty of the people — a process that requires protecting citizens from concentrations of power that threaten fundamental rights.[15]

That reasoning is crucial in considering how *Sullivan* should be understood as preventing government from significantly advantaging or disadvantaging participants in discussion of public affairs. The specific advantage the case addressed was excessive power of government officials to punish citizens for criticizing such officials. The *Sullivan* Court consistently articulated its rationale in terms of maintaining the peoples' speech rights against encroachment by more powerful influences. The Court invoked the ideal of an "unfettered exchange of ideas" not in a manner so as to imply establishing that condition as an absolute or laissez-faire standard but as part of its broader discussion of protecting speech rights of the people in order to further self governance. The Court weighed the interest in unfettered discussion of public issues against the interest in protecting reputation. Then it concluded that the Alabama liability standard was unconstitutional as applied to libel suits brought in response to criticism of government officials because such a standard leads to self-censorship and "thus dampens the vigor and limits the variety of public debate."[16]

Yet, the Court clearly did not conclude that protecting unfettered discussion required a laissez-faire standard *eliminating* libel as a cause of action whenever matters of public discussion are involved — or even eliminating such libel actions by public officials for that matter. Instead, rather than embracing a laissez-faire approach of no standard at all, the Court set the standard higher, requiring actual malice as the level of fault required of public officials in libel actions. The Court expressed its decision to do so in terms of preventing government from significantly advantaging some speakers in a manner so as to diminish public discussion: "It would give public servants an unjustified preference over the public they serve, if critics of official conduct did not have a fair equivalent of the [constitutional] immunity granted to the officials themselves."[17]

Thus, *Sullivan* hardly supports a laissez-faire interpretation of the First Amendment that would bar the government "moderator" from the town meeting and reduce democratic deliberation to what Meiklejohn called "a dialectical free-for-all."[18] Rather, the *Sullivan* Court embraced the procedural function that Meiklejohn's principles hold for the government. It can act as a neutral moderator, ensuring that all citizens can fairly participate in public discussion — rather than granting some speakers a structural advantage that would enable them to dominate the discussion through the relative disadvantaging of others.

MISINTERPRETING MEIKLEJOHN AND *SULLIVAN*

Some scholarly discourse, however — by focusing narrowly upon a laissez-faire interpretation of the right to receive information — argues that government may not regulate corporate political media spending. "According to Meiklejohn, the First Amendment prohibits government from blocking individuals from any opinions or ideas relevant to the governing process," Martin Redish, for example, has written. He has argued that those opinions and ideas should include the political expenditures made by corporate managers with their companies' profits. Redish drew upon Meiklejohnian reasoning to contend that "to exclude corporate expression from the scope of the free speech clause, then, would be unwisely to shut out from public debate a substantial amount of relevant, provocative, and potentially vital information and opinion on issues of fundamental importance to the polity." Indeed, Meiklejohn's principles do bar viewpoint discrimination by government, which would include discriminating against the views of corporate managers. Yet regulation of political spending directly from corporate treasuries by those managers in no way shuts out the information and opinion those managers wish to contribute to public debate as citizens. The Supreme Court has emphasized that such regulation seeks only to deny corporate management the inordinate advantage of tapping into funds generated through the "economically motivated decisions of investors and customers" and then spending that money in the political marketplace so as to "influence unfairly the outcome of elections."[19]

As Daniel Greenwood has characterized it, a business "corporation is not a banding together of citizens but rather best understood as a pot of money, . . . an institution we have created to serve us in a particular area and for a particular purpose." That is, the corporate form of business is endowed through legislative action with powerful economic advantages, such as limited liability, perpetual life, and favorable treatment of the accumulation and distribution of assets. Those advantages are provided so that corporate managers may "enhance their ability to attract capital and to deploy their resources in ways that maximize the return on their shareholders' investments," the Supreme Court has said, not dominate democratic decisionmaking.[20]

Robert Post has argued that Meiklejohn's town-meeting model is flawed as a basis for regulations such as those on corporate political media spending because it undermines personal autonomy to grant government a "managerial" function that violates the "necessary indeterminacy of public discourse." He has contended that government is not capable of assuming a town-meeting moderator's role to "censor public discourse" by distinguishing which speech is relevant/irrelevant, orderly/disorderly, original/repetitious, or rational/irrational. Therefore, "the state ought not to be empowered to control the agenda of public discourse." Such arguments unnecessarily muddy the waters, however. Indeed, some of Meiklejohn's assertions may be construed as attempting to "manage" which speech will be subject to regulation and which will not. But it is hardly necessary for us to do so in order to most legitimately apply his town-meeting model in free-speech jurisprudence today. We can instead focus upon the way that the model enhances democratic deliberation by ensuring that government neither disadvantages nor advantages any speakers so as to significantly diminish the range of ideas in public discussion.[21]

That advances Meiklejohn's objective that "all the alternative lines of action can be wisely measured in relation to one another." But it does not require government to "censor" any discourse on the basis of its degree of relevance, orderliness (unless so disorderly it unfairly impedes opportunities for other viewpoints to be expressed), originality, rationality or any other quality of its content, nor to "control" the agenda of the process. Citizens in a democracy make all such choices, and the moderator's role is limited to neither favoring nor disfavoring any such choices. When government significantly advantages speakers politically — in the manner in which business corporations are advantaged economically — the sovereignty of the people is replaced with the sovereignty of the advantaged speakers. Government is then choosing which voices to favor.[22]

Therefore, regulation of corporate speech in accordance with the town-meeting model cannot be considered viewpoint discrimination. In Meiklejohnian terms, failure to so regulate corporate political media spending in fact amounts to viewpoint *enhancement* on the part of the government. It empowers the views of the few speakers of the corporate managerial class over those of the many speakers outside that class. Meiklejohn said that government "must make sure that its attempts to make men free do not result in making them slaves." As individuals with First Amendment rights, the corporate managers already have the same opportunity as any other citizen in the democracy to fully express all ideas, convey all information, argue all opinions as they may choose. When corporate spending regulation ensures that the significant, government-endowed advantages provided the corporate form in the economic arena not be transferred into the political domain, it appropriately prevents corporate managers from using those advantages to dominate the town meeting.[23]

Thus, it is not regulation of corporate political media spending in this manner that truly represents the imposition of any managerial function upon the content and nature of public discourse. Rather it is the failure to maintain such regulation that does so. In the town meeting, a speaker who is "abusive" of the procedural protections for all viewpoints to be fairly expressed and heard must be ruled out of order. As Meiklejohn articulated his most critical tenet: "The freedom that the First Amendment protects is not, then, an absence of regulation. It is the presence of self-government."[24]

To emphasize again, it is crucial to understand precisely the way concepts like Meiklejohn's are employed whenever a court puts forth any such concept as significant in the reasoning that explains its ruling. The nature of the relationship between Meiklejohn and *Sullivan* remains vitally relevant today because of its continued influence on First Amendment law. No court has any *duty* to consider Meiklejohn's ideas in its decisions. But when a court professes to ground a ruling specifically in Meiklejohn and *Sullivan*, for example, the pivotal question is whether it has done so in a manner truly consistent with those sources.

Five years after *Sullivan*, for example, in another unanimous decision, the Court's *Red Lion Broadcasting v. Federal Communications Commission* ruling was squared resoundingly with Meiklejohnian town-meeting reasoning. Affirming the constitutionality of requiring broadcasters to give individuals attacked on the air an opportunity to respond, Justice Byron White's majority opinion cited *Sullivan* and declared: "It is the purpose of the First Amendment to preserve an uninhibited marketplace of ideas in which truth will ultimately prevail, rather than to countenance monopolization of that market, whether it be by the Government itself or a private licensee." White also cited Justice Brennan's earlier discussion of Meiklejohn on the essential role of public discussion in self governance. It would clearly diminish public discussion to allow access to the public air waves solely to those favored few who receive broadcast licenses from the government, he said. "As far as the First Amendment is concerned those who are licensed stand no better than those to whom licenses are refused," White wrote. "A license permits broadcasting, but the licensee has no constitutional right to . . . monopolize a radio frequency to the exclusion of his fellow citizens."[25]

But a decade later — with four new justices having since joined the Court, led by former corporate attorney Lewis Powell — a considerably divergent interpretation of Meiklejohn and *Sullivan* was employed in *First National Bank of Boston v. Bellotti*. Powell's majority opinion repeatedly cited Meiklejohn and the *Sullivan* case in the Court's decision to provide First Amendment rights to corporate political media spending. However, rather than a town-meeting understanding of the marketplace of ideas, Powell's opinion actually reflects a laissez-faire interpretation. Therein lies the heart of the distorted use of Meiklejohnian principles in *Bellotti* — and in continuing arguments that invoke its laissez-faire approach to related questions in First Amendment law. That approach essentially denies government any role in protecting the *freedom* of the marketplace of ideas. And neither Meiklejohn nor *Sullivan*, the case in which his First Amendment reasoning was so fully embraced by the Court, ultimately supports such an understanding.

Powell's *Bellotti* majority opinion cited Meiklejohn, for example, in asserting that "if the speakers here were not corporations, no one would suggest that the State could silence their proposed speech. It is the type of speech indispensable to decisionmaking in a democracy." That "is no less true," Powell continued, citing *Sullivan*'s emphasis on protecting debate related to self governance from interference by government, "because the speech comes from a corporation rather than an individual." In that reference to *Sullivan*, Powell wrote, "Self-government suffers when those in power suppress competing views on public issues 'from diverse and antagonistic sources.' " Meiklejohn's town-meeting principles do of course ban government suppression based on viewpoint. As Powell cited Meiklejohn in declaring that "the people in our democracy are entrusted with the responsibility for judging and evaluating the relative merits of conflicting arguments,"[26] the moderator in the town meeting has no role in that assessment of the arguments.

However, as discussed in Chapter Five, the *Bellotti* Court accepted a marketplace of ideas in which government provides some participants — and *their* viewpoints — with significantly greater advantages over others. That is, *Bellotti*'s laissez-faire understanding of the marketplace of ideas makes no distinction between the participation of people as citizens and that of corporate management wielding special access to wealth generated through the government-advantaged corporate form of business organization. Powell's opinion argued that banning corporate media spending from referenda campaigns meant "much valuable information" would be lost because corporate management would not be able to participate. However, that sort of regulation did not prevent corporate managers from participating in the way that other citizens participate. What it prevented was the managers spending from their corporations' treasuries and employing the special, wealth-generating advantages that are granted by government to the corporate form — but not to individuals. That allows managers to transfer those advantages from the economic marketplace directly to the political marketplace. To place it in Meiklejohn's town-meeting context, that would be the sort of advantaging of some participants that the moderator would not be allowed to provide. So while professing to advance self governance through more open debate, the *Bellotti* Court actually advanced governance in which the few are advantaged over the many.

Therefore on balance, *Bellotti*'s laissez-faire approach to regulation of corporate political media spending represents a misinterpretation of the central principles from Meiklejohn and *Sullivan*, upon which the ruling purports to rely. As discussed in Chapter Six, that approach prevailed in a series of related Supreme Court cases. Then a new majority formed on the Court and decided another group of cases so as to prevent the transfer of corporate advantages from the economic marketplace to the political marketplace, culminating in the *Austin v. Michigan Chamber of Commerce* ruling in 1990. In the Court's most recent major case involving corporate political media spending, the five-to-four split among the justices showed that the debate between the *Bellotti* and *Austin* lines of reasoning rages on, however.

THE LATEST CORPORATE-POLITICAL-SPENDING BATTLE

In *McConnell v. Federal Election Commission*, the Court's most substantial consideration of corporate political media spending since *Austin* 13 years before, the majority opinion did not cite Alexander Meiklejohn. However, the reasoning and the decision rendered are consistent with a town-meeting understanding of the marketplace of ideas. The majority clearly rejected advantaging of corporate spending in the political marketplace. In doing so, it elaborated upon the power that Congress has to protect democratic processes by prohibiting business corporations from using their treasuries to finance ads targeted at political candidates, a power the *McConnell* Court characterized as "firmly embedded in law."[27]

The *McConnell* case developed in response to the sweeping campaign-finance reforms of the Bipartisan Campaign Reform Act, which was enacted in early 2002 to close loopholes in campaign-finance regulation by amending previous legislative efforts. One major focus of the BCRA was addressing loopholes that had exempted contributions ostensibly used for political party-building activities. Those sort of contributions are commonly referred to as "soft money," and their use and abuse had skyrocketed in the 1990s. Similarly exempted before the BCRA were expenditures for what qualified in law as "issue ads" – political messages that stopped short of expressly advocating the defeat or election of a specific candidate. In practice, such ads had become widely employed in candidate campaigns by calculatingly designing them to observe the letter of the express-advocacy limitation while trammeling the spirit of it. A 1998 Senate Committee Report characterized those and other campaign-finance abuses as creating a "meltdown" of the system designed to protect democratic processes from the influence of corporate, union and other large contributors.[28]

After a number of plaintiffs challenged the constitutionality of the new regulations,[29] the Supreme Court in its 298-page *McConnell* decision upheld virtually all of the BCRA's provisions.[30] The majority opinion by Justices John Paul Stevens and Sandra Day O'Connor emphasized principles consistent with a town-meeting understanding of the marketplace of ideas, highlighting the deeply established interest in preventing corporate domination of democratic processes. The focus on that threat was clear from the opening lines of the majority opinion. It began by recounting how, for more than a century, Congress had repeatedly and aggressively focused upon corporate political activity in campaign-finance legislation. It did so "in order to prevent 'the great aggregations of wealth, from using their corporate funds, directly or indirectly,' to elect legislators who would 'vote for their protection and the advancement of their interests as against those of the public,' " Stevens and O'Connor wrote. Relying heavily on what the opinion characterized as the "disturbing findings" of the Senate report, it pronounced the "post-1990 explosion" in the use of soft money and issue ads to be little more than efforts to evade campaign-finance regulations – with corporate spending figuring prominently in the upsurge of both practices.[31]

The greatest part of the discussion in the majority opinion was devoted to sections of the BCRA that had considerable impact on corporate political activity. Those sections targeted soft money and prohibited corporations and unions from using general treasury funds shortly before elections for issue ads aimed at candidates — defined by the BCRA as illegal electioneering. The Court held that soft-money regulations aimed at preventing the actual or apparent corruption of federal candidates and officeholders were justified, because the record demonstrated how all large soft-money contributions to national parties had been made suspect by the parties trading on their close relationship with federal officeholders.[32]

Also justified, the Court found were the new electioneering regulations aimed at expenditures for issue ads that stopped short of expressly advocating the defeat or election of a specific candidate. The First Amendment does not erect "a rigid barrier between express advocacy and so-called issue advocacy," the majority declared. It made clear that the evidence was overwhelming that ads could easily evade the previous regulations and their purpose. The record had demonstrated the previous legal distinction between candidate ads and issue ads to be "functionally meaningless," the Court said. Further, it asserted, the previous rules allowed corporate and other organized interests to influence federal elections while concealing their identities from the public in such ads. The Court stated that not only does maintaining the distinction "not reinforce the precious First Amendment values that Plaintiffs argue are trampled by BCRA," it "ignores the competing First Amendment interests of individual citizens seeking to make informed choices in the political marketplace."[33]

The Court's reasoning on the matter represented, in town-meeting terms, a powerful demonstration of its refusal to advantage corporate spending over other participation in the marketplace of ideas. In its discussion on the electioneering issue, the Court emphasized its agreement with the lower court that first heard the challenge to the BCRA, before the appeal reached the Supreme Court. The lower court had denounced in scathing terms the extent and nature of the way corporate interests had wielded the advantage of engaging in electioneering in campaigns without revealing who was paying for the ads. "BCRA's disclosure provisions require these organizations to reveal their identities so that the public is able to identify the source of the funding behind broadcast advertisements influencing certain elections," the U.S. District Court for the District of Columbia wrote. It noted in particular how the plaintiffs had challenged the electioneering regulations by citing the priority that *New York Times v. Sullivan* placed on "uninhibited, robust, and wide-open" public discussion. "Curiously, Plaintiffs want to preserve the ability to run these advertisements while hiding behind dubious and misleading names like: 'The Coalition-Americans Working for Real Change' (funded by business organizations opposed to organized labor) [and] 'Citizens for Better Medicare' (funded by the pharmaceutical industry)," the Court observed. "Given these tactics, Plaintiffs never satisfactorily answer the question of how 'uninhibited, robust, and wide-open' speech can occur when organizations hide themselves from the scrutiny of the voting public."[34]

On balance, the Supreme Court's decision in the *McConnell* case can be seen as the continuing survival of a doctrine on corporate political media spending that moves away from the laissez-faire approach of *Bellotti*. That doctrine has moved in a direction consistent with a town-meeting understanding of the marketplace of ideas that more truly advances freedom of the political marketplace and democratic debate. That understanding embraces the long-held legislative and well-established judicial judgment that the special characteristics of the corporate business form require particularly careful regulation in order to protect democratic processes from actual and potential corruption. Yet *McConnell* remains a case decided by one vote. And the justices on the other side denounced the majority ruling in the harshest of terms. The *McConnell* case made clear that the debate among the justices is far from settled as to the conflicting lines of reasoning reflected in the respective *Bellotti* and *Austin* clusters of case law. It suggests that the future of First Amendment law on this matter will be crucially shaped by the struggle on the Court between the laissez-faire and the town-meeting understandings.

"Every man is free to come" to the town meeting, Meiklejohn wrote. "They meet as political equals."[35] Making *that* ideal a literal reality would be beyond the capability of any government — that is, to somehow equalize all the economic, personal, social, and other resources that respective citizens may bring to the political arena. Yet, as this chapter argues, it is both realistic and reasonable for First Amendment law to bar government from choosing to unfairly *provide* resources to some competitors in the political marketplace of ideas. It is both good law and highly principled policy to limit government's role to neither advantaging nor disadvantaging competitors in that marketplace. Whether the Supreme Court's doctrine on corporate political media spending will continue to reflect support for such an understanding is not by any means something that can be taken for granted, however. In fact, as the next chapter will highlight, the chances for that doctrine's survival in the years ahead may already be declining.

[1] For a discussion of the *Bellotti* Court's invocation of Meiklejohn to overcome the "apparent incongruities" of extending First Amendment protection to non-human entities such as business corporations, see Carl E. Schneider, "Free Speech and Corporate Freedom: A Comment on *First National Bank of Boston v. Bellotti*," 59 *Southern California Law Review* 1227, 1234-36 (1986). See Cass R. Sunstein, "Hard Defamation Cases," 25 *William & Mary Law Review* 891, 898 (1984), on the way it has been established as a "relatively uncontroversial working hypothesis that the [*Sullivan*] decision rested on Professor Meiklejohn's conception of the First Amendment." Between 1951 and 1983, Meiklejohn was cited in 27 U.S. Supreme Court opinions — nine times in majority opinions, five in concurring opinions, and thirteen in dissents.

[2] Meiklejohn taught philosophy at Brown University and the University of Wisconsin, and he served as dean at Brown and president at Amherst College. His bachelor's degree at Brown and his Ph.D. at Cornell University were both in philosophy. See Adam R. Nelson, *Education and Democracy: The Meaning of Alexander Meiklejohn, 1872-1964* (Madison: University of Wisconsin Press, 2001), 263-295.

[3] See Alexander Meiklejohn, *Political Freedom: The Constitutional Powers of the People* (Westport, Conn.: Greenwood Press, 1960). 75; James Madison, "Report on the Virginia Resolution," in Gaillard Hunt, ed., *The Writings of James Madison*, vol. 6 (New York: G.P. Putnam's Sons, 1906), 386; *New York Times v. Sullivan*, 376 U.S. 254, 274 (1964). See also Cass R. Sunstein, "Speech in the Welfare State: Free Speech Now," 59 *University of Chicago Law Review* 255 (1992), defending the basic proposition that the understanding of political speech in U.S. law is critically grounded in the "distinctive American understanding of sovereignty."

[4] See U.S. Constitution, Article 1, Section 6 ("The Senators and Representatives . . . for any Speech or Debate in either House . . . shall not be questioned in any other Place."); Meiklejohn, *Political Freedom*, 17, 34-36, 13, 16.

[5] See Meiklejohn, *Political Freedom*, 73-75; *Abrams v. United States*, 250 U.S. 616, 630 (1919) (Holmes, J., dissenting).

[6] See Cass R. Sunstein, "Speech in the Welfare State: Free Speech Now," 59 *University of Chicago Law Review* 255 (1992); Cass R. Sunstein, *The Partial Constitution* (Cambridge, Mass.: Harvard University Press, 1993), 233-42; Lee C. Bollinger, *The Tolerant Society: Freedom of Speech and Extremist Speech in America* (New York: Oxford University Press, 1986); Meiklejohn, *Political Freedom*, 21. See also, in support of Meiklejohn's basic concepts, Robert H. Bork, "Neutral Principles and Some First Amendment Problems," 47 *Indiana Law Journal* 1, 26 (1971); Lillian R. BeVier, "The First Amendment and Political Speech: An Inquiry into the Substance and Limits of Principle," 30 *Stanford Law Review* 299 (1978); Owen M. Fiss, *Liberalism Divided:*

Freedom of Speech and the Many Uses of State Power (Boulder, Colo.: Westview Press, 1996), 117-20.

[7] See, for example, C. Edwin Baker, *Human Liberty and Freedom of Expression* (New York: Oxford University Press, 1989), 25-33; Laurence H. Tribe, *American Constitutional Law* (Mineola, N.Y.: Foundation Press, 1988), 577-78; Paul G. Stern, "A Pluralistic Reading of the First Amendment and its Relation to Public Discourse," 99 *Yale Law Journal* 925, 930-33 (1990); Zechariah Chafee, Book Review, 62 *Harvard Law Review* 891, 896 (1949).

[8] See Meiklejohn, *Political Freedom*, 24, 55.

[9] See Meiklejohn, *Political Freedom*, 24-25 (italics added).

[10] See Meiklejohn, *Political Freedom*, 19-20 (italics added); *Abrams v. United States*, 630 (Holmes, J., dissenting) (italics added for emphasis).

[11] See Meiklejohn, *Political Freedom*, 19-20, 26.

[12] For example, on the recent fortieth anniversary of the *Sullivan* decision, a full issue of the media-law journal *Communication Law & Policy* (Autumn 2004) was devoted to its legacy. See Meiklejohn, *Political Freedom*, 26-27; *New York Times v. Sullivan*, 376 U.S. 254, 264-65, 283 (1964). The lower court had held that because some of the statements in the ad were false, it was libelous per se and did not require proof of fault or damage to reputation under the libel doctrine of strict liability. That doctrine presumed legal injury to a public official from the fact of publication of critical statements alone. See *New York Times Co. v. Sullivan*, 273 Ala. 656, 673, 676 (1962).

[13] See William J. Brennan, Jr., "The Supreme Court and the Meiklejohnian Interpretation of the First Amendment," 79 *Harvard Law Review* 1 (1965); *New York Times v. Sullivan*, 279-84. Justice Brennan did not cite Meiklejohn in the *Sullivan* majority opinion itself. In a concurring opinion, however, Justice Hugo Black cited Meiklejohn in support of the assertion that "freedom to discuss public affairs and public officials is unquestionably, as the Court today holds, the kind of speech the First Amendment was primarily designed to keep within the area of free discussion. . . . An unconditional right to say what one pleases about public affairs is what I consider to be the minimum guarantee of the First Amendment." *New York Times v. Sullivan*, 296-97 (Black, J., concurring).

[14] See Cass R. Sunstein, "Hard Defamation Cases," 25 *William & Mary Law Review* 891, 898-99 (1984); Harry Kalven, Jr., "The New York Times Case: A Note on the Central Meaning of the First Amendment," *Supreme Court Review* 191, 209 (1964); William J. Brennan, Jr., "The Supreme Court and the Meiklejohnian Interpretation of the First Amendment," 14.

[15] See *New York Times v. Sullivan*, 282, 273-77.

[16] See *New York Times v. Sullivan*, 269, 271, 279.

[17] See *New York Times v. Sullivan*, 280-83.

[18] See Meiklejohn, *Political Freedom*, 25.

[19] See Martin H. Redish and Howard M. Wasserman, "What's Good for General Motors: Corporate Speech and the Theory of Free Expression," 66 *George Washington Law Review* 235, 256-57, 235-36 (1998); *Austin v. Michigan State Chamber of Commerce*, 494 U.S. 652, 659, 668-69 (1990).

[20] See Daniel J.H. Greenwood, "Essential Speech: Why Corporate Speech is Not Free," 83 *Iowa Law Review* 995, 1062-63 (1998); *Austin v. Michigan State Chamber of Commerce*, 658-59.

[21] See Robert Post, "Meiklejohn's Mistake: Individual Autonomy and the Reform of Public Discourse," 64 *University of Colorado Law Review* 1109, 1111-19 (1993). See also Morris Lipson, "Autonomy and Democracy," 104 *Yale Law Journal* 2249 (1995), arguing at length, against Post, that regulation enhancing collective self-determination actually advances the autonomy of citizens in a democracy, rather than impeding it.

[22] See Meiklejohn, *Political Freedom*, 26.

[23] See Meiklejohn, *Political Freedom*, 17.

[24] See Meiklejohn, *Political Freedom*, 25; Alexander Meiklejohn, "The First Amendment is an Absolute," *Supreme Court Review* 245, 252 (1961).

[25] See *Red Lion Broadcasting v. Federal Communications Commission*, 395 U.S. 367, 400-01, 389-90 (1969). A broadcaster had challenged the response regulation as an abridgement of its First Amendment rights. The Court upheld the constitutionality of such regulations, when the FCC and Congress deem them necessary. As of this writing, they no longer do so.

[26] See *First National Bank of Boston v. Bellotti*, 435 U.S. 765, 777, 791 (1978).

[27] See *McConnell v. Federal Election Commission*, 540 U.S. 93, 203-04 (2003).

[28] See 26 Senate Report No. 105-167, vol. 4, 4611 (1998).

[29] Immediately after the BCRA was signed into law, U.S. Senator Mitch McConnell and the National Rifle Association filed separate complaints challenging the constitutionality of the new regulations. By the time the case began, nine additional complaints and a total of 75 additional plaintiffs had been consolidated with the complaints of McConnell and the NRA.

[30] The Supreme Court upheld the BCRA's prohibition on national parties raising or spending soft money, ban on federal officeholders or candidates raising or spending soft money, prohibition on political parties transferring or soliciting soft money for tax-exempt political groups, ban on state candidates spending soft money to promote or attack federal candidates, definition of broadcast issue advertisements as electioneering communications when they mention a federal candidate and are targeted at the candidate's electorate within sixty days before an election, ban on corporate and union expenditures for

electioneering from their general treasuries, new disclosure requirements for candidates and for individual expenditures on electioneering communications, and stiffer definition of coordinated expenditures. The Court struck down only provisions prohibiting political contributions by minors and requiring parties to choose between independent expenditures or coordinated expenditures.

[31] See *McConnell v. Federal Election Commission*, 115-42.

[32] See *McConnell v. Federal Election Commission*, 133-59.

[33] See *McConnell v. Federal Election Commission*, 189-98.

[34] See *McConnell v. Federal Election Commission,* 251 F. Supp. 2d 176, 237 (D.D.C 2003).

[35] See Meiklejohn, *Political Freedom*, 24.

CHAPTER EIGHT

A Jurisprudence on the Brink

The outcomes in cases like *Austin v. Michigan Chamber of Commerce* and *McConnell v. Federal Election Commission* should hardly be taken as reason to believe that the corporate free-speech movement has been halted. Although a shift in Supreme Court doctrine was clear in those cases and others, they overturned none of the precedents from *First National Bank of Boston v. Bellotti* and the related rulings establishing First Amendment rights for corporate political media spending. Those specific holdings stand unaltered in the case law. Though the latter cases have limited the full First Amendment rights implied by the earlier cases, a solid faction on the Court argues fiercely against those limits. Only one of the six justices from the 1990 *Austin* majority — John Paul Stevens — remains on the Court, and he is 87 as this is written in late 2007. The preceding three chapters demonstrated how the Court's recent doctrine limiting corporate political spending is more consistent with the free-market principles of Adam Smith, the case law shaped by the late Chief Justice William Rehnquist, and the town-meeting understanding of the First Amendment established by Alexander Meiklejohn. But this chapter will consider the possibility that the corporate free-speech movement at this moment, early in the twenty-first century, could be moving closer to renewed success.

Changes on the Supreme Court in this period, following the retirement of Sandra Day O'Connor and the death of Chief Justice Rehnquist, might well have already provided the needed votes for that success. It will be determined by the positions that ultimately are taken by the most recently appointed justices. Will new Chief Justice William Roberts and Associate Justice Samuel Alito join the bloc of justices firmly opposed to limiting corporate political media spending? If so, it may only be a matter of time before the doctrine Rehnquist fashioned begins to be undermined. Although it is not possible to predict unequivocally how new Supreme Court justices will vote, it is fairly safe to assume that the Court did not grow any *less* favorable toward big business with Roberts and Alito replacing Rehnquist and O'Connor.

"In Nominee, Business Sees Lawyer Who Has Argued Many of Its Cases," read a headline on the Roberts nomination. On Alito: "Court Nominee Has Paper Trail Businesses Like." Headlines, of course, can hardly provide definitive indications of how Roberts or Alito will assess any specific case or issue that may come before them, but it was clear the business community warmly welcomed their arrival on the Court. Roberts — like Justice Powell, the author of the *Bellotti* decision — joined the bench after a highly successful career representing corporate legal interests. But Roberts' judicial record before joining the Supreme Court was too sparse to provide any substantial guide on what to expect from him on the bench. Alito though established an extensive record in fifteen years as a federal judge — one so consistently pro-business that a prominent corporate attorney declared: "We're always happy to see Judge Alito on the panel."[1]

Still, today we can only speculate on the positions that Roberts, Alito, and any other new justices may over time establish in cases involving the agenda of the corporate free-speech movement. However, we know as well as we know anything about the Supreme Court the positions that veteran justices Antonin Scalia and Anthony Kennedy will maintain on the subject. The ferocity with which they have asserted those positions in cases to date makes it clear they can be expected to continue advocating for full First Amendment rights for corporate political media spending. And Justice Clarence Thomas has demonstrated solidarity with the positions of Scalia and Kennedy on the subject. Rather than maintaining the subordination of the economic to the political that Rehnquist advanced in Supreme Court jurisprudence, the current Court may well be more likely to move in the opposite direction.

MISREPRESENTING THE *AUSTIN* RULING

Scalia and Kennedy made clear they held their positions as intensely as ever in their lengthy dissents in the *McConnell* case. Although the case involved an array of complex questions related to legal challenges of the latest overhaul of federal campaign-finance rules, it included the Supreme Court's most substantial consideration of regulations on corporate political media spending since the *Austin* case thirteen years before. Great portions of the dissenting opinions focused on that matter. Kennedy contended that the majority had "compound[ed] the error" made in *Austin* that allowed "the Government to exercise the power to censor political speech based on the speaker's corporate identity" in the first place.[2] Scalia declared it a "casual abridgment of free-speech rights" for the majority to hold "that the particular form of association known as a corporation does not enjoy full First Amendment protection. Of course the text of the First Amendment does not limit its application in this fashion. . . . Nor is there any basis in reason why First Amendment rights should not attach to corporate associations"[3]

Scalia and Kennedy have focused on framing *Austin* as a doctrinal island, as if it suddenly emerged from nowhere, independent of any precursor in case law, any connective tissue between it and related jurisprudence. "*Austin* was the first and, until now, the only time our Court had allowed the Government to exercise the power to censor political speech based on the speaker's corporate identity. . . . In the end the majority can supply no principled basis to reason away *Austin*'s anomaly," Justice Kennedy insisted in *McConnell.*[4] In *Austin*, Scalia had lashed out at the majority for, in his assessment, "permitting Michigan to make private corporations the first object of this Orwellian announcement . . . that too much speech is an evil that the democratic majority can proscribe."[5]

As detailed in Chapter Six, *Austin* was clearly no "anomaly" in the Supreme Court's case law. Led by Rehnquist, the Court had over several years developed a broadly grounded doctrine articulating the constitutionality of restrictions on political expenditures applied to business corporations — based on the threat represented by transferring their special, government-granted, economic advantages to the marketplace of ideas. In that process, the Court's majority moved away from the laissez-faire notions of *Bellotti* toward a doctrine that neither advantages corporate treasuries in the marketplace of ideas nor disadvantages the viewpoints of individuals concerned with corporate interests. The latter are not silenced by regulation consistent with that doctrine because they can be expressed by the individuals themselves or through political action committees – whose funds come not from corporate treasuries but from the contributions of citizens seeking to join together with others specifically to promote their viewpoints.

Thus, although Scalia maligned the majority decision in *Austin* as accepting a form of "New Corruption" that was "hitherto unrecognized" by the Court,[6] the majority in fact had only recognized interests already accepted in the *Federal Election Commission v. National Right to Work Committee* and *Federal Election Commission v. Massachusetts Citizens for Life, Inc.* cases. Further, *Austin*'s grounding ran much farther back than the specific case law on which it drew concerning recent First Amendment cases on corporate political media spending. As the majority emphasized, its *Austin* holding was squarely on point with the long-held "legislative judgment that the special characteristics of the corporate structure require particularly careful regulation" in order to protect democratic processes from actual and potential corruption.[7] That is the point that the case law detailed in Chapter Six emphasizes time and again. Multiple scholarly efforts also have documented evidence of the corrupting influence of corporate spending in democratic processes.[8]

Justice Scalia's *Austin* dissent also argued as "the absolutely central truth of the First Amendment" the principle that "government cannot be trusted to assure, through censorship, the 'fairness' of political debate."[9] Certainly, it may not be possible for government to *assure* the fairness of anything in life. Yet, that hardly suggests that government can therefore not be barred from *creating* unnecessary unfairness by advantaging some participants in public debate. Consistent with the town-meeting model detailed in Chapter Seven, for example, regulations such as the statute challenged in *Austin* (barring corporate political expenditures in candidate campaigns) engage in no censorship of any viewpoint. All citizens remain free under such regulations to express whatever views they may wish to convey in political discourse, concerning the advancement of corporate interests or any other subject. Such regulations only prevent those who do not actually *own* the wealth generated in the economic marketplace through the special advantages of the corporate form — the corporate managers — from deploying it in the political marketplace. That is, under such regulations, the managers of business corporations are not allowed to spend the stockholders' profits on political-campaign advertising.

Granting legal sanction to do so — in the form of First Amendment rights for corporate political media spending — would amount to providing some participants in the "town meeting" with the inestimable advantage of deploying the time and resources of other participants, as well as choosing which viewpoints will be expressed with the others' time and resources. The dimension of such an advantage goes significantly beyond whatever personal qualities any individual may wield through natural talent or personal effort — qualities which do not derive from government-provided advantages. Indeed, it is quite precisely *because* government interference cannot be trusted in political debate that the First Amendment serves to neutralize viewpoint discrimination by government and advance the sovereignty of the people.

In his *Austin* dissent, Scalia conceded that corporations are "to be sure, given special advantages . . . that the State is under no obligation to confer." He argued, however, that "so are other associations and private individuals given all sorts of special advantages . . . ranging from tax breaks to contract awards to public employment to outright cash subsidies. It is rudimentary that the State cannot exact as the price of those special advantages the forfeiture of First Amendment rights."[10] Certainly many circumstances can be hypothesized under which it might be difficult to determine through judicial review whether a particular, government-provided advantage disproportionately enhances the recipients' participation in the marketplace of ideas. Yet the process of complex analysis involved in making crucial distinctions of that sort is a routine element of judicial review. It can be difficult, for example, to determine whether an act of negligence should be considered to reach the level of actual malice in a libel action. Yet courts have been doing that regularly since the *New York Times v. Sullivan* ruling more than four decades ago. Quite simply, judges judge. Assessing complex questions of degree in constitutional law is hardly limited to First Amendment cases on corporate political media spending.

Even more crucially, it is disingenuous at best to dismissively categorize the special advantages of the corporate form as indistinguishable from any other advantage that might be argued to derive from government action. As the majority stressed in *Austin* and the related cases that shaped its reasoning, it has been solidly established by a century of legislative judgment that the advantages provided to the corporate form of organizing business hold alarming potential to corrupt democratic processes. They are not merely on the same order as other advantages that may be argued — indeed may not be similar to *any* others in that context. As detailed in Chapter Two, once the special advantages of incorporation were established as widely available in the United States, that dynamic transformed the way the nation did business so rapidly and sweepingly that it remade the entire American landscape. Those economic advantages have been the driving force behind watershed changes in virtually every aspect of life since that time. In an age when the Supreme Court has declared that " virtually every means of communicating ideas in today's mass society requires the expenditure of money," it strains credulity to pretend that the government-provided advantages at the heart of the most powerful wealth-accumulation device ever invented are indistinguishable from any other advantage arguably deriving from government.[11]

Nevertheless, Kennedy also wrote a lengthy dissent in the *Austin* case, flatly refusing to acknowledge the implications of those advantages. "The Court's hostility to the corporate form used by the speaker in this case and its assertion that corporate wealth is the evil to be regulated is far too imprecise to justify the most severe restriction on political speech ever sanctioned by this Court," he insisted. Kennedy's *Austin* dissent focused on his contention that the challenged regulation "prohibits corporations from speaking on a particular subject, the subject of candidate elections" and "discriminates on the basis of the speaker's identity." He wrote that under the regulation, "any person or group other than a corporation may engage in political debate over candidate elections; but corporations . . . must remain mute.[12] Thus, Kennedy recognized no difference in the First Amendment rights of citizens expressing themselves through their own resources and corporate managers utilizing the resources of others to do so. His acceptance of that advantage for corporate competitors in the marketplace of ideas has held firm in the years since *Austin*, as he demonstrated at some length in the *McConnell* case thirteen years later.

THE CORPORATE FREE-SPEECH MOVEMENT LIVES ON

As detailed in Chapter Seven, the *McConnell v. Federal Election Commission* case addressed a First Amendment challenge to the campaign-finance reforms of the Bipartisan Campaign Reform Act. The majority upheld virtually all of the body of regulations, a significant number of which were targeted at corporate political media spending. The majority found the regulations to be the latest in the century-long legislative effort to prevent " 'the great aggregations of wealth, from using their corporate funds, directly or indirectly,' to elect legislators who would 'vote for their protection and the advancement of their interests as against those of the public.' " However, that majority prevailed by only one vote, with Scalia and Kennedy again denouncing the ruling as infringing corporate First Amendment rights. The five-to-four vote and the intensity of the dissents indicated the great potential for the Court to shift its jurisprudence on corporate political media spending back toward a laissez-faire doctrine that would even more greatly advantage corporate participants in the marketplace of ideas.

Scalia's dissent rejected the principle of preventing corporations from transferring their structural advantages from the economic marketplace to the political marketplace: "In the modern world, giving the government power to exclude corporations from the political debate enables it effectively to muffle the voices that best represent the most significant segments of the economy." He continued to argue that limiting corporate political expenditures to political action committees denied corporations the power to operate with effectiveness politically, utilizing "the organizational form in which those enterprises already exist, and in which they can most quickly and most effectively get their message across."[13] Scalia also joined Kennedy's lengthier dissent, which condemned the majority opinion as having replaced "discrete and respected First Amendment principles with new, amorphous, and unsound rules, rules which dismantle basic protections for speech." Kennedy devoted a significant portion of his dissent to challenging the reasoning that corporate political spending may be constitutionally subjected to regulation in the public interest in order to address real or apparent corruption of democratic processes. "The problem is that the majority uses *Austin*, a decision itself unfaithful to our First Amendment precedents, to justify banning a far greater range of speech," he declared.[14]

Kennedy's assertions on corporate political spending were grounded clearly in a laissez-faire understanding of the marketplace of ideas: "If protected speech is being suppressed, that must be the end of the inquiry" as to whether a regulation of political speech is constitutional. Even more intrinsic to Kennedy's position on corporate political spending is an insistence on a First Amendment jurisprudence that treats government-advantaged corporations as no different in any way from human citizens who are not so advantaged. The *McConnell* majority "diminishes the First Amendment by ignoring its command that the Government has no power to dictate what topics its citizens may discuss," he wrote. Limiting corporate expenditures aimed at influencing candidate elections to PACs rather than allowing such expenditures directly from corporate treasuries amounts to regulation of citizens' speech based on content, in Kennedy's assessment. "The majority can articulate no compelling justification for imposing this scheme of compulsory ventriloquism," he wrote.[15]

Scalia and Kennedy's dismissive characterizations of the use of political action committees that is allowed corporations in campaign-finance regulation suggest that PACs are of little use in expressing corporate political interests. Just how incorrect that is has been abundantly evident ever since the Federal Election Commission ruled in 1975 that corporations may solicit their employees for PAC contributions, as well as use corporate treasury funds to manage their PACs. In the decade after that FEC ruling, the number of corporate PACs mushroomed from 89 to 1,682. Also, organizations such as the Business-Industry Political Action Committee, the National Association of Business Political Action Committees, and the National Chamber Alliance for Politics have developed highly effective systems to coordinate PAC activity among corporations.[16]

In addition to showcasing the unwavering support of Scalia and Kennedy for the objectives of the corporate free-speech movement, the *McConnell* case also left behind something of a mystery — one that, with the subsequent death of William Rehnquist, may never be solved conclusively. The Chief Justice — who had previously been the Court's most unwavering stalwart in defense of regulating corporate political media spending — did not join the *McConnell* majority on the two major holdings. He did join Justice Kennedy's dissent, much of which seems utterly irreconcilable with the doctrinal position Rehnquist had long held so firmly. Yet the Chief Justice's own dissenting opinion clearly did not repudiate the doctrine of corporate political spending regulation that he had championed so fervently and repeatedly in previous cases all the way back to *Bellotti* a quarter-century earlier.

In his dissenting opinion in *McConnell*, the Chief Justice specifically dissented only from majority holdings *other than* those that most substantially focused on corporate political media spending and the related regulatory doctrine. Therefore, Rehnquist's stance in *McConnell* may primarily reflect a concern that the BCRA had too broad an impact in practice, rather than any actual doctrinal shift by him on corporate First Amendment rights per se. That seems quite possible, especially given his position in *Federal Election Commission v. Beaumont* only six months earlier. In that decision, the Chief Justice joined the majority in rejecting a First Amendment challenge to the federal ban on corporate contributions to political candidates. Rehnquist's *McConnell* dissent contended that the critical issue was "whether Congress can permissibly regulate much speech that has no plausible connection to candidate contributions or corruption." He argued that "in reality, Title I is much broader than the Court allows, regulating a good deal of speech that does not have the potential to corrupt federal candidates and officeholders."[17]

Kennedy's dissent was dramatically more sweeping. He wrote that even if he accepted — which he doesn't — the basis of the earlier holdings justifying regulation aimed at preventing the economic advantages of the corporate form being translated into unfair political influence, the BCRA still should have been struck down. In that vein, he too argued overbreadth, contending that the majority's rhetoric suggested "a conflation of the [candidate] anticorruption rationale with the corporate speech rationale. . . . The conflation appears designed to cast the speech regulated here as unseemly corporate speech." Kennedy rejected what he found to be the majority's "referring to the corporate speech rationale as if it were the linchpin of the case," arguing that doing so meant accepting unconstitutional regulation on other political speakers.[18]

On that point, the *McConnell* majority countered that the linchpin of its rationale was not the corporate identity but the established potential for real or apparent corruption of political processes that it represented. It declared that Kennedy's "interpretation of the First Amendment would render Congress powerless to address more subtle but equally dispiriting forms of corruption." Further, the majority argued, "The principles set forth here and relied upon . . . are the same principles articulated in *Buckley* [*v. Valeo*] and its progeny that regulations of contributions to candidates, parties, and political committees are subject to less rigorous scrutiny than direct restraints on speech — including 'unseemly corporate speech.' " In its discussion on the question of overbreadth in the electioneering regulations, the majority noted that the record indicated the "vast majority of ads" in question were exactly the kind justifiably targeted by the regulation. The majority also argued that rather than suggesting that the regulation would have an overly broad impact in practice "the record strongly supports the contrary conclusion."[19]

GETTING BACK TO THE MAIN POINT

The debate on overbreadth can easily pull us into a thicket of related case law on that subject in order to consider it fully. But it is actually a side issue to the focus of this chapter and this book. For even if we grant for the sake of discussion that the *McConnell* dissenters are correct that the regulations upheld are overly broad, that would not in any way invalidate the basis for regulation of corporate political media spending in order to prevent domination of the marketplace of ideas by government-advantaged participants. Certainly, the justification for regulation on that basis cannot also justify regulation that reaches *beyond* corporate political media spending. That is, it is a rationale that cannot simply be extended to justify regulation of the influence of *all* money in political decisionmaking. The influence that wealthy *individuals* may wield in democratic processes, for example, particularly represents a separate and distinct constitutional issue. The case law on corporate political media spending should not be confused with the body of law referenced so succinctly in the *Buckley* case. "The First Amendment's protection against governmental abridgment of free expression cannot properly be made to depend on *a person's* financial ability to engage in public discussion," the Court said in that ruling.[20]

Scalia asked in *Austin*, "Why is it perfectly all right if advocacy by an individual billionaire is out of proportion with 'actual public support' for his positions?"[21] The answer, in terms of the understanding emphasized here, is that the individual billionaire chooses to express viewpoints through the use of the billionaire's own resources — rather than corporate management choosing to express its viewpoints through the use of company treasuries that represent the economic interests of investors, not their political viewpoints. If money is speech, as the Court has held, then *surely* spending someone else's money to espouse political viewpoints must be considered an unconstitutional act — forcing the owners of the money to associate with speech with which they may not agree. In terms of the First Amendment, the two issues – the influence of individual wealth and the influence of corporate wealth — are very different ones that cannot be indistinguishably intertwined, either by regulators or by those who oppose regulation. Yet, just because a regulation cannot solve *all* campaign-finance problems in one fell swoop does not mean that regulation cannot be implemented to resolve *any* such problem. And the bottom line is that a sound basis for justifying the constitutionality of regulating corporate political media spending clearly exists – both in theory and in case law.

It is important to remember that even in the *Bellotti* decision that gave corporate political media spending a foothold in First Amendment law, the support for that action among the Supreme Court justices was thin. Four of them, after all, voted against the holding. And the five-to-four split was marked by disagreement between majority and minority on almost every aspect of the case. So it is quite a distortion to suggest that the cases that later served to narrow the rights *Bellotti* had bestowed upon corporate political media spending were some radical departure from a more broadly established doctrine. Justice Byron White — by almost any measure one of the more conservative jurists to serve on the Court in recent decades — emphasized in his *Bellotti* dissent that the Court had "repeatedly recognized" and treated "with deference" legislation ever since the 1925 Corrupt Practices Act was enacted to "prevent the use of corporate or union funds for political purposes without the consent of the shareholders or union members."

The bottom line was clear, he wrote: "In short, corporate management may not use corporate monies to promote what does not further corporate affairs but what in the last analysis are the purely personal views of the management, individually or as a group." And the constitutional basis justifying such regulation was grounded as centrally in democratic jurisprudence as anything could be, in White's assessment. "The electoral process, of course, is the essence of our democracy," he wrote. "It is an arena in which the public interest in preventing corporate domination and the coerced support by shareholders of causes with which they disagree is at its strongest and any claim that corporate expenditures are integral to the economic functioning of the corporation is at its weakest."[22]

In the *McConnell* ruling a quarter of a century later, the majority on the Court demonstrated strong support for those principles as essential to a functioning democracy. The opening lines of the majority opinion invoked the legacy of early corporate reformers such as Theodore Roosevelt and Senator Elihu Root. President Roosevelt told Congress in 1905 that corporate "directors should not be permitted to use stockholders' money" for political purposes and declared that prohibiting corporate political contributions would be one means of addressing "the evils aimed at in corrupt practices acts." Root — himself a successful corporate attorney before serving in the Senate and the administrations of Presidents McKinley, Roosevelt, and Wilson, in 1916 called the use of corporate spending to dominate democratic processes "a constantly growing evil." He declared that type of spending had "done more to shake the confidence of the plain people of small means of this country in our political institutions than any other practice which has ever obtained since the foundation of our Government."[23]

The years since the BCRA was signed into law have already provided considerable evidence that the measures it put into effect have achieved their objectives, enhancing both greater fairness and broader participation in democratic processes. Longtime political columnist David Broder initially dismissed the BCRA as unlikely to succeed. However, he later concluded that it not only "passed its first test in the 2004 campaign with flying colors" but also "played at least a supportive role in the greatest upsurge ever recorded in the number of small contributors." Anthony Corrado and Thomas E. Mann, editors of the Brookings Institution's *The New Campaign Finance Sourcebook*, have stated flatly that "the doomsday scenario conjured up by critics of the new campaign finance law has not come to pass." Rather than weakening political parties or stifling political debate, they found, the new legislation increased the likelihood that the "emphasis in coming campaign cycles will be on face-to-face contact with voters, . . . expanding the financial base of both parties and using the resources to bring more people into the electorate." Michael Malbin, director of the nonpartisan Campaign Finance Institute declared the BCRA "the most important change in a generation" in campaign-finance regulation.[24]

Nevertheless, just as the Supreme Court was being reconfigured with new justices Roberts and Alito it began signaling an interest in reconsidering elements of campaign-finance law, less than two years after the BCRA was upheld in the *McConnell* decision. In 2005, the Court accepted two new campaign-finance cases, one of which directly challenged a key BCRA provision on corporate political media spending. In that case in early 2006, shortly after Rehnquist's death, the Court directed a lower court to reconsider a Wisconsin campaign-finance case involving the BCRA's restrictions on the use of corporate funds to finance electioneering communications — candidate ads disguised as issue messages shortly before elections. The challenge again reached the Supreme Court the following year, and in a ruling issued in summer 2007, the Court ruled the challenged electioneering provision unconstitutional as applied in that case. In the majority opinion, Roberts wrote that the ruling was a narrow one applying only to the facts at hand and declared the Court's decision did not affect the *McConnell* holding that found the BCRA's electioneering regulations constitutional. In a dissenting opinion joined by justices Kennedy and Thomas, however, Scalia argued the Court should have struck down the electioneering regulations. The other case, while not directly involving the BCRA, struck down Vermont campaign-finance regulations, which beginning in 1997 had imposed the tightest state limits in the nation.[25]

The direction that the Court moved in those cases may well foreshadow its intentions for the next First Amendment case that it considers involving corporate political media spending. As this chapter has made clear, the close split endures on the Court between justices who want to limit the First Amendment rights of such spending and those who want to expand it. Their positions reflect very different understandings of the workings of the marketplace of ideas. The manner in which the Court chooses to interpret that marketplace will determine the future of First Amendment law on corporate political media spending. Ideas have consequences, particularly the ideas of Supreme Court justices. And their ideas will come into play in a major way on other fronts of the corporate free-speech movement as well in the years ahead. That is the focus of the next two chapters.

[1] See Jess Bravin and Jeanne Cummings, "Bush Taps Roberts for Supreme Court; Conservative Nominee, 50, Is Viewed as Pro-Business," *The Wall Street Journal*, 20 July 2005, sec. A, p. 1; Stephen Labaton and Jonathan D. Glater, "As a Lawyer, Court Nominee Was Considered a Skillful Advocate for Corporate Clients," *The New York Times*, 21 July 2005, sec. A, p. 25; Jeanne Cummings, "In Nominee, Business Sees Lawyer Who Has Argued Many of Its Cases," *The Wall Street Journal*, 21 July 2005, sec. A, p. 4; Stephen Labaton, "Court Nominee Has Paper Trail Businesses Like," *The New York Times*, 5 November 2005, sec. A, p. 1; Jess Bravin and Jeanne Cummings, "Nominee's Record Shows Backing of Business Interests, Contracts," *The Wall Street Journal*, 1 November 2005, sec. A, p. 1.

[2] See *McConnell v. Federal Election Commission*, 540 U.S. 93, 323-26 (2003) (Kennedy, J., dissenting).

[3] See *McConnell v. Federal Election Commission*, 256 (Scalia, J., dissenting).

[4] See *McConnell v. Federal Election Commission*, 326 (Kennedy, J., dissenting).

[5] See *Austin v. Michigan State Chamber of Commerce*, 494 U.S. 652, 679 (1990) (Scalia, J., dissenting).

[6] See *Austin v. Michigan State Chamber of Commerce*, 684 (Scalia, J., dissenting).

[7] See *Austin v. Michigan State Chamber of Commerce*, 661.

[8] See, for example, Robert Weissman, "First Amendment Follies: Expanding Corporate Speech Rights," 19 *Multinational Monitor* 15 (1998); David R. Lagasee, "Undue Influence: Corporate Political Speech, Power and the Initiative Process," 61 *Brooklyn Law Review* 1347 (1995); John S. Shockley, "Direct Democracy, Campaign Finance, and the Courts: Can Corruption, Undue Influence, and Declining Voter Confidence Be Found?" 39 *University of Miami Law Review* 377 (1985); Allen K. Easley, "Buying Back the First Amendment: Regulation of Disproportionate Corporate Spending in Ballot Issue Campaigns," 17 *Georgia Law Review* 675 (1983); Randy M. Mastro et al., "Taking the Initiative: Corporate Control of the Referendum Process Through Media Spending and What to Do About It," 32 *Federal Communications Law Journal* 315 (1980).

[9] See *Austin v. Michigan State Chamber of Commerce*, 679-80 (Scalia, J., dissenting).

[10] See *Austin v. Michigan State Chamber of Commerce*, 680 (Scalia, J., dissenting).

[11] See *Buckley v. Valeo,* 424 U.S. 1 (1976).

[12] See *Austin v. Michigan State Chamber of Commerce*, 713, 699-700 (Kennedy, J., dissenting).

[13] See *McConnell v. Federal Election Commission*, 247-65 (Scalia, J., dissenting).

[14] See *McConnell v. Federal Election Commission*, 286-324 (Kennedy, J., dissenting).

[15] See *McConnell v. Federal Election Commission*, 324-33 (Kennedy, J., dissenting).

[16] See David Vogel, *Fluctuating Fortunes: The Political Power of Business in America* (New York: Basic Books, 1989); Jerome L. Himmelstein, Jr., *To the Right: The Transformation of American Conservatism* (Berkeley: University of California Press, 1990); Dan Clawson, Alan Neustadtl, and Mark Weller, *Dollars and Votes: How Business Campaign Contributions Subvert Democracy*, (Philadelphia: Temple University Press, 1998).

[17] See *Federal Election Commission v. Beaumont*, 539 U.S. 146, 151-52 (2003); *McConnell v. Federal Election Commission*, 350-63 (Rehnquist, C.J., dissenting).

[18] See *McConnell v. Federal Election Commission*, 330-37, 290-91 (Kennedy, J., dissenting).

[19] See *McConnell v. Federal Election Commission*, 136-154, 205-07.

[20] See *Buckley v. Valeo*, 49 (italics added for emphasis).

[21] See *Austin v. Michigan State Chamber of Commerce,* 685 (Scalia, J., dissenting).

[22] See *First National Bank of Boston v. Bellotti,* 435 U.S. 765, 819, 813, 821 (1978) (White, J., dissenting).

[23] See *McConnell v. Federal Election Commission*, 115-16, 205-07 (quoting both Roosevelt and Root).

[24] See David Broder, "A Win for Campaign Finance Reform," *The Washington Post*, 3 February 2005, sec. A, p. 27; David Broder, "An Unlikely Campaign Finance Reformer," *The Washington Post*, 10 March 2005, sec. A, p. 21; Glen Justice, "Despite Loss of Soft Money, Parties Are Collecting More Cash," *The New York Times*, 10 August 2004, sec. A, p. 18; Anthony Corrado and Thomas E. Mann, "Despite Predictions, BCRA Has Not Been a Democratic 'Suicide Bill'," *Roll Call*, 26 July 2004, accessed 23 April 2006 at: http://www.brookings.edu/views/op-ed/corrado/20040726.htm; Anthony Corrado, et al., eds., *The New Campaign Finance Sourcebook*, (Washington, D.C.: Brookings Institution Press, 2005); Michael J. Malbin, ed., *The Election After Reform: Money, Politics, and the Bipartisan Campaign Reform Act*, (Lanham, Md.: Rowman and Littlefield, 2006).

[25] See Federal Election Commission v. Wisconsin Right to Life, Inc. 551 U.S. ___ (2007) (No. 06–969), 127 S. Ct. 2652; *Randall v. Sorrell*, 548 U.S. ___ (2006) (No. 04-1528), 126 S. Ct. 2479; Linda Greenhouse, "Supreme Court Takes On Spending Limits for Candidates," *The New York Times*, 28

September 2005, sec. A, p. 1; David Stout, "Court Opens Campaign Law to Challenges," *The New York Times*, 24 January 2006, sec. A, p. 16; Linda Greenhouse, "Vermont Campaign Limits Get Cool Reception at Court," *The New York Times*, 1 March 2006, sec. A, p. 14; Linda Greenhouse, "Justices Reject Campaign Limits in Vermont Case," *The New York Times*, 27 June 2006, sec. A, p. 1; Linda Greenhouse and David D. Kirkpatrick, "Justices Loosen Ad Restrictions in Campaign Law," *The New York Times*, 26 June 2007, sec. A, p. 1.

CHAPTER NINE

Dagger at the Throat of the News Media

There is still another set of dynamics ticking away within the story of the corporate free-speech movement. Call it the Catch-22 of First Amendment jurisprudence on corporate political media spending. That is essentially the way the matter has been put forth in a number of noteworthy forums anyway. In 1978, Warren Burger, then Chief Justice of the U.S. Supreme Court, laid out the basic proposition — though broaching it rather tactfully as a "disquieting" concern. A little over a decade after that, Justice Antonin Scalia brushed aside the tact and bluntly warned American news media that the circumstances represented "a dagger at their throats."

The Catch-22 aspect of the issue lies in the way it has been framed as an inescapable set of choices, none of which would be acceptable to those concerned with corporate influence on democracy. Essentially, this line of judicial reasoning begins with the assertion that corporate political media spending should be an unqualified First Amendment right. However, if legislators and courts *do* decide that such spending can be regulated in order to protect democratic processes — the reasoning goes — then a painful reckoning must be exacted upon news media that engage in political reporting. For almost invariably today, such operations are conducted within the organizational structure of a business corporation. And at present, regulations on the political media spending of business corporations include an exception for news-media corporations. It exempts the latter from regulations that — if they *did* apply to news-media corporations — would likely impose restrictions on all sorts of the political coverage in which they engage. Because when news media make political endorsements, editorialize and comment on political developments, and even report on political activities in the news, they inevitably must make expenditures to pay for producing and disseminating such material.

So the legal question at the heart of it all is this: If a constitutional basis exists for government regulation of political media spending by business corporations, then is there enough of a distinction between news-media corporations and corporations in other lines of business to continue exempting one from that regulation and not the other? When faced with that question thus far, the Supreme Court has said yes. But as on the question of corporate political media spending itself, the Court's deliberations on the matter have been divided and the dissent sharp.

Additionally, many developments of recent decades have only served to make more compelling the argument that there is little, if any, real separation any more between corporations that report the news and those that don't. In effect, the dynamics of the situation create incentive for news media operating as corporations to oppose regulations on corporate political media spending —out of fear that those regulations may someday be applied to news media as well. So the situation works in favor of the corporate free-speech movement, because news media today are organizationally dominated by corporate conglomerates engaged in all sorts of business. Thus, business corporations' general interest in being freed from political media spending regulations dovetails quite neatly with news-media corporations' specific interest in avoiding having such regulations imposed upon their news operations.

It is undeniable that too many news media today are operated with more concern for the bottom line than for the public interest. With the ownership of modern mass communication steadily consolidated within an ever smaller number of corporate entities in recent years, the ultimate control over most news media lies with the management of vast business concerns. That the general public — much less Supreme Court justices — could have reason to question the independence of news media today should come as no surprise. The "dagger" that Scalia warned about would seem to be pressing more sharply than ever against the throats of the free press, the institution intended to serve as a watchdog on government in American democracy.

And yet, as this chapter will argue, it is not truly necessary to frame the problem along either/or lines. Rather than choosing between eliminating the media exception entirely — in effect, throwing the baby out with the bathwater — or continuing to grant the exception to corporations that may warrant it in name only, there is another option. That approach would entail evolving public policy and jurisprudence so as to more effectively advance the intent of the exception — a truly independent news media. As with other sorts of regulation on corporate political media spending discussed in previous chapters, doing that would serve to promote a marketplace of ideas that is more truly a free market.

LITTLE 'PRIVILEGE' FOR NEWS MEDIA IN THE CASE LAW

Exceptions in federal and state regulations on corporate political media expenditures are intended to protect the independence of news media in fulfilling their traditional role of reporting and commenting on government and politics. The significance of that role is reflected in the way the First Amendment specifically articulates protection for the press: "Congress shall make no law . . . abridging the freedom of speech, or of the press." That specific ban (referred to as the Press Clause) on laws abridging freedom of the press — in addition to freedom of speech — has given rise to the argument that the founders intended for the Constitution to "privilege" news media. That is, according to that view, the First Amendment grants distinct protections to the institutional press in order for it to fulfill its role of serving the public interest by keeping citizens informed through independent reporting.

Potter Stewart was one Supreme Court justice who ardently argued the case in favor of constitutional privilege for the institutional press. "The Free Press Clause extends protection to an institution. The publishing business is, in short, the only organized private business that is given explicit constitutional protection," he said. "By including both guarantees [speech and press] in the First Amendment, the Founders quite clearly recognized the distinction between the two." However, more justices have taken positions such as Justice Felix Frankfurter's, expressing skepticism for an institutional press privilege: "The purpose of the Constitution was not to erect the press into a privileged institution but to protect all persons in their right to print what they will as well as to utter it."[1] The Court has never clearly established any broad First Amendment privilege for the institutional press.

For example, in many major cases in which the press has had government restrictions on publishing rejected by the Supreme Court, the ruling was grounded not in a press privilege but in a presumption of the unconstitutionality of prior restraint (government censorship before publication).[2] Similarly, other press-restrictions cases have failed to establish a press privilege. When the Court overturned restrictions on the press entering a trial in *Richmond Newspapers, Inc. v. Virginia*, it focused on a constitutional right of access to courtrooms for *all* citizens. In *Pell v. Procunier*, *Saxbe v. Washington Post Co.*, and *Houchins v. KQED, Inc.*, the Court found no special right of access to prisons and jails for the purposes of news reporting. The Court has held media have no extra protection from police searches (*Zurcher v. Stanford Daily*), no exemption from antitrust laws (*Associated Press v. United States*) or antidiscrimination regulations (*Pittsburgh Press Co. v. Pittsburgh Commission on Human Relations*), and no protection from lawsuits by victims of broken promises (*Cohen v. Cowles Media Co.*).[3]

One arguable exception has developed out of the 1972 *Branzburg v. Hayes* decision. In that ruling, the Court's majority held there is no reporter's privilege to refuse to testify before grand juries, even to protect the identities of confidential sources. However, the four dissenting justices in the five-to-four decision supported at least a limited reporter's privilege that balanced press independence against the needs of law enforcement on a case-by-case basis. And in a concurring opinion, Justice Lewis Powell (who voted with the majority on the major holding) expressed agreement with the four dissenters on that point. So based on the opinions of those five justices, many lower courts have since recognized a *qualified* privilege for reporters refusing to disclose confidential sources. "The press has a preferred position in our constitutional scheme, not to enable it to make money, not to set newsmen apart as a favored class, but to bring fulfillment to the public's right to know," Justice William Douglas contended in his dissenting opinion in the case "Knowledge is essential to informed decisions." Nevertheless, the majority holding in *Branzburg* still stands firmly as the controlling precedent on the subject, and the lower courts that recognize a reporter's privilege not to testify do so only under very limited circumstances.[4]

When the media exception became an issue in regard to corporate political media spending in the 1978 *First National Bank of Boston v. Bellotti* case, the Court avoided the specific question of whether such an exception represented a press privilege. In his majority opinion, Justice Powell dismissed the question of whether media corporations should be subject to any regulations imposed on the campaign expenditures of nonmedia corporations. He wrote that media "corporations need not make separately identifiable expenditures to communicate their views. They accomplish the same objective each day within the framework of their usual protected communications." He carefully walked the line between distinguishing the institutional press and suggesting that any constitutional privilege derived from that distinction. "The press cases emphasize the special and constitutionally recognized role of that institution in informing and educating the public, offering criticism, and providing a forum for discussion and debate. But the press does not have a monopoly on either the First Amendment or the ability to enlighten."[5] However, Chief Justice Burger — while voting with the *Bellotti* majority — made it clear that he did not consider the media-exception question nearly so easily resolved.

CHIEF JUSTICE BURGER SERVES NOTICE

In fact, in the weeks immediately following the handing down of the *Bellotti* decision, the element of it that received the greatest editorial reaction in the national press was not the majority opinion. It was Burger's concurring opinion in which he asserted "the difficulty, and perhaps impossibility, of distinguishing, either as a matter of fact or constitutional law, media corporations from corporations such as the [nonmedia] appellants in this case." By making his argument on that point in such a forceful manner, the Chief Justice "served notice that the First Amendment rights of, say, *The New York Times* may one day be judged legally no greater than those of General Motors," the *Times* concluded on its editorial page.[6]

In his concurring opinion, Burger wrote of what he found to be a particularly "disquieting aspect" of the *Bellotti* case. Any sort of regulation on corporate political media spending, he warned, "may carry the risk of impinging on the First Amendment rights of those who employ the corporate form — as most do — to carry on the business of mass communications, particularly the large media conglomerates." Burger went on to observe the increasing similarities between those large media conglomerates and large nonmedia conglomerates. "Making traditional use of the corporate form, some media enterprises have amassed vast wealth and power and conduct many activities, some directly related — and some not — to their publishing and broadcasting activities," he wrote. If the big nonmedia business corporations posed such a danger to democratic processes that regulations on their media spending were warranted, the Chief Justice said it seemed to him that media corporations might even be *more* dangerous. "In terms of 'unfair advantage in the political process' and 'corporate domination of the electoral process,' it could be argued that such media conglomerates as I describe pose a much more realistic threat to valid interests than do [the *Bellotti*] appellants and similar entities not regularly concerned with shaping popular opinion on public issues." He said that "a result of the growth of modern media empires 'has been to place in a few hands the power to inform the American people and shape public opinion.' "[7]

Burger went on to make clear his belief that the Framers of the Constitution never intended to extend any sort of privilege to the institutional press in the language they employed in the First Amendment. In addition, he wrote, to recognize such a privilege would require the government to then define which media entities qualified for the privilege and which did not. For Burger, that would be "reminiscent of the abhorred licensing system of Tudor and Stuart England — a system the First Amendment was intended to ban from this country." Therefore, Burger declared, the law should no make no distinctions in that regard between (or among) human citizens and corporate citizens. "The First Amendment does not 'belong' to any definable category of persons or entities," he wrote. "It belongs to all who exercise its freedoms."[8]

America's newspaper of record reacted with alarm to Burger's comments — much more so than it did to the *Bellotti* decision itself. In an editorial opinion, the *Times* noted that it did "not particularly object" to the ruling and only mildly admonished the justices not to continue endowing corporations "with more and more of the civil rights that the Constitution reserved for individuals." The editorial vigor was focused largely on the Chief Justice's suggestion that news media operating as corporations could be subject to any regulations imposed on the political media spending of business corporations in general. The *Times* called that and Burger's related assertions a "startling prognosis," expressing the hope that he would "not press them toward resolution too quickly." It argued that business operations such as its own remained quite distinguishable from others outside the news media. "It remains possible to distinguish a company that sells newspapers from a company that sells oil and even from its own parent companies or subsidiaries that mash pulp or bind encyclopedias," the *Times* insisted.[9]

The Wall Street Journal also devoted only a fraction of its editorial comment to the *Bellotti* decision itself. It dismissed with a few sentences the "critics [who] see the decision as opening up the public policy arena to money-laden . . . companies . . . and regard this as a bad thing" as mostly "the likes of Common Cause and the AFL-CIO whose own political clout is likely to be reduced by more intense competition in the marketplace of ideas." Virtually all the remainder of the lengthy editorial focused on Burger's warning for media conglomerates. On that subject, the *Journal* enthusiastically embraced the way the Chief Justice "laid a small trap for anyone who might choose to disagree" with the *Bellotti* decision. In the *Journal*'s view, Burger had asked "a far-reaching question: How could the court have upheld the Massachusetts law [at issue in the case] without . . . 'opening the door to similar restraints on media conglomerates with their greater influence?' " The editorial went on to invoke the most prominent spokesperson of the corporate free-speech movement, asking "Why is it a bad thing for Mobil Oil Corp. to make its public policy views known, but a good thing for The Washington Post Co. to do so?"[10]

It was the *Post* that most fully addressed the implications of the actual decision in *Bellotti*, branding it "a thunderbolt in law and politics" that left unanswered a string of troubling questions concerning the potential of corporate power to threaten democratic processes. Media political spending by corporations created "megaphones for the views of those who own or control them," the editorial contended. "If [the ruling] will mean that the voices of those with the most money will have an unfair advantage over other voices in political debate," the *Post* declared, "we do not see how that would usefully serve the purposes of free speech." In fact, the *Post* did not even mention Burger's concurring opinion in that editorial. In a second editorial two weeks later, it defended its opinion on the subject against both Burger's and the *Journal*'s arguments. Then a month after the *Bellotti* decision, *Post* columnist Charles B. Seib warned that even though it might seem that the case gave the press "nothing to worry about" because "it took nothing away from the media corporations," one vote the other way would have rendered Burger's "musings" far more than theoretical.[11]

RENEWED ASSAULT ON THE MEDIA EXCEPTION

A dozen years later, as detailed in Chapter Six, the Supreme Court made its most important ruling on limiting the First Amendment rights that the *Bellotti* ruling had established for corporate political media spending. The makeup of the justices had changed somewhat, most significantly with William Rehnquist replacing the retired Burger as Chief Justice. Rehnquist's efforts were crucial in shaping the case law that coalesced in the *Austin v. Michigan State Chamber of Commerce* ruling that upheld restrictions on corporate media expenditures in candidate elections. Although the media exception in those regulations did not prove to be the central question in the case, it played a prominent role. As part of its arguments, the Michigan Chamber contended there was no constitutional basis to treat a media corporation differently from a nonmedia corporation in such regulations. The Chamber in fact opened its brief to the Supreme Court with this line: "In Michigan, it is a felony for nonmedia corporations to engage in fundamental First Amendment political speech."[12]

The Supreme Court agreed that because the Michigan regulation treated media corporations differently than nonmedia corporations, it must serve a compelling government interest in order to be constitutional. But in the majority opinion, Justice Thurgood Marshall declared such an interest was clearly served. "Although the press' unique societal role may not entitle the press to greater protection under the Constitution," he wrote, "it does provide a compelling reason for the State to exempt media corporations from the scope of political expenditure limitations." The majority rejected the Chamber's argument on the media exception, ruling that government was justified in maintaining the freedom of news media through such measures. "Although all corporations enjoy the same state-conferred benefits inherent in the corporate form, media corporations differ significantly from other corporations in that their resources are devoted to the collection of information and its dissemination to the public," Marshall wrote. He noted that the Court had "consistently recognized the unique role that the press plays in informing and educating the public, offering criticism, and providing a forum for discussion and debate." The Michigan regulation's "definition of 'expenditure,' conceivably could be interpreted to encompass election-related news stories and editorials . . . [which] might discourage incorporated news broadcasters or publishers from serving their crucial societal role," Marshall pointed out. Therefore, "the media exception ensures that the [regulation] does not hinder or prevent the institutional press from reporting on, and publishing editorials about, newsworthy events."[13]

However, dissenting justices made it clear (among their other objections) that they would have struck down the Michigan regulation on what they considered the unconstitutionality of the media exception alone. Justice Scalia objected to the decision so strenuously that he took the unusual step of reading his dissenting opinion from the bench. Although he emphasized his opposition to limiting First Amendment rights of business corporations, Scalia reserved his sharpest contempt for allowing such regulation to "exclude media corporations, rather than target them specially." He maintained that even if one accepted the Court's rationale for regulating corporate political media spending, "surely that 'unique role' of the press does not give Michigan justification for excluding media corporations from coverage, but provides especially strong reason to include them." Scalia took up even more sharply Burger's argument that media corporations represented a greater threat to democracy than nonmedia corporations. "Amassed corporate wealth that regularly sits astride the ordinary channels of information is much more likely to produce the New Corruption (too much of one point of view) than amassed corporate wealth that is generally busy making money elsewhere," Scalia contended. "Such media corporations not only have vastly greater power to perpetrate the evil of overinforming, they also have vastly greater opportunity."[14]

Scalia observed that while nonmedia corporations such as General Motors would risk lawsuits from stockholders by making a political endorsement unrelated to profitability, "media corporations make money by making political commentary, including endorsements. For them, unlike any other corporations, the whole world of politics and ideology is fair game." Scalia's most chilling comment for "members of the institutional press" was his warning that they should find "little reason for comfort" in the *Austin* decision. "The theory of New Corruption it espouses is a dagger at their throats," he declared. "The Court today holds merely that media corporations may be excluded from the Michigan law, not that they must be. We have consistently rejected the proposition that the institutional press has any constitutional privilege beyond that of other speakers."[15]

And unlike in the *Bellotti* decision, that warning to the institutional press was expressed by more than a lone voice on the Court. Justice Anthony Kennedy authored a second dissenting opinion in which he was joined by Scalia and Justice Sandra Day O'Connor. Kennedy focused a substantial part of his criticism of the decision on the media exception: "An independent ground for invalidating this statute is the blanket exemption for media corporations," he maintained. "The argument relied on by the majority, that media corporations are in the business of communicating and other corporations are not, is unsatisfying. All corporations communicate with the public to some degree, whether it is their business or not."[16]

As Burger had a dozen years before, Kennedy argued that distinguishing between media and nonmedia corporations in First Amendment law had become a dubious proposition. "The web of corporate ownership that links media and nonmedia corporations is difficult to untangle for the purpose of any meaningful distinction," he wrote. "Newspapers, television networks, and other media may be owned by parent corporations with multiple business interests." Kennedy contended that commingling of media and nonmedia operations within such corporate conglomerates represented a particularly troubling threat. "Nothing in the statutory scheme prohibits a business corporate parent from directing its newspaper to support or oppose a particular candidate," he concluded. "I can find no permissible basis under the First Amendment for the States to make this unsupported distinction among corporate speakers."[17]

AN EVEN MORE TANGLED WEB

That the size of the largest media corporations has grown exponentially in the decade since the *Austin* decision is obvious to any casual observer. But even more crucially, media corporations and nonmedia corporations have melded into each other far more than ever before. In that respect, the dynamics fueling the contentions of justices Burger, Scalia, and Kennedy have been supercharged. However much evidence those justices had in 1978 and in 1990 to argue that media corporations and nonmedia corporations were indistinguishable for purposes of regulating their political media spending, they have much more today.

Consider for example General Electric and its vast array of operations, which comprise one of the largest corporations now in existence. G.E. has divisions that manufacture aircraft engines and home appliances and locomotives. It has divisions that practice journalism at NBC News and dozens of television stations in major markets across the country. Its corporate holdings include insurance and finance companies, plastics and lighting operations, and makers of medical-imaging technology and power-generating systems. It reports news around the clock on its CNBC and MSNBC cable-news channels.

Or consider the corporate holdings of the Walt Disney Company. It operates theme parks and resorts. It broadcasts news on its ABC television network and dozens of television and radio stations. It publishes daily newspapers. It makes movies and merchandises related products in great numbers and many venues. It has interests in petroleum and natural gas production. It owns sports franchises and broadcasts sporting events. And it produces news reports on movies and movie companies, petroleum and natural gas production, sports franchises and sporting events, and any number of other activities in which it also has business interests.[18]

Such merging of media and nonmedia operations under the same corporate parent is now commonplace. Ben Bagdikian has been tracking the media corporations that dominate the newspaper, magazine, radio, television, book, and movie industries since 1984 in successive editions of *The Media Monopoly*. He focuses on the conglomerates that control the media on which a majority of Americans say they most rely. In the first edition, his list numbered fifty. By the 2004 edition, that figure had shrunk to five. Bagdikian's work tells him that the impact of that trend has undermined the public-service function of news media. "The handful of dominant corporations have pursued quick, ever-higher profits, mainly by producing more trivialized and self-serving commercialized news," he writes. "The parent firms have pressed their news subsidiaries to cross ethical lines by selecting news that will promote the needs of the owning corporation rather than serve the traditional ethical striving of journalism."[19]

Robert McChesney has published extensively on trends in corporate media holdings and the implications for democracy. He characterizes dominant media corporations as undifferentiated from nonmedia corporations: "The major feature of the global media order is its thoroughgoing commercialism, and an associated marked decline in the relative importance of public broadcasting and the applicability of public service standards. . . . Media outputs are commodified and are designed to serve market ends, not citizenship ends." And, he argues, it's hardly a free market at work: "When they think about it, Americans will fully understand that the existing market is not a flawless indicator of public desires, because it can only address what makes the most short-term profit for the media giants."[20]

One of the most recent and public displays of a media corporation being operated with grossly more concern for short-term business values than for news values played out in 2005 and 2006 when the nation's second-largest newspaper chain was put up for sale. The impetus behind putting the Knight Ridder operation up for bid was pressure from its largest shareholders. Despite strong profits and recent rounds of aggressive cost-cutting and layoffs, the chain's stock price dissatisfied big shareholders (investment companies, in this case), who demanded that the chain be sold to the highest bidder — or else face a hostile-takeover bid. Despite outcries from the journalistic community about the threat such actions represented to newspapers' ability to keep the public informed, the chain was sold to another chain, which immediately began setting up deals to shed many of the Knight Ridder newspapers to other bidders. Similar pressures are leading most newspaper companies to slash expenditures on news operations in an effort to jack their already healthy profit margins sufficiently higher to win favor on Wall Street.[21]

Legal scholars have noted the way that the concerns focused upon in the Burger, Scalia, and Kennedy opinions have only been exacerbated since then. Clay Calvert has written that the courts may well revisit the issues involved. "It may be reality, today, that the Press Clause protects primarily commercial interests," he argued, "keeping the government out of the editorial decision-making processes of the media and allowing increasing concentration of ownership of the news media." Adam Winkler has observed that "while the number of mass media outlets has exploded over the last twenty years, the ownership of those outlets has remained concentrated. This has heightened the power Burger noted as being 'in few hands.' " Lillian BeVier has questioned the *Austin* reasoning that requires nonmedia corporate political expenditures to reflect popular support. "[Media] corporations certainly have resources in their treasuries that do not amount to an 'indication of popular support for' their political ideas," she wrote. "By the Court's definition, therefore, when these corporations use their considerable resources to support particular candidates or political causes, they surely 'distort' debate." Bradley Smith has contended that "restricting private monetary campaign contributions does not empower the 'average constituent,' however defined. Rather, it increases the relative influence of an even smaller elite — media people and others whose skills are directly valuable to a candidate or legislator."[22]

Some equality-based, campaign-finance reform plans have proposed eliminating the media exception. "The owners of newspapers should have no greater opportunity, simply by virtue of owning this property, than any other citizen to attempt to persuade undecided voters how to vote on election day," Edward Foley, for example, has argued. "Equality demands that every individual be given, so far as practical, the same political capital, so that each individual has a roughly equal ability to pursue both an electoral strategy and a legislative strategy," Richard Hasen has contended. "The most important step to ensure such equality is preventing vastly unequal expenditures of money in campaigns," he wrote. "However, assuring roughly equal political access requires ending special treatment for media endorsements as well. Otherwise, media corporations have an advantage over others in securing access."[23]

L.A. Powe has countered that eliminating the media exception would demolish the basic First Amendment principle that government cannot tell news media what to publish or not publish. That is, it might not be possible to limit such regulation, because any such measure could establish precedent for extending regulation beyond editorials and commentary to news stories on politics. "What happens when the inevitable claim is made that, despite our best efforts with campaign finance reform, the press retains its undue influence over elections? Is not the next logical step to reduce that undue influence via additional regulation?" Powe wrote. "After all, to get to this point, there must already have been a decision that gagging the editorial pages is constitutional. Once that interpretation is abroad in the United States Reports, how are we to be sure what is next?"[24]

In the most recent overhaul of federal campaign-finance regulation, the Bipartisan Campaign Reform Act focused on reducing the influence of money in targeted campaign activities, as detailed in Chapter Seven. It maintained a media exception for its provisions relevant to corporate political media spending. That exception was declared "wholly consistent with First Amendment principles" by the Supreme Court in its ruling on the First Amendment challenge to the BCRA in *McConnell v. Federal Election Commission*, which upheld virtually all the regulations in 2003.[25] Justices Kennedy and Scalia reiterated their hostility toward the media exception, and Justice Clarence Thomas devoted part of his dissent to language as threatening as Scalia's in *Austin*. "The chilling endpoint of the Court's reasoning is not difficult to foresee: outright regulation of the press," Thomas wrote, noting again Justice Burger's assertion on the difficulty of distinguishing between media and nonmedia corporations. "What is to stop a future Congress from . . . concluding that the availability of unregulated media corporations creates a loophole that allows for easy 'circumvention' of the limitations of the current campaign finance laws?"[26]

Indeed, during Congressional debate when the BCRA legislation was being hammered out a few years before, sharp criticism of the media exception indicated what a potentially contentious issue it remains. "The media we always sort of carve out of these restrictions because the presumption, I guess, is they have a greater right to the First Amendment than any of us," complained Senator Mitch McConnell of Kentucky — one of the most vocal opponents of the media exception and campaign-finance regulation in general. Senator Oren Hatch of Utah suggested the media exception presented "an equal protection problem," stating that "the media should not have more rights to free speech than any other group, and McCain-Feingold [as the BCRA is often called, in reference to its two original sponsors, Senators John McCain and Russ Feingold] gives the media a monopoly." McConnell cited Hasen's critique of the media exception and argued that the BCRA would add to the power of news media, "which are owned by huge corporations such as AOL-Time Warner and General Electric, are staffed by journalists with their own biases, and are busily clamoring for restrictions on the campaign-related spending and First Amendment rights of everybody else."[27]

In debate on a proposed amendment to the BCRA regarding regulation of issue advertising during elections, McConnell asked Senator Paul Wellstone of Minnesota if he would be willing to eliminate the media exception. "I don't identify the [news] media with the sham issue ads," Wellstone replied. "Whether I agree or disagree, it seems to me, the media are there to inform people." In an earlier debate on the legislation, Senator Trent Lott of Mississippi contended that by maintaining the media exception, the reform plan would allow "the news media to dictate, through their editorial columns and their editorials in their news articles, who will be elected." Senator Paul Coverdell of Georgia maintained that the media exception violates the First Amendment because it "picks corporations that can say anything they want and picks other corporations and says they cannot say anything."[28]

During the March 2001 debate, Senator Fritz Hollings of South Carolina offered a resolution for amending the First Amendment so as to give federal and state governments constitutional authority to regulate campaign contributions and expenditures. The proposed amendment contained no media exception. Senator Arlen Specter of Pennsylvania warned that if the amendment became law, governments "could regulate, restrict, even prohibit, the media's own issue advocacy, independent expenditures and contributions."[29] Hollings's resolution failed, receiving thirty-three votes (of the two-thirds majority of sixty-seven that resolutions for constitutional amendments require to win Senate approval). So just as at the Supreme Court, a majority for altering the media exception had not formed in Congress at that point. Whether that will endure in the years ahead, of course, remains to be seen.

NOT NECESSARILY AN EITHER/OR CHOICE

Clearly, the media exception as currently implemented and the greater body of First Amendment jurisprudence on corporate political media spending are not in harmony. But the real problem is the Catch-22 framing of the situation as one limited to only two choices that cannot be escaped. For a resolution does not need to be framed along the either/or lines that are suggested by the justices most critical of the exception. Basically, that framing holds that the law requires either applying any political-spending restrictions to media corporations — including the news media — in the same manner as they may be applied to nonmedia corporations, or else the restrictions must be abolished on all business corporations. Rather than limiting the question to those two choices, however, there is another way to consider the matter.

That approach would entail evolving public policy and jurisprudence so as to more effectively advance the intent of the exemption — a truly independent news media. Doing so would advance a marketplace of ideas that is more truly a free market, rather than one in which the interest of the profit imperative is advantaged over all others. Essentially, the answer is to move in the direction of better defining the sort of endeavors that will qualify for the media exception — rather than assuming that the best that can be done with the current system is granting the exception to many corporations that may warrant it in name only. Although it would not be easy by any means to define precisely what is a news-media corporation and what is not, that hardly means the current situation cannot be improved upon. We know that it can be done, because the Supreme Court has already accomplished something very similar two decades ago. As discussed in Chapter Six, in a 1986 ruling the Court developed an effective definition for distinguishing *ideological* corporations from business corporations for the purposes of exempting the former from political media spending regulations.

While the Court declared in *Federal Election Commission v. Massachusetts Citizens for Life, Inc.* that government-created advantages enable business corporations to use "resources amassed in the economic marketplace" to obtain "an unfair advantage in the political marketplace," it created an exempt category of those corporations that do not wield that advantage. Citizens who join together specifically for the purpose of supporting political ideas — as had the members of the Massachusetts Citizens for Life, an anti-abortion group — represent a different type of incorporated body. And those types of corporations — because they were formed to disseminate political ideas rather than to amass capital — do not give rise to the concerns underlying regulation of political activity by business corporations, the Court held. Based on that reasoning, the Court established a three-part definition that clearly delineates the characteristics that separate ideological corporations from business corporations.

To qualify as an ideological corporation under that definition, the organization must first be "formed for the express purpose of promoting political ideas, and cannot engage in business activities." That means that its political fundraising efforts must not be business activities but "expressly denominated as requests for contributions that will be used for political purposes." That "ensures that political resources reflect political support." Second, an ideological corporation "has no shareholders or other persons affiliated so as to have a claim on its assets or earnings." That provision "ensures that persons connected with the organization will have no economic disincentive for disassociating with it if they disagree with its political activity." Finally, an ideological corporation cannot be "established by a business corporation or a labor union," and must maintain a policy "not to accept contributions from such entities. This prevents such corporations from serving as conduits for the type of direct spending that creates a threat to the political marketplace."[30]

In articulating that definition, the Court focused on highlighting the reasons for distinguishing that category of corporations from business corporations. Critical to the process was stipulating the independence of such ideological corporations from the influence of business corporations. So, broadly speaking, a definitional effort of that sort for news-media corporations would need to focus on requirements emphasizing their independence from non-media corporate influence. It would also need to focus on qualities that characterize an entity devoted consistently over time specifically to the activities of news media. In fact, the Court in the course of its deliberations in the *Massachusetts Citizens for Life* case discussed the purpose of the media exception and made a beginning of sorts at specifying the sort of elements identified with entities that may qualify for it. Critical among those elements is convincing evidence of ongoing production and distribution to a regular audience. The Court did not attempt to establish a formal definition in that regard, but it stressed that "it is precisely such factors that in combination permit the distinction of campaign flyers from regular publications." It said it regarded "such an inquiry as essential," because "a contrary position would open the door for those corporations and unions with in-house publications to engage in unlimited spending directly from their treasuries to distribute campaign material to the general public."[31]

That line of judicial reasoning could be developed upon toward shaping a more substantiated approach for better distinguishing business corporations that actually are serving the function of news media that the media exception is intended to advance. Such an effort would not bar other business corporations from operating news media. They could do so quite freely, but under the same campaign-finance regulations as all nonmedia business corporations. Such a regulatory framework would need to be tailored so as to be compatible with the First Amendment doctrine well established by the Supreme Court regarding regulations imposed on media companies. The news media, for example, may be taxed in the same way as other industries are. It is only *discriminatory* taxes on media that have been declared unconstitutional on First Amendment grounds. When the state of Louisiana imposed a tax on the advertising revenues of newspapers with a circulation greater than 20,000, the Supreme Court struck it down, because it appeared to be targeted at the state's largest newspapers, which had been critical of Governor Huey Long. The Supreme Court has also struck down a state tax on paper and ink that effectively targeted one large newspaper because the tax exempted the first $100,000 of paper and ink used. The Court has declared that regulations on news media may not discriminate on the basis of content, striking down a tax that exempted religious, professional, and trade and sports journals, and also a tax that exempted only religious periodicals. However, taxes that apply to some but not all media industries can be constitutional. The Court ruled in upholding a sales tax imposed on cable-television companies (but not magazines, newspapers, or home satellite systems) that "differential taxation of speakers, even members of the press, does not implicate the First Amendment unless the tax is directed at, or presents the danger of, suppressing particular ideas."[32]

Tightening the media exception so as to provide it only to business corporations that actually are serving the function of news media that the media exception is intended to advance would not suppress the expression of ideas by other business corporations. It would allow such corporations to finance political spending through political action committees, in order to be consistent with the Supreme Court's broader jurisprudence on such spending regulations on corporations. Still any such measure would be controversial and would certainly be hard fought by those corporations to whom it would apply. Yet it would be fair on principle, given the regulations on other business corporations and the reality that too many corporations with some media operations have evolved in ways so that they are no longer significantly distinct from nonmedia business corporations. The purpose of the media exception is not to provide a free pass to any media operation, regardless how it may be structured as a component of a nonmedia business corporation. It is to foster news media that are independent enough to inform the public and fulfill the function of a free press. Without such independence, that source of information will be denied the public, making a robust and truly free marketplace of ideas impossible.

The recent domination of news media by nonmedia corporate conglomerates tends to foster the notion that such arrangements are the only manner in which news media today can go about their business. And yet the truth is that there are other viable models for maintaining a free press and a free marketplace of ideas. For example, a 2005 Harris survey found that the news media the American public finds most trustworthy are those that are most removed from the demands of the profit imperative. National Public Radio and the Public Broadcasting Service topped the list of media that were rated as providing the most trusted news. The public-service model of structuring news media has proven highly successful and popular in much of the democratic world. The British Broadcasting Corporation, for example, offers extensive news coverage, with correspondents based around the world, a wide range of cultural programs, and free time offered to political parties and candidates during election campaigns.[33]

The BBC is independent of *both* government control and the influence of business-corporation ownership, with funding provided through a fee on television sales. In the United States, Florida's *St. Petersburg Times* operates with similar independence through funding by a private, nonprofit foundation that focuses on a broad mission of journalism education. NPR had its independence as well as its resources for news operations enhanced considerably in 2003 when the late Joan B. Kroc, widow of McDonald's founder Ray Kroc, left the network $235 million with no restrictions or stipulations.[34] Indeed, through such endowments, business corporations could establish a number of truly independent *news*-media operations in the United States. They could qualify for the media exception and serve the public interest free of influence from a corporate business structure, and would generate tremendous goodwill for the corporation — just as other independent, corporate-endowed foundations do. And structurally spinning off news operations in that manner would free corporate media from the obligation of serving the public interest and allow them to focus on the more profitable entertainment programming that too often tends to dominate their news programming today anyway.

Of course, the future may well hold little of that sort of development and simply more of the Supreme Court continuing on a course in which the matter is limited to the two choices discussed earlier in this chapter. In such a case, one possibility would be that the Court could someday strike down on First Amendment grounds the corporate campaign-finance regulations from which corporate media are now exempt. In his *Bellotti* concurrence, Justice Burger argued against regulation of corporate political media spending. "The evolution of traditional newspapers into modern corporate conglomerates in which the daily dissemination of news by print is no longer the major part of the whole enterprise suggests the need for caution in limiting the First Amendment rights of corporations as such," he argued. Or as Senator Coverdell put it more bluntly: "I want to know, what is the difference between corporation A that happens to print a newspaper and corporation B that happens to grow trees? The forefathers said there shall be no difference." Some nonmedia corporations have long pressed a similar case. Herbert Schmertz, the Mobil vice president and creator of the company's influential editorial-advocacy campaign of the 1970s, argued before Congress and elsewhere that the speech of oil companies was as valid as that of newspapers and that corporate media spending should be entitled to the same First Amendment protections as such spending by newspapers and other news media.[35]

Alternatively, instead of taking that course, the Supreme Court could instead at some point rule the media exception unconstitutional while allowing regulation of corporate political media spending to continue. In such a scenario, the greatest impact would be felt by news media with corporate ownership — although even those owned by individuals could potentially become subject to disclosure requirements regarding political editorials, commentary, or perhaps even news stories on politics that might be deemed to represent campaign expenditures. News media owned by corporations would not be allowed to publish or broadcast matter categorized as campaign expenditures, unless paid for by a political action committee or individual at the going advertising rates. Some news operations conceivably might choose to disincorporate in order to avoid corporate campaign-finance regulations, but most likely few would find it viable to give up the considerable advantages of the corporate form of business organization.

The extent to which such limitations would be applied not only to editorials and commentary, but also to news stories on politics, would hinge upon the legal definitions that might be established for the latter in this hypothetical scenario. The current FECA definition of "expenditure" is broad: "any purchase, payment, distribution, loan, advance, deposit, or gift of money or anything of value, made by any person for the purpose of influencing any election for Federal office." If news media were no longer exempt from expenditure limits, the interpretation of which media activities could be considered to fall within that definition would almost undoubtedly become the subject of further litigation and legislative debate. It would be impossible to predict just exactly how far the repercussions might reach in the future, once a precedent were established for imposing regulation of that sort on the institutional press.

Justice Potter Stewart many years ago expressed concern about what such a future would mean for democracy. "It is quite possible to conceive of the survival of our Republic without an autonomous press. . . . The traditional competition between the three branches of government, supplemented by vigorous political activity, might be enough. The press could be relegated to the status of a public utility," he wrote. "Such a constitution is possible; it might work reasonably well. But it is not the Constitution the Founders wrote. . . . Perhaps our liberties might survive without an independent established press. But the Founders doubted it."[36]

[1] See Potter Stewart, "Or of the Press," 26 *Hastings Law Journal* 631, 633-634 (1975); *Pennekamp v. Florida*, 238 U.S. 331, 364 (1946).

[2] See *New York Times Co. v. United States*, 403 U.S. 713 (1971) (in which a government injunction barring publication of the Pentagon Papers was declared unconstitutional); *Nebraska Press Association v. Stuart*, 427 U.S. 539 (1976) (in which restrictions on court reporting were ruled unconstitutional); *Near v. Minnesota*, 283 U.S. 697 (1934) (which clearly established the presumption of unconstitutionality of prior restraint as a core First Amendment principle).

[3] See *Richmond Newspapers, Inc. v. Virginia*, 448 U.S. 555 (1980); *Pell v. Procunier*, 417 U.S. 817 (1974); *Saxbe v. Washington Post Co.*, 417 U.S. 843 (1974), *Houchins v. KQED, Inc.*, 438 U.S. 1 (1978); *Zurcher v. Stanford Daily*, 436 U.S. 547 (1978); *Associated Press v. United States*, 326 U.S. 1 (1945); *Pittsburgh Press Co. v. Pittsburgh Commission on Human Relations*, 413 U.S. 376 (1973); *Cohen v. Cowles Media Co.*, 438 U.S. 1 (1978).

[4] See *Branzburg v. Hayes*, 408 U.S. 665 (1972).

[5] See *First National Bank of Boston v. Bellotti*, 435 U.S. 765, 781-783 (1978).

[6] See *First National Bank of Boston v. Bellotti*, 796 (Burger, C.J., concurring); "Corporate Speech and Media Inc.," Editorial, *The New York Times*, 7 May 1978, sec. A, p. 22.

[7] See *First National Bank of Boston v. Bellotti*, 796-97 (1978) (Burger, C.J., concurring) (quoting *Miami Herald Publishing Co. v. Tornillo*, 418 U.S. 241, 250 (1974)).

[8] See *First National Bank of Boston v. Bellotti*, 798-802 (Burger, C.J., concurring).

[9] See "Corporate Speech and Media Inc.," sec. A, p. 22.

[10] See "Bellotti and Beyond," Editorial, *The Wall Street Journal*, 5 May 1978, sec. 1, p. 12 (quoting *First National Bank of Boston v. Bellotti*, 797 (Burger, C.J., concurring).

[11] See "Money Talks?" Editorial, *The Washington Post*, 2 May 1978, sec. A, p. 18; "Corporate Speech (Cont.)," Editorial, *The Washington Post*, 17 May 1978, sec. A, p. 14; Charles B. Seib, "The First Amendment as Corporate Business," *The Washington Post*, 26 May 1978, sec. A, p. 21.

[12] See Brief for Appellee, 1, *Austin v. Michigan Chamber of Commerce*, 494 U.S. 652 (1990). The Michigan regulation in question exempted media corporations. Violation of the regulation constituted a felony, punishable by a fine of $10,000.

[13] See *Austin v. Michigan Chamber of Commerce*, 668.

[14] See *Austin v. Michigan Chamber of Commerce*, 691 (Scalia, J., dissenting).

[15] See *Austin v. Michigan Chamber of Commerce*, 691 (Scalia, J., dissenting).

[16] See *Austin v. Michigan Chamber of Commerce*, 712 (Kennedy, J., dissenting).

[17] See *Austin v. Michigan Chamber of Commerce*, 712-13 (Kennedy, J., dissenting).

[18] In this age of virtually nonstop corporate mergers, acquisitions, and restructuring, the holdings of any corporate conglomerate are always subject to change. One of the best sources of regularly updated media holdings is *Columbia Journalism Review*'s online media-ownership resource guide: "Who Owns What," *Columbia Journalism Review*, http://www.cjr.org/resources/. See also: Benjamin M. Compaine and Douglas Gomery, *Who Owns the Media? Competition and Concentration in the Mass Media Industry* (Mahwah, N.J.: Lawrence Erlbaum Associates, 2000); William Serrin, ed., *The Business of Journalism* (New York, N.Y.: The New Press, 2000).

[19] See Ben H. Bagdikian, *The New Media Monopoly* (Boston: Beacon Press, 2004); Ben H. Bagdikian, *The Media Monopoly* (Boston: Beacon Press, 2000).

[20] See Edward S. Herman and Robert W. McChesney, *The Global Media: The New Missionaries of Corporate Capitalism* (London: Cassell, 1997); Robert W. McChesney and John Nichols, *Our Media, Not Theirs: The Democratic Struggle Against Corporate Media* (New York: Seven Stories Press, 2002); Robert W. McChesney, *Rich Media, Poor Democracy: Communication Politics in Dubious Times* (Urbana, Ill.: University of Illinois Press, 1999).

[21] See Vikas Bajaj, "Pressured, Knight Ridder Ponders Sale of Company," *The New York Times*, 15 November 2005, sec. C, p. 1; Joseph T. Hallinan and Joe Hagan, "Knight Ridder Sale Could Spark Consolidation in the Industry, but Potential Suitors are Scarce," *The Wall Street Journal*, 3 November 2005, sec. C, p. 1; Steve Outing, "Investigative Journalism: Will It Survive?" *Editor & Publisher*, 16 November 2005, accessed 18 November 2005 at: http://www.editorandpublisher.com/eandp/columns/stopthepresses_display.jsp?vnu_content_id=1001523690; Frank Ahrens, "The News Hounds: Investors and Falling Stock Prices are Dogging the Industry," *The Washington Post*, 3 November 2005, sec. D, p. 1; John McManus, "Don't Let Corporate Raiders Liquidate the Fourth Estate," *Grade the News*, 29 November 2005, accessed 2 December 2005 at: http://gradethenews.org/commentaries/boycott.htm; Todd Gitlin and Olivier Sylvain, "Staff Cuts Are a Disgrace to Journalism," *Newsday*, 12 December 2005, sec. A, p. 37; "SPJ Calls for 'National Debate' Surrounding Sale of Knight Ridder," *Editor & Publisher*, 25 January 2006, accessed 27 January 2006 at: http://www.editorandpublisher.com/eandp/news/a

rticle_display.jsp?vnu_content_id=1001918714; Katharine Q. Seelye and Andrew Ross Sorkin, "Newspaper Chain Agrees to Sale for $4.5 Billion," *The New York Times*, 13 March 2006, sec. A, p. 1.

[22] See Clay Calvert, "And You Call Yourself a Journalist? Wrestling With a Definition of 'Journalist' in the Law," 103 *Dickinson Law Review* 411 (1999); Adam Winkler, "The Corporation in Election Law," 32 *Loyola of Los Angeles Law Review* 1243 (1999); Lillian R. BeVier, "Campaign Finance Reform: Specious Arguments, Intractable Dilemmas," 94 *Columbia Law Review* 1258 (1994); Bradley A. Smith, "Money Talks: Speech, Corruption, Equality, and Campaign Finance," 86 *Georgetown Law Journal* 45, 93 (1997).

[23] See Edward B. Foley, "Equal-Dollars-Per-Voter: A Constitutional Principle of Campaign Finance," 94 *Columbia Law Review* 1204 (1994); Richard L. Hasen, "Campaign Finance Laws and the Rupert Murdoch Problem," 77 *Texas Law Review* 1627 (1999).

[24] See L.A. Powe Jr., "Boiling Blood," 77 Texas Law Review 1667 (1999).

[25] See *McConnell v. Federal Election Commission*, 540 U.S. 93, 208 (2003).

[26] See *McConnell v. Federal Election Commission*, 283-84 (Thomas, J., dissenting).

[27] See *Senate Journal*, 107th Congress, 1st session, 19, 29, 20 March 2001. Senator McConnell later became the lead plaintiff in the First Amendment challenge of the BCRA.

[28] See *Senate Journal*, 107th Congress, 1st session, 26 March 2001; *Senate Journal*, 105th Congress, 1st session, 26 September 1997; *Senate Journal*, 105th Congress, 1st session, 9 October 1997.

[29] See *Senate Journal*, 107th Congress, 1st session, 26 March 2001.

[30] See *Federal Election Commission v. Massachusetts Citizens for Life, Inc.*, 479 U.S. 238, 257-64 (1986). The Court found a section of the Federal Election Campaign Act, which prohibited corporations from using treasury funds to make expenditures in connection with candidate elections, to be unconstitutional when applied to the class of ideological corporations that it defined in the decision.

[31] See *Federal Election Commission v. Massachusetts Citizens for Life, Inc.*, 250-52.

[32] See *Arizona Publishing Company v. O'Neil*, 304 U.S. 543 (1938); *Grosjean v. American Press Company*, 297 U.S. 233 (1936); *Minneapolis Star v. Minnesota Commissioner of Revenue*, 460 U.S. 575 (1983); *Arkansas Writers' Project v. Ragland*, 481 U.S. 221 (1987); *Texas Monthly v. Bullock*, 489 U.S. 1 (1989); *Leathers v. Medlock*, 499 U.S. 439 (1991).

[33] See John Eggerton, "Survey Says: Noncom News Most Trusted," *Broadcasting & Cable*, accessed 11 November 2005 at: http://www.broadcastingcable.com/article/CA6282871.html?display=Breaking+News&referral=SUPP; Steve M. Barkin, *American Television News: The Media Marketplace and the Public Interest* (Armonk, N.Y.: M.E. Sharpe, 2003), 171-81.

[34] See "About Poynter," The Poynter Institute, accessed 21 May 2006 at: http://www.poynter.org/column.asp?id=62; Allan M. Jalon, "Dishing Out the Hamburger Money," *Los Angeles Times*, 16 May 2004, sec. E, p. 1.

[35] See *First National Bank of Boston v. Bellotti*, 802 (Burger, C.J., concurring); *Senate Journal*, 105th Congress, 1st session, 9 October 1997; "Mobil Urges Protection of Constitution for Ads," *The New York Times*, 26 May 1978, sec. D, p. 13; Herbert Schmertz. *Corporations and the First Amendment*. (New York: American Management Associations, 1978).

[36] See Stewart, "Or of the Press," 636-37.

CHAPTER TEN

Cloaking the Commercial as Political

Thus far, this book has focused on First Amendment issues related to regulation of corporate political media spending. This chapter shifts the focus to corporate *commercial* media spending — the promotion of products and services, rather than political messages. The two types of corporate communications — political and commercial — represent distinct bodies of case law in First Amendment jurisprudence. Yet recently, as noted in Chapter One, a major campaign was conducted in the courts to blur the distinction between the two. Essentially, an array of corporate interests contended, First Amendment political rights should be extended to commercial advertising if the sponsor of the message declares that it includes discussion of a public issue. First Amendment rights in that case would mean that advertisers could not be required to show that their claims were truthful.

In the *Nike, Inc. v. Kasky* case that reached the Supreme Court in 2003, for example, the Nike Corporation was accused of false advertising in messages it disseminated concerning labor practices in its overseas factories. The company's lawyers argued, however, that the messages were not subject to false advertising laws on the grounds that they addressed a subject of public concern and therefore were political, not commercial. As such, they contended, First Amendment protections for political speech meant that Nike could not be forced to demonstrate that its statements about its factories were true.[1]

On the face of it, it might strike someone not steeped in the rhetoric of the corporate free-speech movement as a dubious notion that an employer should be protected by the First Amendment from confirming the truth about working conditions in its own factories. It might seem common sense that society should have the means to ensure that the party with the most information about such a situation — as well as a vested interest in presenting that information in the most favorable light — be required to demonstrate the accuracy of its statements on the matter.

In fact, the dispute at the heart of *Nike, Inc. v. Kasky* represents a crucial one in First Amendment law. The facts of the case presented the Supreme Court with what appeared to be an ideal opportunity to answer a question that has snowballed in significance ever since the Court opened the door to First Amendment protection for commercial advertising in *New York Times Co. v. Sullivan.* Over the four decades since that landmark ruling, advertisers and regulators have repeatedly tested the nature and extent of its holding on commercial speech. The process has produced a First Amendment doctrine that permits regulation to restrict false and misleading advertising so as to protect the property rights at stake in the fair-bargaining process from fraudulent practices. If such regulations are challenged on free-speech grounds, the judicial review is conducted under a standard referred to as *intermediate* scrutiny. It is called that because it is neither the easiest nor the most difficult standard of review for challenged regulations to survive in court.

Another First Amendment doctrine requires that restrictions on political speech must meet a judicial standard that is much tougher and is referred to as *strict* scrutiny. Like the doctrine on commercial advertising, the political-speech doctrine is also grounded in the way the Court articulated its broader ruling in *New York Times v. Sullivan.* That ruling emphasized that the fullest First Amendment protection should be maintained for speech involving "debate on public issues."[2]

So the question at the heart of the *Nike* case derives from the crossroads of those two *Sullivan* legacies: When the parties involved disagree about whether the message in question is commercial or political, how should it be assessed in terms of First Amendment protection? This chapter argues that the answer to that difficult and momentous question set in motion more than four decades ago in the *Sullivan* ruling can still be found in the way the Supreme Court laid out its fundamental purpose and reasoning in that far-reaching decision. Understanding those essential principles from *Sullivan* is vital, because as in landmark cases on corporate political media spending, its holdings have been argued to extend First Amendment protections to corporations in cases such as *Nike*. But as the following pages will show, the truth is in fact just the reverse.

THE FACTS OF THE *NIKE* CASE

The *Nike, Inc. v. Kasky* case began to take shape after Nike, Inc., launched a public relations and advertising campaign in response to allegations of unsafe and abusive working conditions in factories where its athletic shoes and apparel are manufactured. Mark Kasky, one of several activists working to pressure the multinational corporation to improve the allegedly substandard working conditions, sued Nike in 1998 for unfair and deceptive practices under California's Unfair Competition Law and False Advertising Law, alleging the communications campaign made false and misleading statements. The case reached the California Supreme Court on the question of whether the Nike messages were subject to regulation under California's commercial advertising laws, as Kasky contended, or were protected as political speech on a subject of public debate, as Nike maintained. The California court ruled for Kasky, and Nike appealed to the U.S. Supreme Court.[3]

The High Court agreed to take the case, accepted a total of thirty-four legal briefs from parties with an interest in the case and heard oral arguments. But then in one of the most anticlimactic moments in Supreme Court history, the justices announced that they had decided, after all, not to decide the case. On the last day of that term, the Court simply handed down a one-sentence, unsigned order dismissing its original acceptance of the case as "improvidently granted." A concurring opinion by Justice John Paul Stevens, joined by two other justices, attributed the dismissal to procedural problems that would make adjudication by the high Court premature.[4]

The Supreme Court's action returned the case to the California courts, ostensibly to proceed with the original case and determine whether Kasky's allegations of false advertising in Nike's communication campaign were correct. The California Supreme Court at that point had considered only whether the messages in question should be considered commercial or political at trial for consideration of First Amendment protection. False commercial advertising receives no constitutional protection. So that court's ruling declaring the Nike messages commercial meant that a crucial issue at trial would have been whether the statements in question were false or misleading. Under California statutes, advertising is subject to misdemeanor punishment if it is "untrue or misleading, and . . . is known, or which by the exercise of reasonable care should be known, to be untrue or misleading."[5]

The case never reached trial, however, because three months after the Supreme Court declined to decide the appeal, Nike announced that the company and Kasky had settled the case out of court.[6] So not only was the truth or falsity of Nike's messages never determined by a court of law, the critical question presented by the *Nike* case remains unanswered by the U.S. Supreme Court. Given the stakes and intense interest in the question though, it seems likely that the matter will be pressed in some future case that sooner or later makes its way back to the nation's highest court for resolution. So the subject remains a vital one, and the debate on it continues quite vigorously.

Indeed, the scholarly discourse on the appropriate standard for commercial advertising in First Amendment law has generated a vast literature. Great swaths of scholars, for example, have criticized the effort to maintain a distinction between commercial and political messages in terms of First Amendment Protection.[7] Many others have articulated arguments in favor of maintaining a subordinate status for commercial messages in First Amendment jurisprudence.[8] And still another considerable number have embraced a middle, less dichotomous approach to the question.[9] The *Nike* case itself and what it means for commercial and corporate First Amendment law also has spawned a substantial and growing body of commentary.[10]

Much concern has been expressed for the implications of the case for corporations. Several scholars have contended that the California court's decision in the *Nike* case will bar corporations from speaking publicly on issues of concern and have criticized the Supreme Court for its failure to decide the case in favor of Nike. In that school of thought, the California Supreme Court should not have "taken a paternalistic approach towards protecting the public against potential false or misleading speech," and "corporations should not be restricted from speaking their mind because they are economically involved."[11] Further, according to that line of reasoning, the California ruling will leave corporations "unable to defend themselves without fear of aggressive and unmerciful prosecution,"[12] and that means "corporate attorneys will advise their corporate clients not to speak at all if they are at risk of being sued every time they may answer a public concern."[13] Given all that, "Corporations will have an incentive to remain silent on important political and business related issues."[14]

As already established in preceding chapters, the current state of affairs in First Amendment law and political culture indicates that American society today has never been *farther* from experiencing corporate silence on public issues. Given the dominance established by big business in the marketplace of ideas over the past quarter-century or so, whatever setback it conceivably may have suffered in the *Nike* case must be considered a very small one in the greater scope of things. So in the context of this book, what is significant about that case is the potential it represents for the future expansion of the corporate free-speech movement. For as law professor Tamara Piety has put it most pointedly: "The next case that the Court accepts may give commercial speakers what Nike hoped to get from this case — a constitutional right to lie."[15]

This chapter does not attempt to weigh in comprehensively on the broader debate over First Amendment jurisprudence concerning commercial advertising. Nor does it wade into the tedium of the various legal maneuvers utilized by Nike in an effort to end the case in its favor.[16] Rather it seeks to focus on what the crucial legacy of *New York Times v. Sullivan* tells us today about the societal value in protecting a degree of false speech in discussion of public issues when doing so serves a greater good. And whether the implications of the *Nike* case justify extending First Amendment protection to *all* false commercial speech that includes any discussion of a public issue. That is the ultimate question that the *Nike* case brought front and center.

The concerns expressed by scholars over the implications for corporate expression must be weighed against the societal interest in protecting the fair-bargaining process from fraud — in this case, by preventing corporations from immunizing false commercial speech from regulation by attaching it to a public issue.[17] From that perspective, as will be discussed, the California Supreme Court's decision was consistent with the *Sullivan* Court's effort to protect political speech — without denying that protection arbitrarily because of the mere *presence* of commercial speech. The California court focused on balancing that interest against the deeply established interest in protecting consumers from false advertising.[18] It is not an easy balance to strike. But when a choice must be made in law between absolute freedom for commercial expression and holding corporate management accountable for false commercial messages in which it has a vested interest in favorable spin, this chapter will show it is in the greatest interests of society to shade jurisprudence toward the latter.

'MATTERS OF THE HIGHEST PUBLIC INTEREST'

As detailed in Chapter Seven, the *New York Times Co. v. Sullivan* case arose in the early sixties from a libel verdict over a full-page advertisement in the *Times*. It described the brutal repression of civil-rights efforts in the South and appealed for contributions to help support the movement.[19] While it was undeniably true that repression as described had occurred repeatedly, some of the statements in the ad were not accurate.[20] Although Montgomery City Commissioner L.B. Sullivan was not named in the text, he contended that charges concerning police activity could be understood to refer to him. The jury was instructed by the trial judge that under Alabama law a publication was considered libelous if it tended to injure the plaintiff "in his public office, or impute misconduct to him in his office, or want of official integrity, or want of fidelity to a public trust," and that general damages were presumed without a showing of "actual intent" to harm or "gross negligence and recklessness."[21]

The Alabama verdict was reversed at the U.S. Supreme Court, which declared that "compelling the critic of official conduct to guarantee the truth of *all* his factual assertions — and to do so on pain of libel judgments virtually unlimited in amount" leads to self-censorship. The Court ruled therefore that the First Amendment requires protecting citizens from such liability unless the public official bringing the libel suit showed the libelous statement was made with "actual malice" — either knowledge that it was false or reckless disregard as to whether it was false or not.[22]

Before the Court could reach that conclusion, however, it had to first of all consider Sullivan's argument that First Amendment protections did not apply to the statements in question because they appeared in a paid advertisement. That argument was based upon the Court's 1942 ruling in *Valentine v. Chrestensen*. That case had established a broad precedent that a "purely commercial advertisement" merited no First Amendment protection from government regulation. In addressing that issue in *Sullivan*, the Court's action altered the *Valentine* precedent enough to begin a process that would dramatically overhaul First Amendment law for commercial advertising a dozen years later. The Court held that the fact that the *New York Times* had been paid for the advertisement in question was "immaterial in this connection." It based that holding on the reasoning that the purpose of the ad in the *Sullivan* case was not evading a law held to legitimately serve the public interest but advancing the cause of "a movement *whose existence and objectives are matters of the highest public interest and concern*."[23] Clearly, the Court considered the motive of the actual speaker involved — the supporters of the civil-rights movement — a material fact. What it deemed *not* material was the motive of the commercial medium in which the message appeared.

Nothing in the *Sullivan* opinion suggests that the Court considered the *Times*' motive to be the same as that of the civil rights supporters who paid for the ad — which of course it wasn't. The *Times*' motive in selling the advertising space for that message was no different than its motive in selling space to all the other advertisers on its pages. In the manner in which the Court distinguished the *Sullivan* context from that of *Valentine*, it deemed the motive of the speaker who was most closely linked to the content of the speech to be material to the question of First Amendment protection — and the motive of the speaker *not* so connected to be immaterial. In so doing, the *Sullivan* Court was engaging for practical purposes in the nuanced sort of test — although it did not articulate it as such — that it would employ in the *Bolger v. Youngs Drug Products Corp.* case some years later. And *Bolger* would be the precedent that the California Supreme Court would rely upon in *Kasky v. Nike, Inc.*[24] Both those cases, which will be further detailed later in this chapter, focused on the question of the appropriate level of constitutional protection to be applied to the commercial messages at issue — in situations involving significantly different fact sets from *Sullivan*.

The Court in *Sullivan* emphasized that the consequence of not protecting the seller of the advertising space in that case would be to discourage such sellers from making their space available to "persons who do not themselves have access to publishing facilities." With such language, the Court stressed its ultimate purpose of protecting the First Amendment rights of citizens. Throughout the *Sullivan* opinion, that overriding purpose resonates. It is grounded, the Court said, in the most fundamental principles that drove the founders' efforts to ensure that the "structure of the government dispersed power in reflection of the people's distrust of concentrated power, and of power itself at all levels." Nothing is more consistent in the language of *Sullivan* than its emphasis on how the decision was intended, above all, to help maintain the sovereignty of the people — a process that requires protecting citizens from concentrations of power that threaten fundamental rights.[25]

PROTECTING THE PEOPLE AS *SULLIVAN* INTENDED

Focusing upon that reasoning is crucial in considering cases like *Nike*, because corporate interests invoke *Sullivan* to justify First Amendment rights for corporate media spending, even in circumstances in which the facts of the case are significantly different.[26] Perfunctorily granting *Sullivan*'s protection for "the people" to Nike, Inc., would represent a virtual inversion of that reasoning. For the threat addressed specifically in *Sullivan* was excessive power of government to punish criticism of government by citizens. The Court's focus on addressing such threats was pronounced in both its framing of the question before it and in its statement of the essential holding. "The question before us is whether this rule of liability, as applied to an action brought by a public official against critics of his official conduct, abridges the freedom of speech and of the press that is guaranteed by the First and Fourteenth Amendments," the Court declared in *Sullivan*. That emphasis on protecting criticism of government was reiterated in the Court's holding that "the rule of law applied by the Alabama courts is constitutionally deficient for failure to provide the safeguards for freedom of speech and of the press that are required by the First and Fourteenth Amendments in a libel action brought by a public official against critics of his official conduct."[27]

Yet, the Court consistently articulated its rationale most broadly throughout *Sullivan* in terms of the great necessity of maintaining the peoples' speech rights against encroachment by more powerful influences. "Debate on public issues should be uninhibited, robust, and wide-open, and . . . it may well include vehement, caustic, and sometimes unpleasantly sharp attacks on government and public officials," the Court declared. It drew upon a federal appellate case that affirmed the dismissal of a libel suit by a member of Congress who had been called anti-Semitic by a newspaper: "Cases which impose liability for erroneous reports of the political conduct of officials reflect the obsolete doctrine that the governed must not criticize their governors." Additionally, in asserting the justification for establishing the actual-malice standard of liability for libel cases brought by public officials, the Court noted that some state courts had already adopted such a standard, one of which had been upheld by the Kansas Supreme Court in a libel suit brought by the state attorney general during a reelection campaign.[28] *Sullivan*'s repeated emphasis on preventing government punishment of its critics accentuates another key distinction between it and the *Nike* case: *Nike* did not involve punishment of the criticism of government. Thus, even if *Sullivan* could be viewed as establishing *only* that the actual-malice standard be applied to protect any criticism of government, then it could not provide authority for corporate parties in cases such as *Nike*. And neither can *Sullivan* be relied upon for that purpose if it is understood more broadly as protecting citizens from concentrations of power that threaten fundamental rights.

In the structure and emphasis of its discourse, the *Sullivan* opinion provides more support for the latter understanding. Other elements of the opinion are not as closely linked to the *Sullivan* holding in factual context, language or reasoning. For example, the discussion of protection for the *Times* and the other defendants via the actual-malice standard was rather brief and focused almost exclusively on considering whether the record in the case indicated that the standard had been met by the public official who brought the suit. No evidence was presented that the individual defendants had any prior knowledge of falsity in the statements at issue. It was determined at trial that the *Times* advertising department could have checked articles by *Times* reporters concerning at least some of what turned out to be minor errors in the ad. Nevertheless, the newspaper was dealing with subject matter occurring completely outside the bounds of its own business operation (another distinction between *Sullivan* and the relationship of Nike, Inc., to the subject matter in the California case). The Court concluded that "the evidence against the *Times* supports at most a finding of negligence in failing to discover the misstatements, and is constitutionally insufficient to show the recklessness that is required for a finding of actual malice."[29] Thus, the Court found that in the context of the greater purpose that it had articulated at length, falsity warranted protection when disseminated without either knowledge of the falsehood or recklessness concerning its verification.

Similarly, the Court's discussion of the "unfettered exchange of ideas" was not articulated so broadly as to imply establishing that condition as an absolute standard. The Court invoked the phrase as part of its broader discussion of protecting speech rights of "the people," certainly not in any proximity to its holding or even its discussion of commercial speech. "The general proposition that freedom of expression upon public questions is secured by the First Amendment has long been settled by our decisions," it said. "The constitutional safeguard, we have said, 'was fashioned to assure unfettered interchange of ideas for the bringing about of political and social changes desired by the people.' "[30] At that point, the Court already had completed its discussion of the commercial-speech question and was well into its discussion on the larger question of whether the Alabama liability standard was constitutional as applied to libel suits brought in response to criticism of government officials.

This analysis shows that on balance the Court's emphasis in *Sullivan* reflected the greatest concern with maintaining the sovereignty of the people from encroachment by centers of concentrated power — represented in that case by the power of government officials to bring libel actions for criticism of their official activities. To the extent that *Sullivan* protected commercial advertising, it went no further — and clearly intended to go no further — than to establish that the advertising format alone could not bar the speech involved from all First Amendment protection. In addition, the Court unequivocally linked that holding with the motive of the speaker involved in relation to the "movement whose existence and objectives are matters of the highest public interest and concern."[31] The Court did not in any way suggest that commercial advertising should be similarly protected in other contexts where different facts and different societal interests were at stake — such as protecting the fair-bargaining process from fraud.[32]

Thus, *Sullivan* in its reasoning and principles is not at odds with efforts by later Courts to distinguish between commercial and political speech for the purposes of resolving very different cases. Despite the many significant Supreme Court rulings that have shaped the evolution of the commercial-speech doctrine, the holdings have not gone beyond protecting truthful commercial speech to also protect *false* commercial speech, not even when it is attached to discussion of public issues. Ultimately, the case law on the subject since *Sullivan* demonstrates a central concern with protecting the fair-bargaining process and the property interests involved from fraudulent practices by permitting regulation aimed at preventing false advertising.

A BRIEF OVERVIEW OF THE CASE LAW

To begin with, the cavalier dismissal of commercial advertising as meriting no protection from government regulation in 1942's *Valentine v. Chrestensen* has long since been rendered obsolete in the case law. However, the Supreme Court has never in fact rejected *Valentine*'s holding that commercial speech should not be able to "to achieve immunity from the law's command" by appending to it "a civic appeal, or a moral platitude."[33] The evolution of the Court's commercial-speech doctrine that began with *New York Times v. Sullivan* has been considerable, but the case law has not gone any farther than protecting *truthful* commercial advertising in First Amendment cases.[34]

The signs that the Court would continue evolving its doctrine on commercial speech were clearly evident in *Pittsburgh Press Co. v. Pittsburgh Commission on Human Relations* in 1973 and *Bigelow v. Virginia* two years later.[35] But neither case's holdings formally expanded First Amendment rights for commercial advertising. That took place in *Virginia State Board of Pharmacy v. Virginia Citizens Consumer Council* in 1976. The facts of the case gave the Supreme Court the opportunity to establish for the first time that speech that does "no more than propose a commercial transaction" is not completely without First Amendment protection. In striking down a state statute prohibiting pharmacists from advertising the price of prescription drugs, the Court emphasized the restraint that the First Amendment places on government against denying truthful information to citizens. "Virginia is free to require whatever professional standards it wishes of its pharmacists," the Court declared. "But it may not do so by keeping the public in ignorance of the entirely lawful terms that competing pharmacists are offering." It grounded that assertion in terms of the public good served by consumers receiving accurate commercial information: "So long as we preserve a predominantly free enterprise economy, the allocation of our resources in large measure will be made through numerous private economic decisions. It is a matter of public interest that those decisions, in the aggregate, be intelligent and well informed. To this end, the free flow of commercial information is indispensable."[36]

In a concurring opinion, Justice Potter Stewart wrote to make clear that the holding did not similarly restrict government's right to regulate false or deceptive advertising. The *Sullivan* principles, he said, "suggest that government may take broader action to protect the public from injury produced by false or deceptive price or product advertising than from harm caused by defamation." He emphasized as critical to that distinction the advertiser's greater relative access to the truth or falsity of its factual statements. "In contrast to the press, which must often attempt to assemble the true facts from sketchy and sometimes conflicting sources under the pressure of publication deadlines, *the commercial advertiser generally knows the product or service he seeks to sell and is in a position to verify the accuracy of his factual representations before he disseminates them*," Stewart pointed out. "The advertiser's access to the truth about his product and its price substantially eliminates any danger that governmental regulation of false or misleading price or product advertising will chill accurate and nondeceptive commercial expression."[37]

Two years later, the Court reinforced that assertion by refusing to invalidate on First Amendment grounds a lawyer's suspension from practice for violation of advertising restrictions. "To require a parity of constitutional protection for commercial and noncommercial speech alike could invite dilution, simply by a leveling process, of the force of the Amendment's guarantee with respect to the latter kind of speech," it said.[38] And the Court even more emphatically demonstrated that false commercial speech would remain completely subject to government regulation two years after that when the Court established a four-part test for assessing the constitutionality of advertising regulations in *Central Hudson Gas and Electric. v. Public Service Commission*. The threshold question in that test is whether the advertising in question concerns lawful activity and is not misleading — with failure to survive that part of the test denying the ad any further consideration of First Amendment protection. "There can be no constitutional objection to the suppression of commercial messages that do not accurately inform the public about lawful activity," the Court stressed, and again emphasized the "extensive knowledge" that commercial speakers have "of both the market and their products."[39]

A year later, the Court struck down a city ban on most outdoor signs, finding that the regulation survived the *Central Hudson* test but still was unconstitutional because it permitted the advertising of goods or services available on sites where the sign was located but did not permit other messages on those signs. The Court emphasized, however, that its ruling was not a departure from *Central Hudson.* On the contrary, it said, by "affording a greater degree of protection to commercial than to noncommercial speech," the regulation in question had inverted the doctrine maintained in *Central Hudson* and related cases. Therefore, the Court struck down the sign regulation because "recent commercial speech cases have consistently accorded noncommercial speech a greater degree of protection than commercial speech"[40]

The Court provided its most substantial guidance for distinguishing between commercial and political speech in 1983's *Bolger v. Youngs Drug Products Corp*. The case required determining whether a condom manufacturer's flyers and pamphlets promoting its products — but also discussing venereal disease and family planning — could be considered commercial messages subject to federal regulation. In order to do that, the Court developed a three-part test that is based upon the combined degree to which messages feature an advertising format, reference to a specific product, and economic motivation for their dissemination. In the *Bolger* case, those elements in combination provided "strong support for the . . . conclusion that the informational pamphlets are properly characterized as commercial speech . . . notwithstanding the fact that they contain discussions of important public issues," the Court concluded. "We have made clear that advertising which 'links a product to a current public debate' is not thereby entitled to the constitutional protection afforded noncommercial speech," the ruling emphasized. It pointed out that advertisers are quite capable of separating their commercial messages from their noncommercial messages. "A company has the full panoply of protections available to its direct comments on public issues," the Court noted, "so there is no reason for providing similar constitutional protection when such statements are made in the context of commercial transactions."[41]

In cases over the years since, the Supreme Court has continued to emphasize the lesser degree of First Amendment protection that is warranted for commercial advertising. But it has not left advertising vulnerable to all government regulation. A number of cases have been decided in favor of advertisers who challenged government regulations because the regulations in question failed to meet the *Central Hudson* standard. In such instances, the Court has focused on striking down regulations that it found were broader than necessary or failed to clearly serve their purpose — particularly when restrictions were imposed upon truthful information concerning legal products and services. For example, in *Edenfield v. Fane* in 1993 the Court ruled unconstitutional a state ban on certified public accountants' personal solicitation of prospective clients, emphasizing that the regulated messages sought "to communicate no more than truthful, nondeceptive information proposing a lawful commercial transaction." But the same year, in *United States v. Edge Broadcasting*, the Court upheld a federal law prohibiting lottery advertising by radio stations located in states where lotteries are not legal.[42]

The Court has also focused on those principles in ruling unconstitutional a federal law prohibiting beer labels from advertising alcohol content and state statutes banning the advertisement of alcohol prices anywhere in Rhode Island except at the point of purchase.[43] Although some justices in those cases and others have criticized aspects of the Court's doctrine on commercial advertising, the majority of them have maintained support for that doctrine, as the Court emphasized in *Lorillard Tobacco v. Reilly*. In that case, the Court noted that the parties challenging state regulations on outdoor tobacco advertising had urged the Court to consider the advertising messages in the same way as fully protected political speech, arguing that some justices had "expressed doubts about the *Central Hudson* analysis and whether it should apply in certain cases." Pointing out that petitioners had made the same argument in *Greater New Orleans Broadcasting v. United States* two years earlier, the *Lorillard* Court said that, as in the earlier case, it saw "no need to break new ground. *Central Hudson*, as applied in our more recent commercial speech cases, provides an adequate basis for decision."[44]

In striking down the tobacco advertising regulations in the *Lorillard* case, the Court declared that although the government interest in preventing use of tobacco by minors was "substantial, and even compelling, . . . it is no less true that the sale and use of tobacco products by adults is a legal activity." That factor once again proved critical in the ruling. "We must consider that tobacco retailers and manufacturers have an interest in conveying truthful information about their products to adults, and adults have a corresponding interest in receiving truthful information about tobacco products."[45] Even while asserting in a concurring opinion that he would subject all of the advertising regulations in question to strict scrutiny rather than *Central Hudson*'s intermediate scrutiny, Justice Clarence Thomas qualified his argument specifically to apply when "the government seeks to restrict truthful speech in order to suppress the ideas it conveys . . . whether or not the speech in question may be characterized as 'commercial.' "[46]

Thus, although justices have at times disagreed about the appropriate level of constitutional protection for commercial messages, the Court's holdings have never wavered on the government's power to regulate false or deceptive advertising. Protecting property interests from fraud by permitting regulation aimed at preventing false advertising has remained a central concern in that jurisprudence. The holdings have emphasized preventing government from denying citizens truthful information, especially when it involves using speech restrictions to discourage activities that government otherwise makes legal.[47] Such a doctrine places a priority on protecting truth in commercial messages. And that principle is completely antithetical to the notion of allowing false commercial speech to be immunized from regulation by attaching it to discussion of a public issue. To the contrary, the Court has repeatedly refused to countenance such an interpretation of the First Amendment.

WHY NIKE LOST ITS ARGUMENT

So in making its decision in the *Nike* case, the California Supreme Court was dealing in well-established law that false or misleading commercial speech receives no protection under the First Amendment. As noted earlier in this chapter, however, the case never reached the point of determining whether the Nike messages were false or misleading. The case before the California Supreme Court was whether the messages were commercial (as Kasky contended) or political (as Nike argued). To that end, the Court's analysis balanced the interest in protecting discussion of public issues against the interest in protecting consumers from false advertising and not allowing such falsity to be immunized from regulation by attaching it to a public issue. "The regulations in question do not suppress points of view but instead suppress false and misleading statements of fact," the court concluded. "To the extent Nike's speech represents expression of opinion or points of view on general policy questions such as the value of economic 'globalization,' it is noncommercial speech subject to full First Amendment protection. Nike's speech loses that full measure of protection only when it concerns facts material to commercial transactions — here, factual statements about how Nike makes its products."[48]

Thus, the California court ruled that Nike's statements were commercial speech for purposes of applying California laws designed to prevent false advertising and other commercial deception. That was the case, its analysis found, by focusing on three critical elements: "Because in the statements at issue here Nike was acting as a commercial speaker, because its intended audience was primarily the buyers of its products, and because the statements consisted of factual representations about its own business operations." The California court rejected Nike's contention that its statements were not commercial speech because they were part of "an international media debate on issues of intense public interest." In doing so, it emphasized the U.S. Supreme Court's assertion in *Bolger v. Youngs Drug Products Corp.* that advertisers "may not 'immunize false or misleading product information from government regulation simply by including references to public issues.' " Nike's allegedly false and misleading messages, the California court declared, "all relate to the commercial portions of the speech in question — the description of actual conditions and practices in factories that produce Nike's products — and thus the proposed regulations reach only that commercial portion." In determining whether the Nike messages were commercial or noncommercial speech, the California court drew extensively on the test established in *Bolger* for that purpose. It further relied on the U.S. Supreme Court's directive in *Board of Trustees, State University of*

New York v. Fox that "commercial and noncommercial messages are not 'inextricable' unless there is some legal or practical compulsion to combine them." The California court pointed out that "no law required Nike to combine factual representations about its own labor practices with expressions of opinion about economic globalization, nor was it impossible for Nike to address those subjects separately."[49]

Crucially, the California court said, Nike made factual representations about its own business operations, addressing consumers on working conditions, wages and other labor practices "within its own knowledge. . . . Nike was in a position to readily verify the truth of any factual assertions it made on these topics." Thus, the ruling declared, "Regulation aimed at preventing false and actually or inherently misleading speech is unlikely to deter Nike from speaking truthfully or at all about the conditions in its factories." To the contrary, the California court emphasized, its ruling held squarely to the case law promoting *truthful* commercial advertising. "To the extent that application of these laws may make Nike more cautious, and cause it to make greater efforts to verify the truth of its statements," it wrote, "these laws will serve the purpose of commercial speech protection by 'insuring that the stream of commercial information flow[s] cleanly as well as freely.' "[50]

As discussed at the beginning of this chapter, the U.S. Supreme Court ultimately declined to rule on Nike's challenge to the California decision and sent the case back to be resolved there. However, the justices seemed to anticipate seeing the crucial questions the *Nike* case presented before the Court again. Not specifically via the *Nike* case, of course, because Nike announced in late 2003 that it had agreed to pay $1.5 million to a worker rights organization to settle the case. As part of the settlement, Nike consented to make the donation to the Fair Labor Association, a Washington-based group that monitors corporate labor practices abroad and helps educate workers. Marc Kasky and Nike said in a joint statement that supporting such programs was preferable to continued litigation. Other terms of the settlement were not disclosed. Jim Carter, general counsel for Nike told reporters that the manner in which its appeal of the California decision was ultimately dismissed "left us with no satisfactory comfort that we could get back to the Supreme Court."[51]

Yet, it is likely that another corporate party in a similar situation will at some point seek to press the central issue of the *Nike* case again. The California Supreme Court gave its full attention to the question of how to address allegedly deceptive speech in the sort of highly sophisticated corporate marketing campaign that is increasingly characteristic of a great deal of commercial communication today. However, because the U.S. Supreme Court deferred on reviewing the California Court's ruling, and because Nike chose to settle its litigation with Kasky rather than pursue the case further, a pronouncement from the nation's highest court will no doubt be sought again in the future. This chapter argues that the Court's *Bolger* test and its broader case law on commercial advertising provide sufficient guidance to resolve such First Amendment questions in the manner in which the California Supreme Court did.

PROTECTING THE ECONOMIC MARKETPLACE

Even under a standard of accountability such as California's, the hardiness of commercial expression will ensure its continued vigor in the very manner in which the Supreme Court envisioned when it first established First Amendment rights for advertising. "The First Amendment, as we construe it today," the Court said in its landmark 1976 *Virginia Pharmacy* ruling, "does not prohibit the State from insuring that the stream of commercial information flow[s] cleanly as well as freely." The standard to which advertising is held in California is hardly as draconian as to put commercial speakers "at risk of being sued every time they may answer a public concern," as it has been portrayed by some scholars. That standard simply makes it a misdemeanor to disseminate advertising that is "untrue or misleading, and which is known, or which by the exercise of reasonable care should be known, to be untrue or misleading."[52] By contrast, for the courts to embrace the broad argument put forth by corporate interests in the *Nike* case could lead to a nightmare scenario in consumer markets. The harms to property interests at stake in protecting the fair-bargaining process from fraudulent practices could be staggering if any false/misleading-advertising regulation could be evaded simply by linking commercial messages to an issue of public interest.

The body of the Supreme Court's rulings on commercial advertising serves to prevent such harms. Despite some disagreement at times over the appropriate level of constitutional protection for truthful commercial messages, the holdings have never wavered on the government's fundamental authority to regulate false or misleading commercial advertising. Even those justices who have argued for a more rigorous level of scrutiny concerning regulation of advertising have not extended their argument to include false or misleading messages. The Court's decisions that have found specific advertising regulations unconstitutional have emphasized denying government the power to deprive citizens of truthful information concerning legal activity — advancing the public good served by consumers receiving accurate commercial information. Most relevant to the critical question in *Nike*, the Court has repeatedly emphasized its long-established holding that advertisers must not be allowed to immunize false commercial messages from regulation simply by linking them to a public issue. For a future court to decide a case like *Nike* in favor of protecting false or deceptive speech from regulation would mean abandoning that vital principle. And it would grossly contradict the purpose for which the Court first declared that a commercial format alone was not sufficient to bar constitutional protection.

In making that declaration in *New York Times v. Sullivan*, the Court deemed the motive of the speaker who was most closely linked to the content of the speech to be material to the related First Amendment questions. The higher purpose that the Court focused upon in distinguishing the message involved — advancing the cause of "a movement whose existence and objectives are matters of the highest public interest and concern" — derived from the civil rights leaders who placed the ad, not the commercial entity (the *Times* advertising department) that merely conveyed the speech.[53] By the same token, the party with the greatest access to the truth of the message was *not* the commercial entity that conveyed it. Yet, in *Nike, Inc. v. Kasky*, the commercial motive and the greatest access to the truth of the message were not located in separate entities, but in the *same* entity: Nike.

The California Supreme Court reflected the significance of that distinction in observing that a fundamental assumption of the relevant First Amendment jurisprudence is that "commercial speech consists of factual statements and that those statements describe matters within the personal knowledge of the speaker or the person whom the speaker is representing and are made for the purpose of financial gain." The *Sullivan* Court found that, in order to protect a cause "of the highest public interest and concern," it was justified to bar punishment for falsehoods made without knowledge or reckless disregard of their falsity. To invert that reasoning in order to deny citizens truthful commercial information would be to render the central purpose of *Sullivan* meaningless. *Sullivan* provides a basis for considering when false speech warrants protection — not for perfunctorily protecting falsity in any message attached to any public issue, regardless the context, regardless the purpose. As Justice Stewart wrote in *Virginia Pharmacy*, "Government may take broader action to protect the public from injury produced by false or deceptive price or product advertising than from harm caused by defamation."[54] In seeking to limit government's authority to punish criticism of government, the *Sullivan* Court sought to protect the sovereignty of the people from the sort of excessive concentration of power that such authority would represent. Citizens subject to such punishment from government officials would be disadvantaged in a manner contradictory to the most fundamental principles of the American Constitution. To provide immensely powerful corporate speakers such as Nike with constitutional protection for false commercial speech would similarly disadvantage citizens.

Thus, in considering any future case like *Nike* the courts should weigh, as the Supreme Court did in *Sullivan,* the greater societal balance at stake. And the decision should similarly focus on protecting the sovereignty of citizens against the encroachment of concentrated power. Enabling immense corporate commercial entities like Nike to immunize false commercial speech from regulation simply by attaching it to a public issue represents a particularly dangerous concentration of power. The Supreme Court in its corporate political media spending cases has articulated a doctrine focused upon preventing actual and potential corruption of the political marketplace of ideas through wealth generated via the government-provided advantages of the corporate form in the economic marketplace. Just as the Court has sought to protect the political marketplace from the dangers of concentrated power represented by the corporate form, so too it would do well to protect the economic marketplace from the threat of false commercial advertising immunized by linkage to public debate.

[1] See *Nike, Inc. v. Kasky*, 539 U.S. 654 (2003).

[2] See *New York Times v. Sullivan*, 376 U.S. 254, 270 (1964).

[3] See *Kasky v. Nike, Inc.*, 27 Cal. 4th 939, 946-948, 969-70 (2002)

[4] See *Nike, Inc. v. Kasky*, 539 U.S. 654, 656-65 (2003) (Stevens, J., concurring).

[5] See *Kasky v. Nike, Inc.*, 27 Cal. 4th 939, 970 (2002); California Business & Professional Code Annotated § 17500 et seq. (West 1997).

[6] See Adam Liptak, "Nike Move Ends Case Over Firms' Free Speech," *The New York Times*, 13 September 2003, sec. A, p. 8.

[7] See, for example, Leo Bogart, "Freedom to Know or Freedom to Say?," 71 *Texas Law Review* 815 (1993); R. H. Coase, "Advertising and Free Speech," 6 *Journal of Legal Studies* 1 (1977); Michael W. Field, "On Tap, *44 Liquormart, Inc. v. Rhode Island*: Last Call For The Commercial Speech Doctrine," 2 *Roger Williams University Law Review* 57 (1996); Daniel Halberstam, "Commercial Speech, Professional Speech, and the Constitutional Status of Social Institutions," 147 *University of Pennsylvania Law Review* 771 (1999); Alex Kozinski & Stuart Banner, "The Anti-History and Pre-History of Commercial Speech," 71 *Texas Law Review* 747 (1993); Alex Kozinski & Stuart Banner, "Who's Afraid of Commercial Speech," 76 *Virginia Law Review* 627 (1990); Martin H. Redish, "First Amendment Theory and the Demise of the Commercial Speech Distinction: The Case of the Smoking Controversy," 24 *Northern Kentucky University Law Review* 553 (1997); Martin H. Redish, "The Value of Free Speech," 130 *University of Pennsylvania Law Review* 591, 630-35 (1982); Rodney A. Smolla, "Information, Imagery, and the First Amendment: A Case for Expansive Protection of Commercial Speech," 71 *Texas Law Review* 777 (1993); Kathleen M. Sullivan, "Cheap Spirits, Cigarettes, and Free Speech: The Implications of *44 Liquormart*," 1996 *Supreme Court Review* 123 (1996); Brian J. Waters, "A Doctrine in Disarray: Why the First Amendment Demands the Abandonment of the *Central Hudson* Test for Commercial Speech," 27 *Seton Hall Law Review* 1626 (1997).

[8] See, for example, C. Edwin Baker, "Commercial Speech: A Problem in the Theory of Freedom, 62 *Iowa Law Review* 1 (1976); C. Edwin Baker, "Realizing Self-Realization: Corporate Political Expenditures and Redish's 'The Value of Free Speech,' " 130 *University of Pennsylvania Law Review* 646 (1982); Vincent Blasi, "The Pathological Perspective and the First Amendment, 85 Columbia Law Review" 449 (1985); Lillian R. BeVier, "The First Amendment and Political Speech: An Inquiry into the Substance and Limits of Principle," 30 *Stanford Law Review* 299 (1978); Ronald K.L. Collins and David M. Skover, "Commerce and Communication," 71 *Texas Law Review* 697 (1993); Ronald K.L. Collins and David M. Skover, "The Psychology of First Amendment Scholarship: A Reply," 71 *Texas Law Review* 819 (1993);

Thomas H. Jackson and John Calvin Jeffries, Jr., "Commercial Speech: Economic Due Process and the First Amendment," 65 *Virginia Law Review* 1 (1979); Sut Jhally, "Commercial Culture, Collective Values, and the Future," 71 *Texas Law Review* 805, 809 (1993); Bruce Ledewitz, "Corporate Advertising's Democracy," 12 *Boston University Public Interest Law Journal* 389 (2003); R. Moon, "Lifestyle Advertising and Classical Freedom of Expression Doctrine," 36 *McGill Law Journal* 76 (1991); Tamara R. Piety, " 'Merchants of Discontent': An Exploration of the Psychology of Advertising, Addiction, and the Implications for Commercial Speech," 25 *Seattle University Law Review* 377 (2001); Robert Post, "The Constitutional Status of Commercial Speech," 48 *UCLA Law Review* 1 (2000).

[9] See, for example, Ronald A. Cass, "Commercial Speech, Constitutionalism, Collective Choice," 56 *University of Cincinnati Law Review* 1317 (1988); Edward J. Eberle, "Practical Reason: The Commercial Speech Paradigm," 42 *Case Western Reserve Law Review* 411 (1992); Daniel Hays Lowenstein, " 'Too Much Puff': Persuasion, Paternalism, and Commercial Speech," 56 *University of Cincinnati Law Review* 1205 (1988); Frederick Schauer, "Categories and the First Amendment: A Play in Three Acts," 34 *Vanderbilt Law Review* 265 (1981); Frederick Schauer, "Commercial Speech and the Architecture of the First Amendment," 56 *University of Cincinnati Law Review* 1181 (1988); Steven Shiffrin, "The First Amendment and Economic Regulation: Away from a General Theory of the First Amendment," 78 *Northwestern University Law Review* 1212 (1983); Nat Stern, "In Defense of the Imprecise Definition of Commercial Speech," 58 *Maryland Law Review* 55 (1999).

[10] See Tamara R. Piety, "Grounding Nike: Exposing Nike's Quest for a Constitutional Right to Lie," 78 *Temple Law Review* 151 (2005); Samuel A.Terilli, "*Nike v. Kasky* and the Running-But-Going-Nowhere Commercial Speech Debate," 10 *Communication Law & Policy* 383 (2005); Ronald K.L. Collins and David M. Skover, "The Landmark Free-Speech Case That Wasn't: The *Nike v. Kasky* Story," 54 *Case Western Reserve Law Review* 965 (2004); David C. Vladeck, "Lessons from a Story Untold: *Nike v. Kasky* Reconsidered," 54 *Case Western Reserve Law Review* 1049 (2004); C. Edwin Baker, "Paternalism, Politics, and Citizen Freedom: The Commercial Speech Quandary in *Nike*," 54 *Case Western Reserve Law Review* 1161 (2004); Deborah J. La Fetra, "Kick It Up a Notch: First Amendment Protection for Commercial Speech," 54 *Case Western Reserve Law Review* 1205 (2004); Rodney A. Smolla, "Free the Fortune 500! The Debate Over Corporate Speech and the First Amendment," 54 *Case Western Reserve Law Review* 1277 (2004); J. Wesley Earnhardt, "*Nike, Inc. v. Kasky*: A Golden Opportunity to Define Commercial Speech — Why Wouldn't the Supreme Court Finally 'Just Do It™'?," 82 *North Carolina Law Review* 797 (2004); Victoria Dizik Teremenko,

"Corporate Speech Under Fire: Has Nike Finally Done It?," 2 *DePaul Business & Communication Law Journal* 207 (2003); Michelle Dobrusin, "Crass Commercialism: Is it Public Debate or Sheer Profit? The Controversy of *Kasky v. Nike*," 24 *Whittier Law Review* 1139 (2003); Amber McGovern, "*Kasky v. Nike, Inc.*: A Reconsideration of the Commercial Speech Doctrine," 12 *Depaul-LCA Journal of Art & Entertainment Law* 333 (2002).

[11] See McGovern, "*Kasky v. Nike, Inc.*: A Reconsideration of the Commercial Speech Doctrine," 346.

[12] See Dobrusin, "Crass Commercialism: Is it Public Debate or Sheer Profit? The Controversy of *Kasky v. Nike*," 1166.

[13] See Teremenko, "Corporate Speech Under Fire: Has Nike Finally Done It?," 244.

[14] See Earnhardt, "*Nike, Inc. v. Kasky*: A Golden Opportunity to Define Commercial Speech — Why Wouldn't the Supreme Court Finally 'Just Do It™'?," 807.

[15] See Piety, "Grounding Nike: Exposing Nike's Quest for a Constitutional Right to Lie," 157.

[16] Nike argued, for example, that rather than addressing the larger issues of the case, the courts should reject such a suit being brought by a private citizen without establishing the suffering of actual injury. See Brief for Appellant, 20, 47-50, *Nike, Inc. v. Kasky*, 539 U.S. 654 (2003). Yet to reject such cases on that basis would require reconsidering the entire body of commercial-speech case law since *Virginia Pharmacy*, the foundation case of current commercial speech doctrine. For none of the plaintiffs in that landmark case, which established constitutional protection for purely commercial advertising, had themselves suffered any injury — as Justice William Rehnquist pointed out at the time. The regulation in question barred pharmacists from advertising the prices of prescription drugs, but it placed no such restrictions on the consumer group that brought the suit. Nothing in the regulation would have prevented the group from "collecting and publishing comparative price information as to various pharmacies in an area. Indeed they have done as much in their briefs in this case," Rehnquist wrote. "Yet . . . the Court finds that they have standing to protest that pharmacists are not allowed to advertise. . . . Here, the only group truly restricted by this statute, the pharmacists, have not even troubled to join in this litigation and may well feel that the expense and competition of advertising is not in their interest." See *Virginia State Board of Pharmacy v. Virginia Citizens Consumer Council*, 425 U.S. 748, 781-84 (1976) (Rehnquist, J., dissenting). Further, questioning in oral arguments before the U.S. Supreme Court in the *Nike* case seemed to suggest some skepticism on that point, with the question arising as to whether a plaintiff like Kasky could establish actual injury simply by showing he had purchased a pair of Nike shoes that he wouldn't have purchased if he had not been misled by the allegedly deceptive

advertising in question. See Oral Arguments, 12-15, 21-28, *Nike, Inc. v. Kasky*, 539 U.S. 654 (2003).

[17] See *Bolger v. Youngs Drug Products*, 463 U.S. 60, 67-68 (1983) (quoting *Central Hudson Gas and Electric Corp. v. Public Service Commission,* 447 U.S. 557, 563 (1980)).

[18] *Kasky v. Nike, Inc.*, 27 Cal. 4th 939, 960-64 (2002).

[19] See *New York Times Co. v. Sullivan*, 376 U.S. 254, 256-258 (1964).

[20] For example, although students had demonstrated on the State Capitol steps, they sang the National Anthem and not "My Country, 'Tis of Thee" as stated in the ad. Although nine students had been expelled by the State Board of Education, it was for demanding service at a lunch counter in the Montgomery County Courthouse, not for leading the demonstration at the Capitol. Most of the student body — though not all, as the ad stated – had protested the expulsion by boycotting classes for one day, rather than by refusing to register for school at Alabama State College in Montgomery. The college dining hall was never padlocked, as the text had stated, and only a few students were barred from eating there, those for failing to have completed appropriate applications or requested temporary meal tickets. Although large numbers of police were deployed near the campus on three occasions, they did not go so far as to literally "ring" the campus. Dr. Martin Luther King, Jr., leader of the movement, had not been arrested seven times, but only four; and an alleged assault on him during one arrest had been disputed by one of the officers involved. See *New York Times Co. v. Sullivan*, 258-59.

[21] See *New York Times Co. v. Sullivan*, 267.

[22] See *New York Times Co. v. Sullivan*, 279-80.

[23] See *Valentine v. Chrestensen*, 316 U.S. 52, 54 (1942); *New York Times Co. v. Sullivan*, 265-66 (italics added for emphasis).

[24] See *Bolger v. Youngs Drug Products Corp.*, 64-68; *Kasky v. Nike, Inc.*, 27 Cal. 4th 939, 960-65 (2002).

[25] See *New York Times Co. v. Sullivan*, 266, 273-77, 282.

[26] See Brief for Appellant, 2, 26, *Nike, Inc. v. Kasky*, 539 U.S. 654 (2003).

[27] See *New York Times Co. v. Sullivan*, 264, 268.

[28] See *New York Times Co. v. Sullivan*, 270, 272, 281 (quoting *Sweeney v. Patterson*, 128 F.2d 457, 458 (D.C. Cir. 1942) and citing *Coleman v. MacLennan*, 78 Kan. 711, 723 (1908)). The Kansas official, who was also a member of a commission that managed and controlled the state school fund, sued a newspaper for criticism relating to his official conduct involving a school-fund transaction.

[29] See *New York Times Co. v. Sullivan*, 286-88.

[30] See *New York Times Co. v. Sullivan*, 269 (quoting *Roth v. United States*, 354 U.S. 476, 484 (1957)).

[31] See *New York Times Co. v. Sullivan*, 266.

[32] See Jeremy J. Ofseyer, "First Amendment Law: Taking Liberties with John Stuart Mill," 1999 *Annual Survey of American Law* 395, 422-26 (1999), for a discussion of the way recent libertarian discourse blurs the distinction between preventing government from presuming an opinion's falsity and the regulation of proven falsity, particularly in addressing fraud: "In contrast to its effects in public discussion, falsity in other contexts, such as commercial fraud, causes pecuniary harm that is direct and tangible. Such pecuniary harm typically involves facts, such as the actual ingredients of a merchant's goods, that the speaker knows or should know are misrepresented. In addition, in commercial contexts subject to duties of honesty and fair dealing, it is easier to prove bad faith."

[33] See *Valentine v. Chrestensen*, 55. This case not only represents the Court's first statement on commercial speech, but the facts involved highlight the deep roots of efforts by commercial speakers to attach commercial speech to statements on public issues. The case involved a promoter who owned a submarine previously belonging to the U.S. Navy and which he wanted to exhibit from a New York pier. When F.J. Chrestensen attempted to distribute a handbill advertising tours of the craft, police informed him that such distribution of commercial and business advertising matter on New York City streets would be in violation of a city anti-littering measure. After Chrestensen printed a message of protest on the back of his handbills and was told the handbills still violated the city ordinance, he challenged the matter in court, leading to the Supreme Court's first pronouncement on First Amendment protection for commercial advertising.

[34] This relatively brief case analysis focuses particularly upon the Supreme Court's First Amendment holdings and rationale concerning falsity in advertising. Numerous articles discuss more broadly the development of the commercial speech doctrine. See, for example, Soontae An, "From a Business Pursuit to a Means of Expression: The Supreme Court's Disputes Over Commercial Speech from 1942 to 1976," 8 *Communication Law & Policy* 201 (2003); Sean P. Costello, "Strange Brew: The State of Commercial Speech Jurisprudence Before and After *44 Liquormart, Inc. v. Rhode Island*," 47 *Case Western Reserve Law Review* 681 (1997); Michael Feldman, "Survey of the Literature: Commercial Speech and Commercial Speakers," 2 *Cardozo Law Review* 659 (1981); Arlen W. Langvardt, "The Incremental Strengthening of First Amendment Protection for Commercial Speech: Lessons from *Greater New Orleans Broadcasting*," 37 *American Business Law Journal* 587 (2000); Mary B. Nutt, "Trends in First Amendment Protection of Commercial Speech," 41 *Vanderbilt Law Review* 173 (1988); Peter J. Tarsney, "Regulation of

Environmental Marketing: Reassessing the Supreme Court's Protection of Commercial Speech," 69 *Notre Dame Law Review* 533 (1994).

[35] See *Pittsburgh Press Co. v. Pittsburgh Commission on Human Relations*, 413 U.S. 376 (1973); *Bigelow v. Virginia*, 421 U.S. 809 (1975).

[36] See *Virginia State Board of Pharmacy v. Virginia Citizens Consumer Council*, 762, 765, 770.

[37] See *Virginia State Board of Pharmacy v. Virginia Citizens Consumer Council*, 776-78 (Stewart, J., concurring) (italics added for emphasis).

[38] See *Ohralik v. Ohio State Bar Association*, 436 U.S. 447, 456 (1978). A year before that, in another case involving regulation of advertising by attorneys, the Court ruled that the First Amendment barred a *total* ban on such advertising, but emphasized why untruthful commercial speech in the same context remained completely subject to regulation: "We, of course, do not hold that advertising by attorneys may not be regulated in any way. . . . Advertising that is false, deceptive, or misleading of course is subject to restraint. Since the advertiser knows his product and has a commercial interest in its dissemination, we have little worry that regulation to assure truthfulness will discourage protected speech. . . . Indeed, the public and private benefits from commercial speech derive from confidence in its accuracy and reliability. Thus, the leeway for untruthful or misleading expression that has been allowed in other contexts has little force in the commercial arena." See *Bates v. State Bar of Arizona*, 433 U.S. 350, 383 (1977).

[39] See *Central Hudson Gas and Electric. v. Public Service Commission*, 563-66. The Court articulated its four-part test in this manner: "At the outset, we must determine whether the expression is protected by the First Amendment. For commercial speech to come within that provision, it at least must concern lawful activity and not be misleading. Next, we ask whether the asserted governmental interest is substantial. If both inquiries yield positive answers, we must determine whether the regulation directly advances the governmental interest asserted, and whether it is not more extensive than is necessary to serve that interest." The ruling struck down a state ban on advertising that promoted use of electricity after determining that the ban failed the fourth prong of the test.

[40] See *Metromedia, Inc. v. City of San Diego,* 453 U.S. 490, 503-17 (1981).

[41] See *Bolger v. Youngs Drug Products Corp.*, 62-68 (quoting *Central Hudson Gas and Electric. v. Public Service Commission*, 563).

[42] See *Edenfield v. Fane*, 507 U.S. 761, 765-73 (1993); *United States v. Edge Broadcasting*, 509 U.S. 418, 426-35 (1993). See also *Cincinnati v. Discovery Network*, 507 U.S. 410 (1993), in which the Court ruled the government had failed to show how a ban on commercial news racks (that

exempted noncommercial news racks) on city streets served its interest in maintaining esthetics.

[43] See *Rubin v. Coors*, 514 U.S. 476 (1995); *44 Liquormart v. Rhode Island*, 517 U.S. 484, (1996).

[44] See *Lorillard Tobacco v. Reilly*, 533 U.S. 525, 554-67 (2001); *Greater New Orleans Broadcasting v. United States*, 527 U.S. 173, 184 (1999). In *Greater New Orleans Broadcasting* the Court ruled unconstitutional federal regulations that prohibited advertisements for casino gambling that were broadcast by stations located in states where such gambling was legal. Scholarly articles assessing the Court's recent consideration of its *Central Hudson* test more fully include Elizabeth Blanks Hindman, "The Chickens Have Come Home to Roost: Individualism, Collectivism and Conflict in Commercial Speech Doctrine," 9 *Communication Law & Policy* 237 (2004); Susan Dente Ross, "Reconstructing First Amendment Doctrine: The 1990s Revolution of the *Central Hudson* and *O'Brien* Tests," 23 *Hastings Communication & Entertainment Law Journal* 723 (2001); Brian J. Waters, "A Doctrine in Disarray: Why the First Amendment Demands the Abandonment of the *Central Hudson* Test for Commercial Speech," 27 *Seton Hall Law Review* 1626 (1997).

[45] See *Lorillard Tobacco v. Reilly*, 564.

[46] See *Lorillard Tobacco v. Reilly*, 572 (Thomas, J., concurring).

[47] Scholarly articles assessing more fully the Court's developing doctrine that limits government's right to restrict non-misleading commercial communication about lawful products and services include Timothy R. Mortimer, "*44 Liquormart, Inc. v. Rhode Island*: A Toast to the First Amendment," 32 *New England Law Review* 1049 (1998); Michael Hoefges and Milagros Rivera-Sanchez, " 'Vice' Advertising under the Supreme Court's Commercial Speech Doctrine: The Shifting Central Hudson Analysis," 22 *Hastings Communication & Entertainment Law Journal* 345 (2000); Nicholas P. Consula, "The First Amendment, Gaming Advertisements, and Congressional Inconsistency: The Future of the Commercial Speech Doctrine after *Greater New Orleans Broadcasting Association v. United States*," 28 *Pepperdine Law Review* 353 (2001); Michael Hoefges, "Protecting Tobacco Advertising Under the Commercial Speech Doctrine: The Constitutional Impact of *Lorillard Tobacco Co.*," 8 *Communication Law & Policy* 267 (2003).

[48] See *Kasky v. Nike, Inc.*, 27 Cal. 4th 939, 967 (2002).

[49] See *Kasky v. Nike, Inc.*, 27 Cal. 4th 939, 960-67 (2002) (quoting *Bolger v. Youngs Drug Products Corp.*, 68; and *Board of Trustees, State University of New York v. Fox*, 492 U.S. 469, 474 (1989)).

[50] See *Kasky v. Nike, Inc.*, 27 Cal. 4th 939, 963-64 (2002) (quoting *Virginia State Board of Pharmacy v. Virginia Citizens Consumer Council*, 425 U.S. 748, 772 (1976)).

[51] See *Nike, Inc. v. Kasky*, 539 U.S. 654, 656-65, 665-84 (2003) (Stevens, J., concurring) (2003) (Breyer, J., dissenting); Adam Liptak, "Nike Move Ends Case Over Firms' Free Speech," *The New York Times*, 13 September 2003, sec. A, p. 8.

[52] See *Virginia State Board of Pharmacy v. Virginia Citizens Consumer Council*, 771-72; Teremenko, "Corporate Speech Under Fire: Has Nike Finally Done It?," 244; California Business & Professional Code Annotated § 17500 et seq. (West 1997).

[53] See *New York Times v. Sullivan*, 266.

[54] See *Kasky v. Nike, Inc.*, 27 Cal. 4th 939, 962 (2002); *Virginia State Board of Pharmacy v. Virginia Citizens Consumer Council*, 776-77 (Stewart, J., concurring).

CHAPTER ELEVEN

An Age Still in Spin

We live in times in which far too much public discourse consists of instant analysis pronounced with unwavering certainty. That is particularly true in such venues as talk radio, the blogosphere, and far too much of broadcast and cable television. In those ever more dominant spheres it is possible — indeed virtually required — to maintain the posture that absolutes are easy to come by. To pretend that finality is the rule in the body of human knowledge, rather than the exception. The electronic blitz feeds our understandable impulse to believe that we — or at least *someone* — can spell out precisely what is happening in our world at any given time. And do so in a relatively few and unambiguous words.

But Justice Holmes launched America's great age of free speech on precisely the opposite proposition. "Every year if not every day we have to wager our salvation upon some prophecy based upon imperfect knowledge," he said — in the same breath that he articulated his marketplace-of-ideas concept, which would prove more influential than any other in First Amendment Law. He grounded that concept in a couple of humbling but historically enduring verities: Human beings seldom possess more than imperfect knowledge. And the passing of time tends to discredit the "fighting faiths" that drive our certitudes of the moment.[1]

The preceding chapters offer much evidence in support of the argument that a watershed change took place in the marketplace of ideas over roughly the final quarter of the twentieth century. They also argue that the change shifted American political culture and society in ways that were in many respects more feudal than democratic. Nevertheless, that body of evidence and argument remains subject to the mortal limitations that Justice Holmes articulated so tellingly. Though this book is the product of years of research and reflection, its author believes that all historians and philosophers do best to acknowledge Hegel's reminder that "the owl of Minerva spreads its wings only with the falling of the dusk." The influential nineteenth-century philosopher's pronouncement on the difficulty of truly knowing the meaning of an age, while it is still in progress, remains a caution for any who would honestly seek to explain their times.[2]

How much longer the age of cognitive feudalism may have before dusk falls upon it is, at this writing, something yet to be known. The central argument here is that governmental advantaging of corporate political media spending in the marketplace of ideas is the most significant variable in the matter. So the direction of the Supreme Court in its First Amendment jurisprudence will be crucial. Given the ongoing agenda of the corporate free-speech movement and the changing makeup of the justices on the Court, it may be only a matter of time before full First Amendment rights are extended to corporate political media spending. For government to so fully advantage the corporate profit imperative in the marketplace of ideas would mean the end of the latter as a truly free market, this analysis argues. It would represent a fundamental undermining of the sovereignty of the people, advancing the feudalization of American democracy exponentially.

But a society can move in many ways as time goes by. Certainly other variables, other trends, other events may well also come into play significantly in the years ahead. At this very moment, competing forces of consequence may be taking shape, and change may be under way that is not yet recognizable. Just as it was not widely apparent in the 1970s that the corporate free-speech movement was about to coalesce with such sweeping impact, so too is our current view of what comes next an imperfect one. At least, we do not know with certainty what events now in play will mean until after they unfold more fully. The most ardently held fighting faiths of this day may or may not ultimately have much to do with which seeds will take root and flourish, which ideas will prevail and shape the course of human history.

Those qualifying comments are not intended as a hedge on the larger thesis of this book. Rather they represent an effort to conclude this volume on a note of dynamism, rather than the illusion of finality. With the historical era examined on these pages still in spin, the remainder of this chapter will briefly take note of a sampling of trends that could potentially alter the course of the age of cognitive feudalism. Indeed, the degree to which the following ideas — and others — get a viable hearing in the years ahead will in itself help show us how much freedom remains in the marketplace of ideas.

A FEW OF THE POSSIBILITIES

One current school of thought holds that just as history has over time diminished the influence of other dominant institutions — such as the church, the monarchy, any number of empires — so too will that eventually be the fate of the business corporation as we know it today. Activist attorney Joel Balkan has articulated that line of reasoning at some length. He contends that just as governments grant corporations essential rights such as corporate personhood and limited liability, "governments can pursue social values — such as democracy, social justice, citizens' health and welfare, environmental integrity, cultural identity — that lie beyond the narrow goals of self interest and wealth maximization that dictate the behavior of corporations and markets." He argues that more people are reaching the conclusion that the corporation as the dominant institution of our age "has failed to solve, and indeed has worsened, some of the world's most pressing problems: poverty, war, environmental destruction, ill health." As a result, he writes, "growing numbers of people — activists, Main Street Americans, the globe's poor and disenfranchised, and even business leaders — believe that rationalized greed and mandated selfishness must give way to more human values." Ultimately, Balkan grounds his optimism in human nature: "Though individualistic self-interest and consumer desires are core parts of who we are and nothing to be ashamed of, they are not all of who we are."[3]

There are those involved in a variety of reform efforts who argue that it is the unprecedented corporate excesses of recent years that will drive change, including further campaign-finance reform and renewed support for corporate regulation. Mark Green, a veteran of legal and political activism in public-interest causes, for example, points to the Bipartisan Campaign Reform Act and the Sarbanes-Oxley Corporate Accountability Act, both enacted in 2002. He sees such legislation as the beginning of a potential shift driven by public outrage over corporate scandals of the early 2000s such as those at Enron, Adelphia, Global Crossing, Tyco, and WorldCom, etc. Indeed, even the threat of impending government regulation may motivate changes in individual corporate behavior. After a major government-commissioned study concluded that advertising contributes significantly to childhood obesity and bills were launched in Congress to regulate advertising aimed at children, for example, Kraft Foods announced in 2005 that it would halt the advertising of many of its products to children under 12, and other corporate players in the food industry have reported plans for similar measures. A number of Fortune 500 companies have begun to express support for action addressing global warming, in part to avoid having regulation imposed without their input.[4]

Much commentary contends that there are even broader signs of an emerging movement dedicated to reconstructing the corporation in fundamental ways. Entrepreneur Ted Nace compares the effort to the way the American Revolution reengineered government: "Just as it was necessary to innovate and implement specific new features in order to democratize and constrain state power, the same applies to corporate power." He proposes a multi-faceted effort that over time would return the corporation to the legally restrained status maintained roughly through America's first century — not in an anti-capitalist fervor, but in the way society would constrain the destructive potential of any runaway technology. In the same spirit, economist David Korten articulates his vision of an evolving movement to reform the corporation in the way that earlier generations reformed the monarchy. He writes that he approaches the issue from the perspective of "a traditional conservative in the sense that I retain a deep distrust of large institutions and their concentrations of unaccountable power."[5]

There are some signs that such a movement may be gaining traction. For example, the events that led to the Supreme Court case discussed in Chapter Ten were by no means the only public effort to address working conditions in Nike's factories. The issue generated waves of media reports, letters of protest to the company, Web sites, demonstrations, and boycotts. A similar process seems to be playing out in relation to other corporate giants, particularly ExxonMobil and Wal-Mart. After a six-year struggle, a small farm-worker organization in 2005 succeeded in its campaign to persuade Yum Brands, the world's largest fast-food company (operator of Taco Bell, Pizza Hut, and others) to help enforce humane working conditions among growers and to pay slightly more for tomatoes so the workers who picked them could earn a living wage. McDonald's has since entered into a similar accord. In 2006, the World Wildlife Fund completed an agreement with a Singapore corporation known for clear-cutting trees in tropical rainforests to preserve one of the last large stands of natural forest in Indonesia. *The Wall Street Journal* called it part of a trend in which "more multinational corporations have shifted from warring with environmentalist groups to negotiating agreements with them."[6]

On another front, some evangelical leaders have begun to question whether their loyalty to the dominant political culture of recent decades is in fact advancing their values. The Rev. Jim Ball of the Evangelical Environmental Network, has gone so far as to motor a hybrid vehicle cross-country while preaching a "What Would Jesus Drive?" campaign. He and other prominent leaders of large organizations of evangelicals have urged action to combat global warming as a cause of poverty and a failure to maintain stewardship of God's creation. A movement some have called "Eco-Christianity" or "Green Religion" seeks to promote efforts to stop environmental destruction. Columnist David Brooks has argued that the only two key constituencies whose joint effort could fundamentally address poverty today would be socially conservative evangelicals and socially liberal nongovernmental organizations. The Network of Spiritual Progressives, which rejects being labeled either liberal or conservative, petitioned Congress in 2006 to consider its Spiritual Covenant With America. The Covenant includes a Social Responsibility Amendment that would require review of corporate charters every ten years for demonstration of social responsibility.[7]

In mainstream politics, recent years have begun to produce relatively more frequent examples of discourse that challenges the ideology of the corporate citizen as it has been constituted in recent decades. One of the most compelling examples has been central to the way recently elected New York Governor Eliot Spitzer has framed his political agenda on establishing "a capital market system based on integrity." Though his prosecutions of corporate fraud while New York State Attorney General were criticized sharply by powerful business voices, he has repeatedly argued in speeches across the country that it is good business to enforce basic business rules on fiduciary duty, transparency, accountability, and fair play. By freeing honest corporations from competing with those that gain advantages through wrongdoing, preventing misallocation of capital in companies that misrepresent their profits, maintaining investor confidence, and forcing lawbreaking companies to reform, Spitzer has argued, enforced regulation can advance "full, fair . . . true competition to the markets." Other efforts to articulate competing visions to the ideology of the corporate citizen and the diminished role it has meant for human citizens have focused on framing the American story as one in which the people have advanced multiple values through the democratic process. "Our economic dominance has depended on individual initiative and belief in the free market," Illinois Senator and presidential aspirant Barack Obama has told audiences. "But it has also depended on our sense of mutual regard for each other — the idea that everybody has a stake in the country. That we're all in it together and everybody's got a shot at opportunity. That's what's produced our unrivaled political stability."[8]

Spitzer and Obama are of course ambitious politicians, who may or may not ultimately find such visions expansively embraced by voters, and who may or may not significantly advance legislation that translates such principles into action. And of course the other trends noted in this chapter may also realize wider success in the years to come, or they may fade. Even between the time these words are written and the time this book comes off the presses, matters potentially will have evolved in one way or another. At this moment for example, in late 2007, the previous year's shift in political fortunes in the U.S. Congress may have signaled the beginning of significant societal change, or it may mean little beyond momentary partisan gain.[9] The point is that any one election is unlikely to alter the larger trends detailed in this study. For that to happen will require the ongoing advancement of many developments along the lines highlighted in this chapter.

LET A *TRULY* FREE MARKETPLACE DECIDE

So these last few lines are not an attempt to actually predict what impact any of that will have on the course of the American future. What *can* be said here unequivocally is what this book has sought to articulate throughout. The fate of developments such as those noted in this chapter — and of countless others — depends crucially on the degree to which the marketplace of ideas is truly a free market. Such developments may represent a new direction for the nation's political culture. If the interests they represent have the opportunity to compete in a marketplace of ideas in which government does not advantage the few over the many, then we shall find out whether they can win favor among the people. They may, or they may not. But we will never know, this study argues, with a marketplace of ideas that is more feudal than free.

In the analysis presented over the course of this book, the age of cognitive feudalism has been argued to be one in which the interests of most Americans have not been advanced. Even if Americans should disagree with that assessment and are happy with the direction of recent decades, then at the least they should be able to voice that preference in a free political marketplace. American democracy has its best chance of flourishing when all ideas have a fair opportunity to compete. And when democracy governs the corporation, instead of the corporation governing democracy.

[1] See *Abrams v. United States*, 250 U.S. 616, 630 (1919) (Holmes, J., dissenting).

[2] See Georg Wilhelm Friedrich Hegel, *The Philosophy of Right*, trans. T. M. Knox (1821; reprint, Oxford: Clarendon Press, 1942), 13.

[3] See Joel Balkan, *The Corporation: The Pathological Pursuit of Profit and Power* (New York: Free Press, 2004), 140-167.

[4] See Mark Green, *Selling Out: How Big Corporate Money Buys Elections, Rams Through Legislation, and Betrays Our Democracy* (New York: Harper Collins, 2002), 8-25; Sarah Ellison, "Why Kraft Decided to Ban Some Food Ads to Children," *The Wall Street Journal*, 31 October 2005, sec. A, p. 1; Miguel Bustillo, "A Shift to Green," *Los Angeles Times*, 12 June 2005, sec. C, p. 1; Stephanie Strom, "Businesses Try to Make Money and Save the World," *The New York Times*, 6 May 2007, sec. BU, p. 1.

[5] See Ted Nace, *Gangs of America: The Rise of Corporate Power and the Disabling of Democracy* (San Francisco: Berrett-Koehler, 2003), 197-228; David C. Korten, *When Corporations Rule the World*, 2ed. (Bloomfield, Conn.: Kumarian Press, 2001), 3-20.

[6] See Naomi Klein, *No Logo* (New York: Picador, 1999), 365-79; Felicity Barringer, "Environmental Groups Planning To Urge Boycott of Exxon Mobil," *The New York Times*, 12 July 2005, sec. A, p. 14; David Staba, "A Message Aimed at Big Oil, or Pain for the Little Guy?" *The New York Times*, 7 May 2006, sec. A, p. 39; Dan Mitchell, "The Campaign Against Wal-Mart," *The New York Times*, 6 August 2005, sec. C, p. 5; Transcript, *NOW*, 27 May 2005, accessed 22 July 2005 at: http://www.pbs.org/now/transcript/transcriptN OW121_full.html; "McDonald's to Pay Tomato Farmers More," *The Wall Street Journal*, 10 April 2007, sec. A, p. 9; Steve Stecklow, "Paper Mates: Environmentalists, Loggers Near Deal On Asian Rainforest," *The Wall Street Journal*, 23 February 2006, sec. A, p. 1.

[7] See "Our Commitment to Jesus Christ Compels Us to Solve the Global Warming Crisis," Advertisement, *The New York Times*, 9 February 2006, sec. A, p. 11; Laurie Goodstein, "86 Evangelical Leaders Join to Fight Global Warming," *The New York Times*, 8 February 2006, sec. A, p. 10; Laurie Goodstein, "Evangelical Leaders Swing Influence Behind Effort to Combat Global Warming," *The New York Times*, 10 March 2005, sec. A, p. 16; "A Shepherd Protects His Own Backyard," *Newsweek*, 29 August/5 September 2005, p. 51; David Brooks, "A Natural Alliance," *The New York Times*, 26 May 2005, sec. A, p. 29; "A Spiritual Covenant with America," The Network of Spiritual Progressives, accessed 24 May 2006 at: http://www.spiritualprogressi ves.org/rabbi_lerner/news_item.2006-05-15.7487741783.

[8] See Don Mecoy, "Law & Order: New York AG Brings His Message to City," *The Oklahoman*, 13 January 2005, sec. B, p. 1; Eliot Spitzer, "Strong

Law Enforcement is Good for the Economy," *The Wall Street Journal*, 5 March 2005, sec. A, p. 18; "Remarks of U.S. Senator Barack Obama at the Knox College Commencement," Galesburg, Illinois, 4 June 2005, accessed 12 February 2006 at: http://obama.senate.gov/speech/050604-remarks_of_us_senator_barack_obama_at_the_knox_college_commencement/.

[9] For discussion of the way such questions concerning the actual meaning of the 2006 elections began to be raised virtually as soon as the votes were counted, see Robin Toner and Kate Zernike, "For Incoming Democrats, Populism Trumps Ideology," *The New York Times*, 12 November 2006, sec. A, p. 1; David D. Kirkpatrick, "As Power Shifts in New Congress, Pork May Linger," *The New York Times*, 26 November 2006, sec. A, p. 1; Robert Pear, "Time to Party in the Capital. Just Bring the Checkbook," *The New York Times*, 8 December 2006, sec. A, p. 26 (in which one powerful lobbyist predicted confidently, "There will be some changes on the margins that will be relatively short-lived.").

References

Abrams v. United States. 250 U.S. 616 (1919).

Akard, Patrick J. "Corporate Mobilization and Political Power: The Transformation of U.S. Economic Policy in the 1970s." *American Sociological Review* 57:5 (October 1992): 597-615.

Anderson, Annelise, and Martin Anderson, eds. *Reagan in His Own Hand: The Writings of Ronald Reagan That Reveal His Revolutionary Vision for America*. New York: Free Press, 2001.

Aune, James Arnt. *Selling the Free Market: The Rhetoric of Economic Correctness*. New York: Guilford, 2001.

Austin v. Michigan State Chamber of Commerce. 494 U.S. 652 (1990).

Backman, Clifford R. *The Worlds of Medieval Europe*. New York: Oxford University Press, 2003.

Bagdikian, Ben H. *The New Media Monopoly*. Boston: Beacon Press, 2004.

Baker, C. Edwin. "Paternalism, Politics, and Citizen Freedom: The Commercial Speech Quandary in *Nike*." 54 *Case Western Reserve Law Review* 1161 (2004).

_____. *Human Liberty and Freedom of Expression*. New York: Oxford University Press, 1989.

Balkan, Joel. *The Corporation: The Pathological Pursuit of Profit and Power*. New York: Free Press, 2004.

Barkin, Steve M. *American Television News: The Media Marketplace and the Public Interest*. Armonk, N.Y.: M.E. Sharpe, 2003.

Barlow, Frank. *The Feudal Kingdom of England, 1042-1216*, 5th ed. New York: Addison Wesley Longman, 1999.

Bassiry, G.R., and Marc Jones. "Adam Smith and the Ethics of Contemporary Capitalism." *Journal of Business Ethics* 12, no. 8 (August 1993).

Bates v. State Bar of Arizona. 433 U.S. 350 (1977).

Beatty, Jack, ed. Colossus: *How the Corporation Changed America*. New York: Broadway, 2001.

Bello, Walden, with Shea Cunningham and Bill Rau. *Dark Victory: The United States, Structural Adjustment, and Global Poverty* Oakland, Calif.: Institute for Food and Development Policy, 1994.

Bergsten, C., et al. *China: The Balance Sheet.* Hoboken, N.J.: Public Affairs, 2006.

Bernays, Edward L. *Crystallizing Public Opinion*. New York: Liveright, 1923.

_____. *Propaganda*. New York: Liveright, 1928.

_____. *The Engineering of Consent.* Norman: University of Oklahoma Press, 1955.

BeVier, Lillian R. "Campaign Finance Reform: Specious Arguments, Intractable Dilemmas." 94 *Columbia Law Review* 1258 (1994).

_____. "The First Amendment and Political Speech: An Inquiry into the Substance and Limits of Principle." 30 *Stanford Law Review* 299 (1978).

Bishop, John D. "Adam Smith's Invisible Hand Argument," *Journal of Business Ethics.* 14, no. 3 (March 1995): 165.

Black, Edwin. *Internal Combustion: How Corporations and Governments Addicted the World to Oil and Derailed the Alternatives.* New York: St. Martin's Press, 2006.

Board of Trustees, State University of New York v. Fox. 492 U.S. 469 (1989).

Bok, Derek. *Universities in the Marketplace: The Commercialization of Higher Education.* Princeton, N.J.: Princeton University Press, 2003.

Bolger v. Youngs Drug Products. 463 U.S. 60 (1983).

Bollinger, Lee C. *The Tolerant Society: Freedom of Speech and Extremist Speech in America.* New York: Oxford University Press, 1986.

Bork, Robert H. "Neutral Principles and Some First Amendment Problems." 47 *Indiana Law Journal* 1 (1971).

Bowman, Scott R. *The Modern Corporation and American Political Thought*. University Park: The Pennsylvania State University Press, 1996.

Bratton, William W., Jr. "The New Economic Theory of the Firm: Critical Perspectives from History." 41 *Stanford Law Review* 1471 (1989).

Brennan, William J., Jr., "The Supreme Court and the Meiklejohnian Interpretation of the First Amendment." 79 *Harvard Law Review* 1 (1965).

Buckley v. Valeo. 424 U.S. 1 (1976).

Butler, Henry N. and Larry E. Ribstein. *The Corporation and the Constitution.* Washington, D.C.: AEI Press, 1995.

Calvert, Clay. "And You Call Yourself a Journalist? Wrestling With a Definition of 'Journalist' in the Law." 103 *Dickinson Law Review* 411 (1999).

Carter, Dan T. *From George Wallace to Newt Gingrich: Race in the Conservative Counterrevolution, 1963-1994*. Baton Rouge: Louisiana State University Press.

Central Hudson Gas & Electric Corp. v. Public Utilities Commission. 447 U.S. 557 (1980).

Cincinnati v. Discovery Network. 507 U.S. 410 (1993).

Clawson, Dan, Alan Neustadtl, and Mark Weller. *Dollars and Votes: How Business Campaign Contributions Subvert Democracy*. Philadelphia: Temple University Press, 1998.

Coates, John C., IV. "State Takeover Statutes and Corporate Theory: The Revival of an Old Debate." 64 *New York University Law Review* 806 1989.

Collins, Denis. "Adam Smith's Social Contract: The Proper Role of Individual Liberty and Government Intervention in Eighteenth Century Society." *Business and Professional Ethics Journal* 7, no. 3-4 (Fall-Winter 1988).

Collins, Ronald K.L., and David M. Skover, "The Landmark Free-Speech Case That Wasn't: The *Nike v. Kasky* Story." 54 *Case Western Reserve Law Review* 965 (2004).

Compaine, Benjamin M., and Douglas Gomery. *Who Owns the Media? Competition and Concentration in the Mass Media Industry*. Mahwah, N.J.: Lawrence Erlbaum Associates, 2000.

Conrad, Keith. "Media Mergers: First Step in a New Shift of Antitrust Analysis?" 49 *Federal Communication Law Journal* 675 (1997).

Consolidated Edison v. Public Service Commission. 447 U.S. 530 (1980).

Corak, Miles, ed. *Generational Income Mobility in North America and Europe.* Cambridge, U.K.: Cambridge University Press, 2004.

Corrado, Anthony, et al., eds. *The New Campaign Finance Sourcebook*, Washington, D.C.: Brookings Institution Press, 2005.

Cutlip, Scott M. *The Unseen Power: Public Relations, A History.* Hillsdale, N.J.: Lawrence Erlbaum, 1994.

Dartmouth College v. Woodward. 17 U.S. 518, 636 (1819.

Deffeyes, Kenneth S. *Hubbert's Peak: The Impending World Oil Shortage.* Princeton, N.J.: Princeton University Press, 2001.

Dodge v. Ford Motor Co. 204 Mich. 459 (1919).

Dobrusin, Michelle. "Crass Commercialism: Is it Public Debate or Sheer Profit? The Controversy of *Kasky v. Nike.*" 24 *Whittier Law Review* 1139 (2003).

Drucker, Peter F. "The New Meaning of Corporate Social Responsibility." *California Management Review* 26, no. 2 (Winter 1984): 62.

Earnhardt, J. Wesley. "*Nike, Inc. v. Kasky*: A Golden Opportunity to Define Commercial Speech — Why Wouldn't the Supreme Court Finally 'Just Do It™'?" 82 *North Carolina Law Review* 797 (2004).

Easley, Allen K. "Buying Back the First Amendment: Regulation of Disproportionate Corporate Spending in Ballot Issue Campaigns." 17 *Georgia Law Review* 675 (1983).

Easterbrook, Frank H., and Daniel R. Fischel. *The Economic Structure of Corporate Law.* Cambridge, Mass: Harvard University Press, 1991.

Edenfield v. Fane. 507 U.S. 761 (1993).

Edsall, Thomas Byrne. *The New Politics of Inequality.* New York: W.W. Norton, 1984.

Edwards, Chris. *Downsizing the Federal Government.* Washington, D.C.: Cato Institute, 2005.

Ehrenreich, Barbara *Nickel and Dimed: On (Not) Getting By in America.* New York: Metropolitan Books, 2001.

_____. *Fear of Falling: The Inner Life of the Middle Class.* New York: Pantheon, 1989.

Ewen, Stuart *PR! A Social History of Spin.* New York: Basic, 1996).

Falkner, Robert. *A Conservative Economist? The Political Liberalism of Adam Smith Revisited.* London: Mill Institute, 1997.

Faux, Jeff. *The Global Class War: How America's Bipartisan Elite Lost Our Future — And What It Will Take to Win it Back.* New York: John Wiley & Sons, 2006.

Federal Election Commission v. Massachusetts Citizens for Life. 479 U.S. 238 (1986).

Federal Election Commission v. National Right to Work Committee. 459 U.S. 197 (1982).

First National Bank of Boston v. Bellotti. 435 U.S. 765 (1978).

Fishman, Ted C. *China, Inc.: How the Rise of the Next Superpower Challenges America and the World.* New York: Scribner, 2005.

Fiss, Owen M. *Liberalism Divided: Freedom of Speech and the Many Uses of State Power.* Boulder, Colo.: Westview Press, 1996.

Fitzgibbons, Athol. *Adam Smith's System of Liberty, Wealth, and Virtue: The Moral and Political Foundations of "The Wealth of Nations."* New York: Oxford University Press, 1995.

Foley, Edward B. "Equal-Dollars-Per-Voter: A Constitutional Principle of Campaign Finance." 94 *Columbia Law Review* 1204 (1994).

44 Liquormart v. Rhode Island. 517 U.S. 484 (1996).

Frank, Thomas. *What's the Matter with Kansas? How Conservatives Won the Heart of America.* New York: Metropolitan Books, 2004.

_____. *One Market Under God: Extreme Capitalism, Market Populism, and the End of Economic Democracy.* New York: Doubleday, 2000.

Friedman, Kenneth S. *Myths of the Free Market.* New York: Algora, 2003.

Friedman, Milton. "The Social Responsibility of Business is to Increase its Profits." *The New York Times Magazine.* 13 September 1970.

Friedman, Thomas L. *The World is Flat: A Brief History of the Twenty-first Century.* New York: Farrar, Straus and Giroux, 2005.

Gelbspan, Ross. *Boiling Point: How Politicians, Big Oil and Coal, Journalists, and Activists are Fueling the Climate Crisis.* New York, N.Y.: Basic Books, 2004).

Giles, Allison C. "The Value of Nonlegislators' Contributions to Legislative History." 79 *Georgetown Law Journal* 359 (1990).

Ginzberg, Eli. *The House of Adam Smith* New York: Octagon, 1964.

Goodstein, David. *Out of Gas: The End of the Age of Oil.* New York: W.W. Norton & Company, 2004.

Greater New Orleans Broadcasting v. United States. 527 U.S. 173 (1999).

Green, Mark. *Selling Out: How Big Corporate Money Buys Elections, Rams Through Legislation, and Betrays Our Democracy.* New York: Harper Collins, 2002.

Greenwood, Daniel J.H. "Essential Speech: Why Corporate Speech is Not Free." 83 *Iowa Law Review* 995 (1998).

Hamilton, James T. *All the News That's Fit to Sell: How the Market Transforms Information into News.* Princeton, N.J.: Princeton University Press, 2004.

Hasen, Richard L. "Campaign Finance Laws and the Rupert Murdoch Problem." 77 *Texas Law Review* 1627 (1999).

Head, Simon. *The New Ruthless Economy: Work and Power in the Digital Age.* (New York: Oxford University Press, 2003.

Hegel, Georg Wilhelm Friedrich. *The Philosophy of Right.* trans. T. M. Knox 1821; reprint, Oxford: Clarendon Press, 1942).

Hill, John E. *Revolutionary Values for a New Millennium: John Adams, Adam Smith and Social Virtue.* Lanham, Md.: Lexington, 2000.

Herman, Edward S., and Robert W. McChesney. *The Global Media: The New Missionaries of Corporate Capitalism.* London: Cassell, 1997.

Himmelstein, Jerome L., Jr. *To the Right: The Transformation of American Conservatism.* Berkeley: University of California Press, 1990.

Hirschman, Albert O. *The Passions and the Interests: Political Arguments for Capitalism before Its Triumph.* 20th anniv. ed. Princeton: Princeton University Press, 1997.

Hopkins, W. Wat . "The Supreme Court Defines the Marketplace of Ideas." *Journalism & Mass Communication Quarterly* 73, no. 1 (Spring 1996): 40-52.

Horwitz, Morton J. "Santa Clara Revisited: The Development of Corporate Theory." 88 *West Virginia Law Review* 173 (1985.

Hurst, James Willard. *The Legitimacy of the Business Corporation in the Law of the United States, 1780-1970.* Charlottesville: University of Virginia Press, 1970.

Imfeld, Cassandra, and Victoria Smith Ekstrand. "The Music Industry and the Legislative Development of the Digital Millennium Copyright Act's Online Service Provider Provision." 10 *Communication Law and Policy* 291 (2005).

Johnston, David Cay. *Perfectly Legal: The Covert System to Rig Our Tax System to Benefit the Super Rich — and Cheat Everybody Else.* New York: Portfolio, 2003.

Kalven, Harry, Jr. "The New York Times Case: A Note on the Central Meaning of the First Amendment." *Supreme Court Review* 191 (1964).

Kaysen, Carl, ed. *The American Corporation Today.* New York: Oxford University Press, 1996.

Kerr, Robert L. "Justifying Corporate Speech Regulation Through a Town-Meeting Understanding of the Marketplace of Ideas." *Journalism & Communication Monographs* 9:2 (Summer 2007) 58-113.

_____. "Subordinating the Economic to the Political: The Evolution of the Corporate Speech Doctrine." *Communication Law and Policy* 10:1 (Winter 2005) 63-99.

_____. *The Rights of Corporate Speech: Mobil Oil and the Legal Development of the Voice of Big Business.* LFB Scholarly: New York, 2005.

_____. "Creating the Corporate Citizen: Mobil Oil's Editorial-Advocacy Campaign in *The New York Times* to Advance the Right and Practice of Corporate Political Speech, 1970-80." *American Journalism* 21:4 (Fall 2004) 39-62.

_____. "From *Sullivan* to *Nike*: Will the Noble Purpose of the Landmark Free Speech Case be Subverted to Immunize False Advertising?" *Communication Law and Policy* 9:4 (Autumn 2004) 525-566.

_____. "Is What's Good for General Motors Good for the First Amendment? Corporate Media Concentration's 'Dagger at the Throat' of the Press Clause." Chap. 13 in *Media, Profit, and Politics: Competing Priorities in an Open Society*. Thom Yantek and Joseph Harper, eds. (Kent State University Press: Kent, Ohio, 2003).

_____. "Impartial Spectator in the Marketplace of Ideas: The Principles of Adam Smith as an Ethical Basis for Regulation of Corporate Speech." *Journalism and Mass Communication Quarterly* 79:2 (Summer 2002) 394-415.

Klein, Naomi. *No Logo*. New York: Picador, 1999.

Korten, David C. *When Corporations Rule the World*, 2ed. Bloomfield, Conn.: Kumarian Press, 2001.

Krugman, Paul. *The Age of Diminished Expectations: U.S. Economic Policy in the 1990s*. 3d ed. Cambridge, Mass.: MIT Press, 1998.

Kuttner, Robert. *Everything for Sale: The Virtues and Limits of Markets*. New York: Alfred A. Knopf, 1997.

La Fetra, Deborah J. "Kick It Up a Notch: First Amendment Protection for Commercial Speech." 54 *Case Western Reserve Law Review* 1205 (2004).

Lagasee, David R. "Undue Influence: Corporate Political Speech, Power and the Initiative Process." 61 *Brooklyn Law Review* 1347 (1995).

Lamb, Robert Boyden. *Property Markets and the State in Adam Smith's System.* New York: Garland, 1987).

Lammers, Nancy, ed. *Dollar Politics*. 3d ed. Washington, D.C.: Congressional Quarterly, 1982.

Lindgren, J. Ralph. *The Social Philosophy of Adam Smith.* The Hague, Netherlands: Martinus Nijhoff, 1973.

Lipson, Morris. "Autonomy and Democracy." 104 *Yale Law Journal* 2249 (1995).

Lorillard Tobacco v. Reilly. 533 U.S. 525 (2001)

Luntz, Frank. *Words That Work: It's Not What You Say, It's What People Hear.* New York: Hyperion, 2007.

Malbin, Michael J., ed. *The Election After Reform: Money, Politics, and the Bipartisan Campaign Reform Act.* Lanham, Md.: Rowman and Littlefield, 2006.

Manning, Robert D. *Credit Card Nation: The Consequences of America's Addiction to Credit.* New York: Basic Books, 2000.

Marchand, Roland, *Creating the Corporate Soul: The Rise of Public Relations and Corporate Imagery.* Berkeley: University of California Press, 1998.

Mastro, Randy M., et al. "Taking the Initiative: Corporate Control of the Referendum Process Through Media Spending and What to Do About It." 32 *Federal Communications Law Journal* 315 (1980).

Matasar, Ann B. *Corporate PACs and Federal Campaign Financing Laws: Use or Abuse of Power.* New York: Quorum, 1986.

Mayton, William T. "Law Among the Pleonasms: The Futility and Aconstitutionality of Legislative History in Statutory Interpretation." 41 *Emory Law Journal* 113 (1992).

McChesney, Robert W. and John Nichols. *Our Media, Not Theirs: The Democratic Struggle Against Corporate Media.* New York: Seven Stories Press, 2002.

McChesney, Robert W. *Rich Media, Poor Democracy: Communication Politics in Dubious Times.* Urbana, Ill.: University of Illinois Press, 1999.

McConnell v. Federal Election Commission. 540 U.S. 93 (2003).

McCraw, Thomas K. "Business & Government: The Origins of the Adversary Relationship." *California Management Review* 26, no. 2 (Winter 1984): 33-52.

_____. *Prophets of Regulation: Charles Francis Adams, Louis D. Brandeis, James M. Landis, Alfred E. Kahn.* Cambridge: Belknap Press of Harvard University Press, 1984.

McGovern, Amber. "*Kasky v. Nike, Inc.*: A Reconsideration of the Commercial Speech Doctrine." 12 *Depaul-LCA Journal of Art & Entertainment Law* 333 (2002).

Meiklejohn, Alexander. *Political Freedom: The Constitutional Powers of the People.* Westport, Conn.: Greenwood Press, 1960.

_____. "The First Amendment is an Absolute." *Supreme Court Review* 245 (1961).

Metromedia, Inc. v. City of San Diego. 453 U.S. 490 (1981).

Millon, David. "Theories of the Corporation." 1990 *Duke Law Journal* 201 (1990.

Milton, John. *Areopagitica: A Speech of Mr. John Milton, for the Liberty of Unlicensed printing, to the Parliament of England.* (1644; reprint, London: A. Millar, 1738).

Muller, Jerry Z. *Adam Smith in His Time and Ours: Designing the Decent Society.* New York: Free Press, 1993.

Nace, Ted. *Gangs of America: The Rise of Corporate Power and the Disabling of Democracy.* San Francisco: Berrett-Koehler, 2003.

Navarro, Peter. *The Coming China Wars: Where They Will Be Fought and How They Can Be Won.* Upper Saddle River, N.J.: Financial Times Press, 2007.

Nelson, Adam R. *Education and Democracy: The Meaning of Alexander Meiklejohn, 1872-1964.* Madison: University of Wisconsin Press, 2001.

New York Times v. Sullivan. 376 U.S. 254 (1964).

Nike, Inc. v. Kasky. 539 U.S. 654 (2003).

Nimmer, David. "Appreciating Legislative History. The Sweet and Sour Spots of the DMCA's Commentary." 23 *Cardozo Law Review* 909 (2002).

Ofseyer, Jeremy J. "First Amendment Law: Taking Liberties with John Stuart Mill." 1999 *Annual Survey of American Law* 395 (1999).

Ohralik v. Ohio State Bar Association. 436 U.S. 447 (1978).

Pacific Gas & Electric Co. v. Public Utilities Commission. 475 U.S. 1 (1986).

Pascal, Roy. "Property and Society — The Scottish Historical School of the Eighteenth Century." *Modern Quarterly* 61, no. 1 (1938): 167-78.

Phillips, Kevin. *Boiling Point: Republicans, Democrats, and the Decline of Middle-Class Prosperity.* New York: Random House, 1993.

Phillips, Michael J. "Reappraising the Real Entity Theory of the Corporation." 21 *Florida State University Law Review* 1061 (1994).

Piety, Tamara R. "Grounding Nike: Exposing Nike's Quest for a Constitutional Right to Lie." 78 *Temple Law Review* 151 (2005).

Post, Robert. "Meiklejohn's Mistake: Individual Autonomy and the Reform of Public Discourse." 64 *University of Colorado Law Review* 1109 (1993).

Powe, L.A., Jr. "Boiling Blood." 77 *Texas Law Review* 1667 (1999).

Power, Richard. *Gain*. New York: Picador, 1999.

Red Lion Broadcasting v. Federal Communications Commission. 395 U.S. 367 (1969).

Redish, Martin H., and Howard M. Wasserman. "What's Good for General Motors: Corporate Speech and the Theory of Free Expression." 66 *George Washington Law Review* 235 (1998).

Reynolds, Susan. *Fiefs and Vassals: The Medieval Evidence Reinterpreted.* New York: Oxford University Press, 1994.

Ritter, Kurt, and David Henry. *Ronald Reagan: The Great Communicator*. New York: Greenwood Press, 1992.

Rosenkranz, E. Joshua, ed. *If Buckley Fell: A First Amendment Blueprint for Regulating Money in Politics*. New York: The Century Foundation Press, 1999.

Rubin v. Coors. 514 U.S. 476 (1995).

Schacter, Jane S. "The Confounding Common Law Originalism in Recent Supreme Court Statutory Interpretation: Implications for the Legislative History Debate and Beyond." 51 *Stanford Law Review* 1 (1998).

Schneider, Carl E. "Free Speech and Corporate Freedom: A Comment on *First National Bank of Boston v. Bellotti*." 59 *Southern California Law Review* 1227 (1986).

Serrin, William, ed. *The Business of Journalism.* New York, N.Y.: The New Press, 2000.

Shockley, John S. "Direct Democracy, Campaign Finance, and the Courts: Can Corruption, Undue Influence, and Declining Voter Confidence Be Found?" 39 *University of Miami Law Review* 377 (1985).

Singleton, Loy A. and Steven C. Rockwell. "Silent Voices: Analyzing the FCC 'Media Voices' Criteria Limiting Local Radio-Television Cross-Ownership," 8 *Communication Law and Policy* 385 (2003).

Singman, Jerry L. *Daily Life in Medieval Europe.* Westport, Conn.: Greenwood Press, 1999.

Smith, Adam. *The Theory of Moral Sentiments.* 1759; reprint, Amherst, N.Y.: Prometheus, 2000.

_____. *An Inquiry into the Nature and Causes of the Wealth of Nations.* vol. 2 1776; reprint, London: Penguin, 1999.

Smith, Bradley A. "Money Talks: Speech, Corruption, Equality, and Campaign Finance." 86 *Georgetown Law Journal* 45 (1997).

Smith, Jeffery A. *Printers and Press Freedom: The Ideology of Early American Journalism.* New York: Oxford University Press, 1988.

Smith, Mark A. *American Business and Political Power: Public Opinion, Elections, and Democracy.* Chicago: University of Chicago Press, 2000.

Smolla, Rodney A. "Free the Fortune 500! The Debate Over Corporate Speech and the First Amendment." 54 *Case Western Reserve Law Review* 1277 (2004).

Solomon, Robert C. *Ethics and Excellence: Cooperation and Integrity.* New York: Oxford University Press, 1992.

Stefancic, Jean, and Richard Delgado. *No Mercy: How Conservative Think Tanks and Foundations Changed America's Social Agenda.* Philadelphia: Temple University Press, 1996.

Stern, Paul G. "A Pluralistic Reading of the First Amendment and its Relation to Public Discourse." 99 *Yale Law Journal* 925 (1990).

Sunstein, Cass R. *The Partial Constitution.* Cambridge, Mass.: Harvard University Press, 1993.

_____. "Speech in the Welfare State: Free Speech Now." 59 *University of Chicago Law Review* 255 (1992).

_____. "Hard Defamation Cases." 25 *William & Mary Law Review* 891 (1984).

Tanner, Michael D. *Leviathan on the Right: How Big-Government Conservatism Brought Down the Republican Revolution.* (Washington, D.C.: Cato Institute, 2007.

Teremenko, Victoria Dizik. "Corporate Speech Under Fire: Has Nike Finally Done It?" 2 *DePaul Business & Communication Law Journal* 207 (2003).

Terilli, Samuel A. "*Nike v. Kasky* and the Running-But-Going-Nowhere Commercial Speech Debate." 10 *Communication Law & Policy* 383 (2005).

Tribe, Laurence H. *American Constitutional Law*, 2d ed. Mineola, N.Y.: Foundation, 1988.

Tye, Larry. *The Father of Spin: Edward L. Bernays and the Birth of Public Relations.* New York: Crown, 1998.

Uchitelle, Louis. *The Disposable American: Layoffs and Their Consequences.* New York: Alfred A. Knopf, 2006).

United States v. Edge Broadcasting. 509 U.S. 418 (1993).

Urofsky, Melvin I. *Money and Free Speech: Campaign Finance Reform and the Courts.* Lawrence, Kan.: University Press of Kansas, 2005.

Valentine v. Chrestensen. 316 U.S. 52 (1942).

Virginia State Board of Pharmacy v. Virginia Citizens Consumer Council. 425 U.S. 748 (1976).

Vladeck, David C. "Lessons from a Story Untold: *Nike v. Kasky* Reconsidered." 54 *Case Western Reserve Law Review* 1049 (2004).

Vogel, David. *Fluctuating Fortunes: The Political Power of Business in America.* New York: Basic, 1989.

Warren, Elizabeth, and Amelia Warren Tyagi. *The Two-Income Trap: Why Middle-Class Mothers and Fathers are Going Broke.* New York: Basic Books, 2003.

Watts, Charles D., Jr. "Corporate Legal Theory Under the First Amendment: *Bellotti* and *Austin*." 46 *University of Miami Law Review* 317 (1991).

Weissman, Robert. "First Amendment Follies: Expanding Corporate Speech Rights." 19 *Multinational Monitor* 15 (1998).

Werhane, Patricia H. *Adam Smith and His Legacy for Modern Capitalism.* New York: Oxford University Press, 1991.

Wilson, James. "Adam Smith on Business Ethics." California Management Review 32, no. 1 (Fall 1989).

Winkler, Adam. "The Corporation in Election Law." 32 *Loyola of Los Angeles Law Review* 1243 (1999).

Wormser, I. Maurice. *Frankenstein Incorporated.* New York: Whittlesey House, 1931.

Zweig, Michael, ed., *What's Class Got to Do With It? American Society in the Twenty-First Century.* Ithaca, N.Y.: Cornell University Press, 2004.

Index